Mixed Race Children

A STUDY OF IDENTITY

ANNE WILSON

London
ALLEN & UNWIN
Boston Sydney Wellington

Allen & Unwin, the academic imprint of
Unwin Hyman Ltd
PO Box 18, Park Lane, Hemel Hempstead, Herts HP2 4TE, UK
40 Museum Street, London WC1A 1LU, UK
37/39 Queen Elizabeth Street, London SE1 2QB, UK

Allen & Unwin, Inc.,
8 Winchester Place, Winchester, Mass. 01890, USA

Allen & Unwin (Australia) Ltd.,
8 Napier Street, North Sydney, NSW 2060, Australia

Allen & Unwin (New Zealand) Ltd in association with the Port
Nicholson Press Ltd,
60 Cambridge Terrace, Wellington, New Zealand

First published in 1987

British Library Cataloguing in Publication Data

Wilson, Anne
    Mixed race children: a study of identity.
1. Race awareness in children
2. Children of minorities———Psychology
I. Title
305.2′3   BF723.R3
ISBN 0–04–370168–X
ISBN 0–04–370169–8 pbk

Library of Congress Cataloging-in-Publication Data

Wilson, Anne, 1955–
    Mixed race children.
Bibliography: p.
Includes index.
1. Children of interracial marriage———Great Britain.
2. Identity (Psychology) in children———Great Britain.
I. Title.
HQ777.9.W55 1987   155.4′24   86–28732
ISBN 0–04–370168–X (alk. paper)
ISBN 0–04–370169–8 (pbk. : alk. paper)

Typeset in 10 on 11 pt Garamond by Columns of Reading
and printed in Great Britain by
Billing and Sons Ltd, London and Worcester

Contents

Acknowledgements

The original research that this book is based on was supported financially by the Social Science Research Council (now the Economic and Social Research Council) and was supervised at the London School of Economics by Professor Percy Cohen and Dr E. I. Hopper. Several other people have been involved in the preparation of the book. Mike Herbert reduced the 'unnecessary isolation' of doing a PhD and gave unflagging friendship and support. Ros Schwartz read the manuscript at various stages and offered her usual intelligent and constructive criticism. Mark Wilson made the book possible in every kind of way – financial, intellectual, emotional – and my parents were, as ever, kind and understanding about the whole endeavour. Carol Carnall, formerly of the national organization for interracial families called Harmony, helped me to get started on the study by giving me some initial contacts. The greatest debt of all is to the mothers and children who took part in the study. In the text their names are fictional but they allowed me into their homes, they gave me hospitality and they shared their experiences with patience and generosity. I hope I have done them justice.

For my parents,
J. L. Riley and E. P. Riley,
who have always believed
in children being themselves.

Introduction

Where do 'mixed race' children feel they belong in our world of black and white? How can their parents and teachers help them to develop a positive racial identity? These are the questions posed by this study, which was conducted in the late 1970s, on a sample of fifty-one children who had one black and one white parent. The research attempted to trace connections between the way British 'mixed race' children perceive their place in the racial structure and certain characteristics of their parents, school and neighbourhood.

Methodologically, the study was similar to the United States 'doll' studies, which used dolls and pictures to elicit the racial identity of black children, but it differed from these studies in one important respect. Whereas the US research gave children a choice between two racial categories, 'black' and 'white', this study allowed the children to *set their own racial categories* before making an identification choice. Previous research on black US (and on black British) children seemed too rigid in its view of racial categorization. The mixed race children who took part in the present study were allowed to express their identity in terms of the categories used in everyday speech, such as 'brown', 'mixed race', 'half-caste' and 'coloured'.

The results of the study, overall, were hopeful and positive. Contrary to the popular stereotype of mixed race people as torn between black and white, many children seemed to have found a happy and secure identity for themselves as 'black mixed race'. This was particularly true of children in multiracial areas who were able to draw support from the existence of other mixed race and 'brown' children in their area. In a multi-ethnic setting, mixed race children were part of a subjectively agreed local pecking order which might include Asian, Cypriot, Arab, Spanish, Jewish and Moroccan children as well as 'black' and 'white'. For these children, there was nothing odd about having one black and one white parent. As one 7-year-old said with a nonchalant shrug: 'A black dad and a white mum is the usual mixture at our school.'

The children who lived in white areas were less able to construct a viable categorization system and so were more prone to racial identity conflict; they were more reliant on their parents to encourage a black/mixed race identity. Most mothers struggled heroically to do this, and some of them seemed to have been successful. Despite the white bias with which their children were surrounded they managed, through a variety of strategies, to put across the idea that it was good to be black and good to be mixed race. These families were determined not to be denied out of existence by a rigid demarcation between black and white. 'We are what we are,' said one mother. 'We must give the children space to be themselves.'

A word should be said about the use of the term 'mixed race' in the book. 'Mixed race' is used to describe the respondents simply because it is widely understood to refer to children who have one white European parent and one black Afro-Caribbean parent. I apologize in advance to people who find it offensive, perhaps because it implies that there is such a thing as a pure race which can be mixed with another pure race. Terms such as 'mixed origin', 'Anglo-Jamaican' or simply 'black' may be less offensive to some, but their meaning is not so clear. One of the main points made in the book is that our racial terminology in Britain is vague and confused and that people vary widely in the meanings they attach to different labels. If I sacrifice clarity in order to please one set of people, I am likely to offend another. Suffice it to say that throughout the text the terms 'race' and 'mixed race' are meant to be read in inverted commas even when they appear without them, because they are categories which are *socially* rather than *biologically* defined.

There is a further misunderstanding which I should like to pre-empt. The point of this book is *not* to suggest that mixed race children either do, or should, separate themselves in some way from the black community. On the contrary, it is one of the basic premises of the study that, like other black children, they must accept and be proud of their blackness and incorporate it into the core of their identity. However, in the book I distinguish between the primary (black or white) and secondary racial identification. It is on this second, 'private' level of identification that many children seem to take account of the fact that they have one white and one black parent and to include it in the way they see themselves. It seems to me desirable that mixed race children accept both sides of their dual heritage, provided that in doing so they do not lose sight of the fact that white society sees them as black and metes out to them the same degree of disadvantage that it does to all black people. An identity which includes *both* black *and* white elements may seem like a contradiction, but on an individual level this need not be so; for the categories used by white and black people to construct their racial and cultural identities appear to be far more complex than the simple 'black' and 'white' of institutional racism.

Taking interracial families out of the 'problem' mould into which they have been cast by sociological research will be, I hope, one of the main effects of the book. Perhaps, too, the substantive findings of the study will stimulate further research into the racial categorization and identity of all black British children. But my main hope in writing the book is that it will be of practical use to those who are involved in the welfare and care of mixed race children – be they parents, foster parents, social worker, health visitors, or teachers. The main message of the book for carers of all kinds is simple: don't prejudge the state of a child's identity just because he or she is of mixed race; listen to the children, however young they are, because they have their own views of the racial structure and of where they belong within it.

Many assertions are made about the racial identity of black and mixed race children without any reference to what the children themselves think, feel, believe, or want. I hope this book will highlight how little is really known about mixed race children's identity, about the factors which influence it and about the process by which it develops. More information in this area, based on talking to children and parents directly about their racial attitudes, will mean better decisions about mixed race children's welfare and better guidelines for parents about how a positive black/mixed race identity can be encouraged.

In this study, three aspects of the mother's attitudes seem to exert a major influence on the child's identity: her attitude to her own and to her child's identity and her views about the extent of racism in Britain. The children with the most positive and secure identities had mothers who were open and secure about their own racial identity (whether black or white), who encouraged their children to think of themselves as black *and* mixed race and represented racism realistically to their children, as a force which would affect them personally. Children who were more prone to identity conflict tended to have mothers who were in conflict about their own identity, who saw the children as 'coloured' or 'almost white' and underplayed racism as a factor in the children's lives. These children were told, 'Work hard enough and you will achieve your goals, regardless of the colour of your skin.'

These results have significant implications for the way parenting needs are assessed in fostering and adoption placement. They suggest, for example, that it is not enough for prospective parents to be black; they must also feel good about being black and be able to transmit that feeling to the child. The results also show that the parenting factors which influence a mixed race child's identity are not all obvious or commonsense. One might think that a 'no punches pulled' approach to teaching the child about racism would drive them firmly into identity conflict, but this does not appear to be the case, perhaps because mothers with such an approach also reassured the child that he or she was not being singled out for racist treatment. Mothers who adopted this line told their children that racism was being countered by *collective action by the black community* and they took pains to divorce this struggle from the child's *personal endeavours for achievement*. Racism meant that all black people united to oppose an unfair system, but it did not mean that you stopped trying your best at school. Telling mixed race children that racism would affect their lives seemed to confirm what they knew already and to put well-defined limits on what had been previously a vague and amorphous fear. On the other hand, children whose mothers told them that they had as good a chance at white children were thrown into a morass of guilt and confusion. How could that be true when white people seemed to have the monopoly on weath and power – or when white children called black children names at school and got more of the teacher's attention?

The parenting qualities which were important for mixed race children's identity were not exclusive to the black mothers. Results suggested that white mothers, too, could create conditions in which a black/mixed race identity could flourish, provided they were willing and able to become involved in a black community and life-style. The white mothers who were most successful in encouraging a black/mixed race identity had abandoned *full* membership of the white group. They saw themselves as somewhere between black and white and were often part of a network of interracial families. Because of this they did not feel threatened or rejected by their children's black identity – indeed, they encouraged it more fully. Like the black mothers who had children with a positive identity, these mothers believed that racism was rife and they made sure that their children were prepared to face and to fight it. As one white woman said: 'We all know that the system isn't fair, but the children have to learn to challenge that, alongside other black people.'

This study of mixed race children was carried out on a small scale with limited resources and it left many areas unexplored, but it also uncovered a vast area of research in which more work is needed. If the book stimulates greater interest in British children's racial categorization and identity, it will have achieved something. But if it can also show, to the people that matter, that mixed race children have their own views of who they are which do not necessarily conform to popular stereotypes, and that, given the right environment, they can be both black *and* mixed race *and* proud of it, then the study will have been more than worthwhile.

Chapter One

Between Black and White

The prevailing view of mixed race children is that they have identity problems because of their ambiguous social position. It is said that, where one parent is black and one white, the children are bound to suffer from a divided loyalty. They belong simultaneously to both races and to neither. Suggestions vary as to how the identity conflict of mixed race children can be resolved, but they usually come down to three alternatives: to be black, to be white, or to be forever racked between the two. The more modern literature suggests that the only realistic solution is for mixed race children to consider themselves full members of the black community, since any attempt to adopt a white identity is likely to bring conflict and rejection.

Where did these ideas come from and how accurate a picture do they give of the racial identity of British mixed race children? To some extent, the sociological view of mixed race children has come from popular ideas about the problems they are likely to suffer. Despite the liberalization of attitudes to intermarriage, mixed race children are still regarded as a psychologically disadvantaged group; and sociological thought has inevitably been influenced by this view. Of course, the sociological analysis of the position of mixed race children differs from the popular view in its explanation of *why* the children suffer. Sociology attributes it to white institutional racism, whereas society blames the parental relationship. None the less, the idea that mixed race children suffer from identity confusion is partly derived from the prevailing popular wisdom on the subject.

This is not to say that the view is entirely without empirical sociological foundation. Mixed race children have been considered in passing in a number of studies from the 1950s onwards, and from this literature a fragmented picture emerges of a group caught in the crossfire of racial conflict. The 'problem' perspective

1

also finds support from early United States research on marginality and the 'mulatto', which suggested that individuals who had claim to membership of both the black and the white group would inevitably suffer some degree of identity confusion.

However, the evidence is scanty, and one important point is often overlooked; the question of whether or not British mixed race children *are* particularly prone to racial identity conflict has never been fully investigated. The stereotype of the 'tortured misfit' has certainly captured the imagination of sociologists and psychologists alike, but it sometimes appears to be based more on popular belief than on the observations of social scientists in Britain. This first chapter looks at the origins of the 'problem' perspective on British mixed race children and explores the evidence upon which it is based.

Interracial Relationships and Mixed Race Children in Britain

As far back as the earliest black/white contacts, there have been mixed race children in Britain. James Walvin (1973), in his study of the black British population from 1555 to 1945, noted that when the white planters returned from the colonies to their homeland in the eighteenth century they were shocked by the extent of interracial sex in England. Because the black British population before the twentieth century was predominantly male, these relationships tended to involve black men and white women; but they occurred in all classes of society. Cartoonists of the eighteenth century took great delight in depicting upper-class women saucily enjoying the attentions of their black male servants, and relationships between black and whites in the poorer classes were inevitable in the absence of black women.

The upper-class affairs were regarded as scandalous, but they were also seen as relatively harmless. The lower-class relationships, on the other hand, were more stable and more egalitarian and usually produced a large interracial family. By the end of the eighteenth century these families were being labelled as a serious problem, and the question of how they could be stopped was openly discussed. According to Walvin (1973), the scheme to recruit poor London blacks to the new colony of Sierra Leone in 1787 was partly inspired as a way of preventing these 'unnatural connections' in England. As Walvin notes: 'There can be no doubt ... that, by a substantial and influential section of English society, miscegenation was regarded as a threat to the structure of

2

that society. Consequently, racial mixing became a central issue in the opposition to the development of a black community in Britain' (Walvin, 1973).

Myths and stereotypes concerning mixed race people revolved upon white fears of the 'pollution' of their race with 'Negro blood'. The idea that Negroes were intellectually inferior was firmly entrenched and it was feared that mixed race people represented the beginnings of a new 'breed' of people which was of a lower order than either race. This type of biological racist thinking reached its height in the late nineteenth century with the advent of Social Darwinism and of 'scientific' theories of white superiority, but in 1772 Edward Long was writing about mixed race children in hysterical eugenic terms. Miscegenation was, he said,

a venomous and dangerous ulcer that threatens to disperse its malignancy far and wide until every family catches infection from it ... The English blood will become so contaminated with this mixture ... till the whole nation resembles the Portugese and Moriscos in complexion of skin and baseness of mind.

(Long, 1772)

The idea of the mixed race person as a social problem and as a biologically inferior being was particularly strong at the end of the nineteenth and beginning of the twentieth centuries. All the strands of dizzy colonial power, sexual repression and a widely accepted theory of evolution came together to produce virulent and extreme reactions to mixed race people in Britain. 'Half-castes' were regarded as not only a threat to moral standards and to the race, but a threat to the British Empire as well. In 1937 Cedric Dover, reviewing the literature since the turn of the century, depicted British attitudes to mixed race people as a kind of fearful contempt:

The half-caste appears in a prodigal literature. It presents him, to be frank, mostly as an undersized, scheming and entirely degenerate bastard. His father is a blackguard, his mother a whore. But more than all this, he is a potential menace to Western Civilization, to everything that is White and Sacred and majusculed.

The second half of the twentieth century brought a number of changes in white attitudes to intermarriage. Slowly but surely, biological arguments against miscegenation were discredited, and the idea that black/white unions produced genetically inferior children was abandoned, at least by the scientific community. In its place, however, came the 'compassionate common-sense'

3

approach, which justified disapproval of intermarriage on the grounds of the 'suffering of the children'. It is all very well, went this argument, if a couple from different races choose to marry – but what about the children? Mixed race children do not choose to be born, it was said, and their lives will be fraught with misery because of the vastly different backgrounds of their parents.

A good example of this twentieth-century 'commonsense' can be found in the wartime health manual for women which contained specific advice against marrying 'coloured' men. Speaking from the medical man's professional viewpoint, Sir W. Arbuthnot Lane stated that

Marriages between coloured and white races are almost certain to be unhappy and even if the couple themselves are fairly happy, life is very hard for the children of such unions. It is hardly necessary to say anything more about the problem here, as most people agree that such marriages are unwise; unfortunately they appear to be on the increase ... It is the children ... who suffer most in mixed marriages, even between people of the same colour, and they are often unhappy and ever conscious of the struggle within themselves of two different nationalities, to neither of which they belong.

(Arbuthnot Lane, 1939)

It is interesting that, although the good sense of this advice is taken to be self-evident, the author none the less felt compelled to issue it with the most authoritative tone he could muster. It was perhaps meant as a stern warning to white middle-class women who might succumb to the 'dangerous' attraction of black, American GIs.

The twentieth-century argument, that because mixed race children would be the victims of racial prejudice they should not be brought into the world in the first place, was a flimsy replacement for the strident biological bigotry of the previous centuries. But the racists need not have worried, for pseudo-scentific eugenic theories were lurking just beneath the surface. Susan Benson notes that many newspapers and magazines still reflected in the 1950s the view that miscegenation was 'harmful to the race' and that mixed race children were 'a great problem' (Benson, 1981). In 1961 the Rev. Clifford Hill had more direct experience of such views when he said on a radio programme that he would allow his daughter to marry a 'coloured' man, provided that the couple appeared to be compatible (Hill, 1965). Hill received a deluge of hate mail, accusing him of being unfit to be a father and of sanctioning the production of 'a race of unhappy creatures who have ignored God's and Nature's rules' (Hill, 1965);

a Manchester woman declared that 'Interbreeding is evil and nobody could be proud of half-caste children'. The whole incident culminated in an attack on Hill's house during the night, when slogans such as 'nigger lover' and 'race-mixing priest' were daubed over its doors and walls.

The late 1960s brought a shift towards more liberal attitudes to intermarriage in the sense that theories of racial purity were confined more and more to extreme right-wing groups. Some whites even began to see mixed race children as the key to racial harmony, the idea being that, if black and whites blended peacefully into one, there could be no more racial conflict. These new ripples of tolerance were widely felt and they began to change the way interracial relationships were depicted in the media. Susan Benson (1981) exemplified the change in attitude by the kind of advice that was given in the 'agony' columns of women's magazines, to readers who brought up the 'problem' of interracial relationships. In 1955, *Glamour* replied to a reader:

many coloured men are fine people, but they do come from a different race with a very different background and upbringing. Besides, scientists do not yet know if it is wise for two such very different races as white and black to intermarry, for sometimes the children of mixed marriages seem to inherit the worst characteristics of each race.

In 1969, however, Honey advised: 'Only if you are so much in love and can't be bothered with the odd cold shoulder can differences in race, background and skin colour be overcome.'

The second attitude is a good illustration of what Benson (1981) calls the 'love against the odds' genre of feature, where romantic attachment overcomes opposition from friends and family. This now seems to be the most common treatment of interracial relationships in the media. 'True romance' slots on radio often feature black/white couples whose 'love has brought them through', and the agony columns of magazines continue to take the stance that 'love conquers all'. Yet despite the relatively tolerant view of boyfriend/girlfriend relationships, the media still tend to endorse the earlier 'common-sense' approach when it comes to the question of marriage and children. Apart from the occasional attempt to treat the subject sensitively and seriously, plays, magazine articles, novels and television programmes all tend to return to the same theme: that interracial marriages are fraught with problems and that mixed race children are crazy, mixed-up kids who are rejected by both black *and* white communities.

This idea is sometimes portrayed in a subtle or implicit way. For example, in the late 1970s the *Sunday Times Magazine*

5

interviewed a black/white couple for a feature on mixed marriages. Their reported comments about their own and their children's lives were bravely positive, but we were left in no doubt that they had encountered all the 'obvious' problems: Ros and John admit that for their children belonging to two races was difficult. It was particularly hard for Ann, of whom John's mother wrote with obvious relief after her birth: "She's beautiful; she is pure white." '

The stereotype of the unhappy mixed race child was portrayed more directly in a play called *Scrape off the Black* by Tunde Ikoli, first performed at Riverside Studios in London in August 1980. The play highlighted the plight of a young man with a white mother and a black father who could not come to terms with the fact that he was 'neither black nor white'. Similarly, an episode of the short-running black television soap-opera *Empire Road* (by Michael Abbensetts) featured a 'half-caste' girl who displayed all the classic signs of racial identity conflict. The fact that a person has one black and one white parent is often seen as sufficient to define his or her character; that they will have psychological problems is taken to be self-evident.

A development which has taken place over the last twenty-five years is the addition of black voices to the intermarriage debate. Before about 1960, black people's views on sexual relations with whites were largely ignored, but were generally assumed to be favourable. This assumption was based partly on white ethnocentric arrogance and partly on the idea that Afro-Caribbean people thought marrying a light-skinned person was highly desirable. Yet in the 1960s and 1970s black people in Britain began to speak out against black/white relationships. Susan Benson (1981) cites a heated correspondence in the newspaper *West Indian World* in spring 1974, which began when a woman reader complained that too many black men seemed to prefer white women. Subsequent letters argued to and fro, and the issue seemed to touch on a raw nerve in the new black outlook. Because the Black Consciousness movement of this period stressed black pride and the rediscovery of the aesthetic and cultural value of blackness, sexual attraction to white people was seen as disloyal and psychologically unsound. Then, as now, the more radical sections of the black community saw black/white relationships as an impediment to the development of a strong, cohesive black community.

Throughout their history, mixed race children in Britain have aroused strong feelings in the people around them. Attitudes have ranged from 'common-sense' doubt to extreme persecution, but they have never been indifferent. Why is it that, even in the present climate of relative tolerance of intermarriage, reactions of doubt and disapproval towards the children endure? The answer seems to be that mixed race children strike at the very heart of a racist system. They threaten its existence by calling into question the categories upon which it is based. As Susan Benson says: 'To study the everyday life of interracial families ... is to study the nature of British race relations' (1981).

The Sociological View

Sociological thought about intermarriage and mixed race children has both influenced and been influenced by the 'problem' persepective taken by the media. Most of the existing research suggests that mixed race children are prone to identity conflict, but this is seen as a reflection of the depth of racialist feeling in British society. The plight of mixed race children demonstrates the rigid racial boundary imposed by our society; these children *must* choose between black and white, for it is impossible to maintain a dual allegiance to both racial groups. According to the accepted sociological view, interracial relationships and mixed race children arouse strong emotions in white people because they pose a threat – to the system of white domination, to the culture of white values and to the sexual repression which a puritanical religion has traditionally imposed.

The most direct threat posed by mixed race children is that of blurring the physical categories upon which white status and power depend. Where two groups are hierarchically arranged and where physical differences are used as a 'marker' to delineate the boundary, the group which has greater access to privilege and reward will fight hard to preserve the status quo. Racial exogamy threatens a fiercely guarded social division. The white reaction to it is in proportion to the amount whites feel they have to lose if the division breaks down.

The black reaction to interracial marriage and mixed race children might seem like a contradiction of this idea, but this too can be understood through the ideas of power and oppression. In the last twenty-five years, the black minority in Britain has changed its tactics in the fight against white racism. Although the white majority still thinks that it will lose its power through racial intermarriage, many black people no longer believe this. The black response to white rejection is now to fight for power *within the existing system* rather than to seek integration. Many black

7

people want a society in which they are recognized as a political force in their own right, rather than one which promises vaguely to treat everyone the same. Mixed race children symbolically undermine the new black strength. They signal the return of the 'melting-pot' ideology with its dream of gradual, harmonious integration into a white-controlled society.

A second reason why mixed race children arouse strong emotions in white people is that the contrast between black and white has great psychological significance in Western culture. Black is associated with negative and dangerous things, whereas white is linked with all that is good and safe. European and North American literature abounds with this kind of colour symbolism – the works of Shakespeare, Chaucer, Milton, Hawthorne, Poe and Melville all use white in expressing good and black in expressing evil – and it has also been used to great effect in the Bible (see Bastide, 1967). Luckiesh (1967), who made a study of the symbolic meanings of black and white in the West, found that the things most commonly associated with black were death, horror, wickedness and mortification, whereas white was frequently used to represent life, joy, innocence, purity and happiness. The link between these associations and white racism may seem tenuous, but many writers argue that its importance should not be underestimated (Williams and Morland, 1976). If colour symbolism does influence racial attitudes then we can be sure that it plays a part in white people's disapproval of mixed race children. The idea that 'black equals bad' tends to confirm the deep-seated fear that interracial contact is potentially 'dangerous' and that mixed race children have a 'corrupting' or 'polluting' effect on the 'white race'. A common expression of these fears is the view that mixed race people are unpredictable because of their 'black blood'. The blackness is perceived as more dangerous because it is hidden and is likely to emerge unexpectedly ('blood will out').

A third source of white disapproval of mixed race children can be found in the powerful eroticism with which the black race is invested. Theories abound as to why myths of black sexuality are given so much credence, but one widely accepted view is that the puritan tradition has encouraged white people to attribute the black group with *their own* repressed sexuality. If this is the case, then this is yet another reason for them to find interracial families threatening. Sexual contact with black men and women arouses white fears of loss of control in a *psychological* as well as in a *political* sense. Mixed race children are the result of relationships which whites perceive as highly sexual; for this reason they are often regarded with a mixture of shame, disgust and secret curiosity.

8

Despite sociological interest in mixed race people as a microcosm of the wider racial conflict, empirical research on British mixed race children has been scanty. Most of the data have been collected by sociologists *en passant*, while conducting studies of other aspects of race relations. In earlier studies (from 1940 onwards) it was *assumed* that mixed race children suffered from identity conflict and attention was directed towards analysing *which aspects of their situation caused them the most distress.* A common conclusion was that white prejudice and discrimination were among the main causes of the problem; in particular, the attitude of the white extended family. The amount of tolerance shown by whites towards mixed race children's 'unusual' social background was believed to be crucial in determining how much rejection and confusion the child experienced. The situation of mixed race children was also seen as being dependent on area to a certain extent; in some areas of Britain the children might find acceptance with the black or the white group, whereas elsewhere they might be rejected by both communities.

Another contributing factor suggested by these earlier studies was mixed race children's lack of ties with a culture outside Britain. When white society rejected them, these children of black seamen could not easily fall back on African or Caribbean culture for an alternative value system. Britain was their homeland; without another set of roots to turn to, the children felt psychologically isolated and filled with self-doubt.

More recent studies of mixed race children have been influenced by the greater emphasis which is now placed on race and racism in the study of minority groups in Britain. Since the late 1960s, sociologists have tended to see the problems of mixed race children as a more acute version of those suffered by black children – that is, the problem of being black in a white-controlled society. Like children with two black parents, mixed race children must accept and embrace their blackness in spite of the societal pressure to identify as white. This task is even more difficult if one has a 'legitimate claim' (such as one white parent) to membership of the white group. However, although this is the implicitly accepted stance of modern race relations *theory*, the few empirical studies which have treated mixed race children as a separate group offer little evidence to support the view. If any conclusion can be drawn from the one or two studies which have considered mixed race children directly, it is that such children in Britain have a positive view of their racial position and tend to think of themselves as belonging to a separate, mixed race group.

9

The Dockland Studies

The largest mixed race communities in Britain after the Second World War were to be found in the dockland areas of the larger ports: Liverpool, Cardiff, Newcastle and London. The black population of Britain was also concentrated here, so it is not surprising that the first sociological studies of British race relations were conducted in these areas. In 1954 Anthony Richmond published a study of 'colour prejudice' in Liverpool, in which he mentioned briefly the 'plight' of mixed race children. Taking it as read that mixed race people had psychological problems, Richmond suggested that their suffering was caused by the extensive discrimination that was practised against them. According to Richmond, white people's prejudice against intermarriage was transferred to mixed race children, thus affecting both their job opportunities and their psychological development:

There is no inherent reason why mixed marriages should not be successful, or why coloured children should not grow up into healthy, well-adjusted citizens. That mixed marriages are less often successful than others, and that the children of such marriages sometimes become severely maladjusted, must be attributed to the widespread existence of colour prejudice and the practice of discrimination.

(Richmond, 1954)

The following year Michael Banton supported Richmond's view from his research in Stepney:

It is impossible to say how much the children born of racially mixed marriages do suffer. In all probability they suffer less on account of the colour factor than on account of the disadvantages entailed by their position in the economic and social structure. The argument that a mixed marriage is inadvisable because it entails suffering for the children has some validity in the individual case but in the aggregate is invalid, for there are bound to be mixed marriages. It would be easier in the long run to change the climate of opinion than to prevent them.

(Banton, 1955)

Clifford Hill, who made a study of thirty-six interracial couples in the London area during the 1960s (Hill, 1965), also assumed that mixed race children had identity problems. But he attributed these not to the white population at large (who saw them unequivocally as black) but to the attitudes of their white extended family. Hill argued that it was the family of the white spouse who felt most afflicted by the 'shame' of mixed race children, for it seemed to put their own white identity in jeopardy. In Hill's sample, grandparents who had just about been able to tolerate a black husband for their daughter, shunned the whole interracial family after the arrival of the first child. The black spouse, suggested Hill,

is not a *blood* relative. The children on the other hand are in a very different category. They are full blood relatives, members of the family *by right of birth*, and thus the real racial crisis is provoked not by marriage of one member of the family to a coloured man but by the birth of the first child. This child must either be accepted or rejected. He cannot be viewed with detachment... He *belongs* to the family.

(Hill, 1965, original emphasis)

In another 1950s dockland study, Kenneth Little described the mixed race adolescents he met in Cardiff as 'typical marginal men', whose personalities had been greatly affected by their ambiguous social position (Little, revised, 1972). In Little's view, the social and psychological unease of these adolescents derived from the fact that they had neither ties with a 'homeland' nor the acceptance of the society into which they were born. Unlike their fathers, these boys could not defend themselves against white rejection by retreating spiritually to their cultural roots, yet neither did they have the educational or emotional resources to confront the reality of their position and fight against the injustices they suffered. In psychological terms, their choice of identification presented them with a painful dilemma; as mixed race people, they could either identify with their black father and take on, by association, an antagonistic attitude to white people, or else they could identify with their mother and accept the values of the white community. If he chose the latter, a mixed race boy must 'learn to regard his father with good-humoured contempt' (Little, 1972). Many of the individuals observed by Little appeared to have found the choice impossible to make and so remained ambivalent, isolated and rootless.

Sydney Collins (1957) added one proviso to the view that mixed race children's problems were an inevitable consequence of their racial position. Racial identity, he argued, can vary from area to area. To some extent, mixed race children's social position will depend on the structural and cultural nature of the immigrant community in their area and on its relationship with the white host community. Comparing the three areas in which his study was conducted, Collins distinguished three distinct types of social position and racial identity among the mixed race people he met:

The Lancashire Negro community is in an extreme state of flux, with numerous short-lived emergent associations. Informal social control is extremely weak. Here the Anglo-Negro is in a position of marginality *par excellence*, experiencing extreme forms of insecurity. But the Welsh Negro community is highly integrated internally, and informal social control is effectively maintained. Here the relationship of the community vis-à-vis the host society is one verging on a rigid caste-like separation, and the Anglo-Negro, being without status in the white section of the town, tends to confine himself to his own community for social security. Of the three communities, the Tyneside Negroes are the most highly integrated into the structure of the host society. Anglo-Negroes here have a positive attitude towards life and a feeling of greater social security than their counterparts in the other two communities.

(Collins, 1957)

In effect, Collins's analysis suggested the same choices for the mixed race *group* as Little had put forward for the mixed race *individual*: to be white (or integrated into the white group), to be 'coloured', or to be transient and marginal, accepted by neither group. However, Collins appeared to view the mixed race person's dilemma less as a matter of choice and more as a matter of the restrictions imposed by the particular degree of prejudice to be found in the local white community.

More Recent Studies

Unlike the studies of the 1950s and 1960s, more recent works on British race relations have tended not to distinguish mixed race people from the main black group. This change of emphasis is the result of a general shift in the focus of sociological research. Whereas in the 1950s most studies centred on the cultural characteristics of the various immigrant groups and on their interactions with white society, social scientists are today concerned with second- and third-generation ethnic minority Britons, for whom *race* is a more crucial issue than culture. Race relations research now tends to centre on white institutional racism rather than on the 'problem' of single minority groups, the argument being that black, mixed race and Asian people are all equally affected by the predominance of white power in political and economic institutions.

This change in the approach of race relations research has been extremely important for the way sociologists analyse the British racial identity. A person's view of themselves in racial terms now tends to be seen as a clear choice between 'black' and 'white' rather than as a more esoteric choice between 'homeland culture' and 'the British way of life' in a particular area of the country.

Because 'black' and 'white' are the categories through which white institutional racism operates, they are also often assumed to be the terms in which *individual racial identity* is expressed.

The implications of this argument for the study of the British mixed race identity will be discussed in full in the chapter following. In the present consideration of empirical studies, it must be noted simply that very few data are available to support this view. Out of five recent studies (Bagley and Young in Verma and Bagley, 1979, 1984; Benson, 1981; Durojaiye, 1970; Kannan, 1972) of mixed race children's identity, only one suggested that these children experience their situation as a painful clash of loyalties between black and white; and there is no research to support the argument that mixed race children have higher levels of self-esteem if they identify with the black group.

Kannan's research, conducted in London in the late 1960s, was a study of one hundred intercultural families, including twenty families where one parent was African or Afro-Caribbean and one was white (Kannan, 1972). Kannan's study should have been able to offer valuable insights into the racial identity of the children, but the work is marred by a lack of methodological explanation and an abundance of statements which seem to go beyond the bounds of the data. Kannan clearly does not support the view that mixed race children are a 'problem' but his claims that being of mixed race is a positive experience appear to come from nowhere. For example, Kannan informs us, apparently referring to the whole sample, that

The children are not generally any problem for the neighbours. In the playground they behave well and in turn there is not any apparent discriminatory treatment meted out to them. They get generally ample love and affection and good care at home, except in a very few cases in which the parents have developed some trouble for themselves.

Durojaiye's 1970 study was a more careful sociological analysis but it was narrow in its scope. Durojaiye set out to study patterns of friendship choice in an ethnically mixed junior school and in doing so gathered some data on the friendships of a sample of thirty-three mixed race children. He found that, although mixed race children were quite frequently chosen as companions by members of the black and the white groups, they themselves showed a strong preference for companions who were also of mixed race. Durojaiye concluded:

The fact that both white and coloured children, boys and girls, show less ethnic self-preference in relation to children of mixed parents than the whites show to the coloured and the coloured to the whites, would

13

appear to contradict the fears often expressed about children of mixed parents belonging to neither 'camp'. It will appear that they have 'the best of both worlds'.

(Durojaiye, 1970)

Durojaiye's study was conducted in just one school in the Manchester area and did not attempt to measure racial identity in any way except by companion choice. None the less, it is one of the few studies of British children's racial attitudes which specifically mentions mixed race children and it is interesting in that it contradicts the accepted wisdom of more theoretical inquiries.

Christopher Bagley and Loretta Young have made two studies of British mixed race children's identity – one of adopted children and the other of children living with their natural parents (in Verma and Bagley 1978, 1984). Yet as with Durojaiye's and Kannan's studies, Bagley and Young's research adds only a very small piece to a fragmented picture of the British mixed race identity. Each of their studies is described in one chapter, in a book on wider educational themes; and because of this they offer little methodological detail and even less qualitative information on the children's thoughts and feelings about themselves. Like Kannan, Bagley presents a highly positive view of mixed race children's position; but one is still left with no clear idea of how the children feel about their racial situation or how they place themselves in the racial structure.

In the study of sixty-four mixed race children (aged 4–7) living with their natural parents, Bagley and Young (in Verma and Bagley, 1984) gave the children two tests devised by the US researchers Williams and Morland to measure racial attitudes. In the first 'colour meanings test' (CMT) subjects were asked to examine and evaluate pairs of identical animals, white and black; in the second, the 'pre-school racial attitudes measure' (PRAM), they were asked to evaluate pairs of adults and children who were identical in every respect except for race – black or white. Replies were categorized as showing either 'white bias', 'black bias', or 'lack of bias'. In addition, Bagley and Young gave the children a test which was intended as a measure of self-esteem. This test relied on the spatial positioning of three cardboard figures: the 'good girl' (or boy), the 'bad girl' and 'me'. The way the subject placed him- or herself in relation to the 'good' and 'bad' figures was taken to be a measure of self-image.

Mixed race children tested by Bagley and Young had a high degree of 'no bias' in their responses to PRAM and CMT when compared with other studies of black and white children using identical techniques. This was because the children were positively evaluating adults 'like their parents' – that is, a black man if they had a black father and a white woman if their mother was white. The children also displayed high levels of self-esteem. The researchers concluded that mixed race children 'do not have the negative colour biases which many black children display and their evaluation of colour seems to be based on positive evaluations of their black and white parents. This positive identification is reflected in high levels of self-esteem' (Verma and Bagley, 1984).

Susan Benson's conclusions from her study of twenty interracial families in Brixton (Benson, 1981) were not so optimistic and were more in line with those of the dockland researches in the 1950s. Benson was overt in her endorsement of the 'problem' perspective; even without reference to her empirical data, she suggested that the position of mixed race children in Britain involved some inherent contradictions which were detrimental to their racial identity. She argued that 'In a racially divided society, where differences of ethnic origin are of primary significance in establishing social identity, the future lives of children must, inevitably, be fraught with difficulties.' (Benson, 1981). The ages of the twenty-seven 'children' in Benson's study ranged from a few months to 20 years. Information about their identity was gained from either incidents Benson witnessed or accounts given by the parents. Benson reported that several of the children in the sample had 'overt identity problems', as indicated by either open verbal rejection of a black identity, by the 'washing syndrome' (trying to 'wash off' blackness in the bath), by an expressed desire to change their appearance, or by abusive behaviour towards black children. In addition, the majority of the younger children had almost exclusively white friends, even though many were attending schools which had a very high proportion of black pupils.

Benson's study gave a highly detailed account of the lives of interracial families in Brixton in the early 1970s, but the data on the children should perhaps be treated with some caution. The primary focus of the research was on the *couples* rather than on the children's identity; so, on the basis of very little data, Benson has tended to draw rather hasty conclusions. Information on the children's friendships and identity was gathered somewhat unsystematically from second-hand sources; we cannot be sure, then, how accurately the findings reflect the views of even this small number of mixed race children in one area of London.

It is impossible to draw any clear conclusions from these studies of the racial identity of British mixed race children, for they all either were confined to one small aspect of the children's lives or else attempted to confirm a previously formulated view of mixed race children on the basis of rather scanty evidence. Far more research is needed in this area before any patterns can emerge. Yet this in itself is an important conclusion. Up to the present time, there have been only a handful of studies which have attempted to investigate the racial attitudes and racial identity of mixed race children. This means that the statements about mixed race children's identity problems which have been made with such confidence for decades, if not centuries, have no sound empirical basis. They appear to have been drawn from a mixture of impressionistic observation, popular myth and theoretical analysis of race and racism in Britain.

However, there is one source of the 'problem' perspective on mixed race children which does have some empirical foundation. In the latter half of the twentieth century, our ideas about British mixed race children have been partially rooted in studies of mixed race people in other parts of the world. In particular, they have been based on a whole body of theory and research which has come across the Atlantic, from the United States.

The 'Problem' Perspective and the United States Experience

Sociology textbooks which mention mixed race people frequently refer to them as 'marginal'. The term has become a convenient shorthand to describe any person who does not fit into the mainstream mould and who, for whatever reason, straddles two or more conflicting social identities. In its connotations, marginality comes across as both dangerous and exotic. On the one hand, the marginal individual threatens the fabric of an existing social order and so risks being ostracized or oppressed; on the other, he or she is liberated from adhering to one given code of behaviour and is thus able to view normal social life from an unusual perspective. The contemporary 'problem' approach to mixed race children can be traced to the work of the first US 'marginality' theorists: Robert Park (1937) and Everett Stonequist (1937). They suggested that individuals who were caught between two conflicting social groups were particularly prone to feelings of social unease, divided loyalty and psychological distress.

Park's theory stemmed primarily from his interest in human

migration and in the process by which immigrant groups became incorporated into the host society. Park hypothesized that, when individuals were attempting to move into a new group or cultural setting that was reluctant to accept them, at some time during the process they would find that they were strangers to *both* cultures – their former one and the new one. This could be extremely disruptive emotionally and cause them to experience

spiritual instability, intensified self-consciousness, restlessness and mal-aise . . . The marginal man is a personality type that arrives at a time and a place where, out of the conflict of races and cultures, new societies, new peoples and cultures are coming into existence. The fate which condemns him to live, at the same time, in two worlds is the same which compels him to assume, in relation to the worlds in which he lives, the role of cosmopolitan and stranger.

(Park, 1937)

The Jew, newly emancipated from the European ghetto and trying to enter Gentile American life, exemplified for Park the marginal individual who was caught by prejudice between two social worlds, while attempting to move from one to the other. However, Park also believed that the concept of marginality could extend to people who belonged to two antagonistic groups by virtue of *birth* rather than *migration* – such as the American 'mulattos', the Anglo-Indians and children of Jewish-Gentile parentage. In both these cases, the tensions and feuds between two different cultures were played out in microcosm in one individual; the external conflict was internalized and experienced personally as a crisis of identity.

Park emphasized that, although these 'marginal men' were faced with a stressful psychological uncertainty, their fate was not wholly negative. Being in a marginal situation gave them unusual insight into the workings of both cultures which they could often use to advantage as community leaders, philosophers and social commentators. It was Stonequist (1937) who laid emphasis on the potential trauma of marginality when he attempted to analyse the characteristics which made up the 'marginal personality'. Stonequist chose to see marginality as a problematic stage from which the individual may or may not move on to some form of 'adjustment'. Whereas Park was equivocal about the merits of marginality, seeing it as something which could be both positive and negative depending on how the individual used it, Stonequist explicitly represented it as a painful state, from which people would seek any means of escape. His definition of marginality included the idea of an internal battle which must be resolved if

17

peace of mind is to be attained: 'So the marginal man as conceived in this study is one who is poised in psychological uncertainty between two (or more) social worlds; reflecting in his soul the discords and harmonies, repulsions and attractions of those worlds, one of which is often "dominant" over the other' (Stonequist, 1937). Drawing on biographies and first-hand accounts given by people from a variety of cultural groups, Stonequist suggested that there was a 'typical life cycle' which applied to most people in marginal situations.

The first 'pre-marginal' stage was in childhood, when 'the barriers of the adult world have not yet been fully experienced' and the child is 'partially assimilated into the dominant culture' (Stonequist, 1937). In the case of the American 'mulatto', the pre-marginal phase involved a strong identification with the white group. The American mixed race child began his or her life believing, hoping and wishing that he or she was white. But the pre-marginal phase was quickly curbed by rejection, and the child was suddenly forced to realize that he or she was not accepted as a member of the white group. According to Stonequist, this 'crisis of rejection' was a dramatic turning-point in the life of the marginal individual: 'The individual finds his social world disorganized. Personal relations and cultural forms which he had previously taken for granted suddenly become problematic. He does not know how to act. There is a feeling of confusion, of loss of direction, of being overwhelmed' (Stonequist, 1937).

This crisis experience heralded the phase of the life cycle in which the true marginal personality emerged. The painful shock of rejection had estranged the mixed race person from both the black and the white group. A dual self-image developed, but the marginal individual did not simply see him- or herself from two standpoints (for this is common enough) but from two *conflicting* standpoints. 'It is as if', wrote Stonequist, 'he were placed simultaneously between two looking glasses, each presenting a sharply different image of himself' (1937). Stonequist described the development of this second phase thus:

The making of a new racial or national identification is forced by the violent emotional reaction against the old. The old identification, however, though shaken, continues to exist and trouble the mind. It will not be stilled or easily thrust aside. On the other hand, a new racial identification cannot be formed by the mere willing of it. It must grow, if at all, with time and experience. In the interval of transition the individual suffers from a divided loyalty − an ambivalent attitude.

The truly marginal 'mulatto' embraced the values and attitudes of

18

both the white *and* the black group, yet his or her view of each veered from devotion to derision. Whiteness was idealized and despised at the same time; the black group was seen now as a haven and a refuge, now as a hated prison. There was inner turmoil, pain and tension. In Stonequist's words:

From an earlier, spontaneous identification with the white man, he has, under the rebuffs of categorical race prejudice, turned about and identified himself with the Negro race. In the process of so doing, he suffers a profound inner conflict. After all, does not the blood of the white man flow in his veins? Does he not share in the higher culture in common with the white American? And yet he finds himself condemned to a lower caste in the American system!

(1937)

The final phase of the life cycle was that of response or adjustment. The marginal condition of ambivalence could be permanent, but it could equally be a brief period of transition leading to a more stable period of identification and acceptance. Stonequist suggested three possibilities for this less volatile arrangement: assimilation into the dominant group, assimilation into the subordinate group, or 'some form of accommodation ... between the two groups' (Stonequist, 1937). Assimilation into the subordinate group, as either a community leader or as a mediator between the black and white groups, was the most obvious choice for the American 'mulatto'. Education and an intimate knowledge of white affairs meant that 'lighter-coloured' Negroes were often regarded as spokespeople for the black community.

In becoming a champion of the Negro cause, the marginal individual relinquished all claims to membership of the white group. By throwing themselves into the defence of the Negro people, they could objectify their own rejection by whites. The personal issue was redefined as a group issue, and all energy could then be directed towards overthrowing the oppressive rule of the dominant group. The role of intermediary also involved identification with the minority group, but here there was more sense of security and of real belonging. 'Mulattos', who became intermediaries felt they had found their 'true identity' as black and now wished to resolve the group conflict peacefully. The marginal individual, in their capacity as 'interpreter, conciliator, reformer, teacher', sublimated the wider cultural conflict and used their insight into the two cultures to promote better understanding between them.

Stonequist's (1937) description of the marginal personality and its application to the American 'mulatto' has undoubtedly influenced the modern sociological view of mixed race people. Kenneth Little referred to the mixed race adolescents he interviewed in Cardiff as 'typical marginal men' (Little, 1972). More recently, Benson (1981) has used the concept to sum up the position of interracial families in Britain. Yet Stonequist's influence is perhaps more general than specific. Marginality, like the whole 'problem' view of mixed race children, appeals to sociologists' sense of the tensions which exist between the individual and society. Research on marginality legitimized what many sociologists already believed to be the case: that, when a group of people falls foul of society's rigid categorization system, the only possible outcome is for the individual to suffer a crisis of identity.

It is curious that in the plethora of literature which followed Park and Stonequist there was almost exclusive emphasis on the sufferings of marginal people rather than on the creative potential of the role. One reason for this may be that sociologists themselves occupy an ambiguous place in society and so have an intuitive understanding of the problems such a position entails. Having felt the pressures of being detached from society merely through being sociologists, they have perhaps a greater tendency to exaggerate the predicament of people whose in-betweenness is more visible and more obvious. What is seen to be creative tension in our own lives can easily be thought of as destructive schism in the lives of others. This is merely conjecture; a more demonstrable argument is that the description of British mixed race people as 'marginal' is part of a much wider influence of US ideas on British race relations theory. In the next chapter it will be suggested that the 'problem' perspective on British mixed race people is intimately bound up with an essentially American model of the racial structure. The model dictates that British racial categorization is strictly dichotomous and that British people conceive of their identity purely in terms of 'black' and 'white'.

Chapter Two

Who Thinks in Terms of Black and White?

'Identity' is a vague and all-embracing label for a subject which has been the focus of a vast amount of social and psychological research. As David Milner says: 'The term "identity" has been a repository for a variety of imprecise ideas about what people are and how they see themselves. It has been all things to all theorists' (Milner, 1975).

When people say that mixed race children have 'identity problems', what they usually mean is that mixed race children have problems fitting themselves into socially defined categories; more specifically, that the children have difficulty discovering where they belong in relation to the black and to the white group. When 'identity' is used in this sense, it is being viewed from an *interactionist*, rather than from a purely psychological, perspective. It refers not to some aspect of intrinsic personality, but to the 'social self'. The racial identity of mixed race children is seen as the result of a complex interaction between *individual* and *social* definition.

As children develop in social awareness, they come to realize that who or what they are to some extent depends on how society defines them. In the words of E. Hughes: 'All societies emphasize some series of individual characteristics and assign people social identities accordingly. A good deal of each person's inner drama is discovery of the identity given him by others and his reactions to it and to the people who define him so' (Hughes and Hughes, 1952). The dictates of society become an intrinsic, though distinct, part of each child's identity. Berger and Luckmann describe this as being when 'a segment of the self is objectified in terms of the socially available typifications. This segment is truly the "social self", which is subjectively perceived as distinct from

21

and even confronting the self in its totality' (Berger and Luckmann, 1966). The process by which identity is formed comes both from within the individual and from society. It entails 'a dialectic between identification by others and self-identification, between objectively assigned and subjectively appropriated identity' (Berger and Luckman, 1966).

Some 'objectively assigned' identities are more central to the self than others. Whereas some attributes are important in only one circumscribed sphere ('consumer', 'commuter', 'confidant(e) to a friend') other are more relevant in nearly all social situations. Race, like age and sex, is one of the latter 'core' attributes which are significant in almost every social encounter. Race forms a consistent part of the ongoing sense of self which individuals abstract from social situations. The task which confronts mixed race children (and, indeed, all children in our society) is to unravel the complexities of British racial classification and then to locate the 'racial typification' which best applies to them. All children in Britain are expected to have some knowledge of racial classification and to be able to locate themselves 'accurately' within the racial structure.

But the complication to this process is that society does not present all racial ·identities as equally desirable. Only whiteness tends to guarantee status, value and material reward. This means that children have not only to find out where society places them racially, but also to reconcile this definition with what they themselves would like to be. Thus, mixed race children's identity problems may be of two kinds. They may result from being unable to extract a clear-cut identity from society's categorization system; or their identity problems, like those of black children, may come from a desire to belong to a more valued category than the one to which white society assigns them.

Racial identity, then, is a process of negotiation between the individual and those in the immediate social environment, the idea being to reconcile society's view of a person's social position with the individual's own conception of self. A *successful* outcome to this process must be defined as one which is both psychologically satisfying for the individual *and* socially approved: one which maintains a congruence between the socially defined and the subjectively appropriated identity. At the very least, a successful racial identity must be tolerable for the individual and acceptable to society; at best, it provides the individual with high levels of self-esteem while simultaneously satisfying the rigid, ordering impetus of the wider racial structure. This ideal identity can be described as one which is both *socially and psychologically*

22

viable – where *social viability* refers to the constraints imposed upon an individual's identification by the racial structure, and *psychological viability* is defined as the limitations stemming from the individual's personality and threshold of psychological resistance.

For the sociologist who wishes to study racial identity, the first task is to establish what constitutes a viable racial identity for the group or individuals in question. Before he or she can do this, the sociologist must first have a clear idea of which categories are 'available' for racial identity choice in that particular society. Certain prior assumptions must be made about the number and names of categories which are in current usage and also about the pecking order of those categories.

It became clear in the previous chapter that most identity researchers in Britain worked with a dichotomous model of the British system of racial thought. They assumed that, because *institutionalized racism* was structured in a dualistic way, most people also *thought* in terms of two racial categories and that they saw identity in terms of a choice between 'black' and 'white'. According to these sociologists, the only viable identity for mixed race children was for them to consider themselves members of the black group. Basing their assumptions on the US literature, most researchers argued that, since mixed race children would not be accepted by the white group as white, their best source of self-esteem would be a black identity. The warmth of black strength and black unity would protect them, together with other 'black' children, from the chill of white exclusion. Preliminary investigation, in the form of conversations with a number of interracial families who were not included in the study, made me uneasy about this assumption that the racial identity choices of people in Britain were identical to those of Americans. The mixed race children and adults I spoke to did not seem to see their identity that way. Terms such as 'brown', 'mixed race', 'half English, half Jamaican' cropped up regularly in their conversations. Moreover, these terms appeared to describe identities which had meaning and significance to the people who used them. I was also surprised at the lack of consensus about using the term 'black'. It was 1979, yet many of the black, white and mixed race people I spoke to still found 'coloured' a more acceptable term for people who were not white. The idea that British racial categorization is both varied and confused was borne out by the comments of the mothers who took part in the study (see Chapter 6). Collectively, they provided no less than three distinct meanings of the term 'black', and their feelings about the term ranged from vehement dislike to complete approval.

This chapter looks briefly at the historical and theoretical origins of current sociological assumptions about British racial thought and suggests that they can provide only a partial view of the total range of racial identities which are possible in Britain today. The black/white model appears to cover only those aspects of British racial categorization which come closest to the US experience. Later on in the chapter, some modifications to this model of British racial categorization are suggested which make it more appropriate to the empirical study of the mixed race identity in Britain.

The Dichotomous Racial Structure: the United States and Britain

Since the first Negro slaves arrived in the European colonies, America has been a dichotomous society, divided into a white and a black group. The slave economy was based on this distinction. From the beginning, blackness in American was the unmistakable mark of oppression – the symbol of a life spent in harsh servitude, propping up the edifice of white affluence and power. In the USA today, the categories used in racial *thought* follow the historical antecedents of the country's racial *system*; 'one drop' of Negro blood makes a person socially black, unless that person chooses to 'pass' as white.

Yet racial *thought* in the USA has not always followed the black/white pattern. In the eighteenth and early nineteenth centuries the offspring of white planters and black female slaves occupied a distinct intermediate category in US society which was greatly favoured by the dominant class. It was not unknown for a white father to provide education, freedom and even property for his 'mulatto' child. Joel Williamson (1980), in his recent historical study of the American 'mulattos', suggested that the distinction which was made by whites between 'Negroes' and 'mulattos' was not just a quirk of racial labelling; in the South, it meant real differences between the two groups in terms of status, education and wealth:

Before 1850 in South Carolina and in the lower South generally the master class was at the same time especially harsh upon the black slave class and especially lenient toward the relatively few free mulattoes. In short, mulattoness did count, real distinctions were made, and the one-drop rule did not always prevail. Before 1850 race relations in the lower South partook of the character of race relations among its Latin American and especially its West Indian neighbors, where the harshest slavery somehow bred the greatest freedom for free mulattoes and mulattoes used their freedom to purchase and achieve white culture.

(Williamson, 1980)

The rest of America had, according to Williamson, arrived at the 'one-drop' rule much earlier – in the case of most states, in the early eighteenth century. But in the South, whites seem to have felt secure enough in their slave economy to be able to make certain categorical concessions. The presence of 'white blood' in Negro bodies was acknowledged in a series of finely graded categorizations – 'mulatto', 'quadroon', 'octaroon' – and different levels of status were assigned accordingly.

The racial categorization system of the lower South came in line with that of the rest of the USA after 1850, as slavery disintegrated and US society went through the violent changes of industrialization and Civil War. White racism grew apace, and there was no longer any room for an intermediate status group, between black and white. Williamson describes the change thus:

Under heavy fire from a seemingly universal racism, the previous ambivalence of mulattoes towards both whites and blacks turned during the Civil War toward a steadily growing affinity with blacks. In Reconstruction the engagement of mulattoes and blacks was firmly cemented, though obvious vestigates of a preference for lightness lingered for two or three generations. By the 1920s the great mass of mulattoes saw their destiny as properly united only with that of their darker brothers and sisters. They saw themselves as fusing with blacks and together forming a whole people in embryo.

(Williamson, 1980)

The fusion of mulattos and Negroes resulted in the emergence of a new Negro group. Independent, educated and Americanized, Negroes of the 1930s evolved for themselves a unique blend of cultural traditions which was different from both their African and slave roots and the white mainstream. The Civil Rights movement of the 1950s and 1960s politicized this cultural development. What had been dubbed the 'brown' group in the 1930s now became the more vehement and self-affirming 'black'. The label proclaimed a group which was no longer prepared to be treated by whites as a political and economic underclass. American blacks declared themselves different from, but equal to, American whites. This, argues Williamson, brought about the emergence of 'the near perfect paradox in which white could be unblinkingly black. The drive for a biracial society had reached its culmination, finally not by white dictation, but rather by the eager embracement of "blackness" by American Negroes' (Williamson, 1980).

This 'near perfect' paradox is a constant source of surprise to foreigners having their first taste of US life. They are often puzzled by the number of people who are white, blue-eyed and Caucasian in appearance, yet define themselves as 'black' and move in an exclusively black social world. This is the 'one-drop' rule taken to its logical extreme. It is perhaps most poignantly illustrated by the story of an actress in Mississippi in the 1920s, who was to be charged with contravening the state's miscegenation laws by taking a blond, blue-eyed white lover. Just as the sheriff was about to arrest them both, the boy used his knife to prick the woman's finger and then sucked and swallowed some of her blood. The couple was allowed to go free because, as the sheriff had to admit, in Mississippi one drop of Negro blood made anyone a Negro.

The idea that *British* society is divided into a black and a white group is much more recent than the US 'one-drop' rule. Only in the last twenty years or so have historical contrasts between the USA and Britain given way to modern similarities which have led British theorists to make comparisons with the US race relations literature. When Commonwealth immigration was at its height in Britain in the 1950s and 1960s, the prevailing opinion among social scientists was that the position of 'the coloured immigrant' was quite different from that of the US Negro. The latter, they argued, was originally brought to the USA by force, in slavery and lived in the patriarchal atmosphere of the plantation; the former, on the other hand, was an immigrant who came voluntarily from Asia or the Caribbean to seek a measure of prosperity from the economic boom in Britain. The only common denominator between the two situations was the dark skin of the two minorities concerned, a fact which seems to be overshadowed by cultural and historical differences.

However, as the new generation of British-born 'coloureds' grew up, arguments explaining discrimination, prejudice and community tension in terms of cultural differences or 'strangeness' became less convincing. This was particularly true of the West Indian group who, it was argued, had a culture highly influenced by the British way of life even before they arrived. Unlike most Asians, the Caribbean minority spoke English as their first language and shared many moral and religious beliefs with the resident British. Faced with overt discrimination against 'coloured' immigrants alone, sociologists began to see the euphemistic nature of British 'cultural' classification. Whereas the Americans spoke directly of 'the Negro', the British hid their racial consciousness under the blanket conceptions of 'foreigners' and 'immigrants'. Persistent prejudice against the new minorities brought physical differences more and more into focus. British sociologists began to talk of *racial* prejudice and discrimination and, in recognition of the growing similarities between the countries, looked to US theories of race relations in the analysis of British society. As Michael Banton wrote in the late 1960s: 'Since the middle of the 1950s, the immigration perspective has become less appropriate to studies of the British scene and the racial one more so' (Banton, 1967).

In the 1950s sociologists wrote about 'coloured immigrants' 'Asians' and 'West Indians'. By the 1960s and 1970s they were writing of the 'black British community'. The change in terminology was due partly to the growing numbers of young black people who had been born in Britain, but the emphasis on 'community' came from black British radicals who had been influenced by the Black Power movement in the United States. The vibrancy and energy of US blacks who were confronting the social, legal and political strictures with which they had been shackled since Reconstruction spread like giant waves across the Atlantic. The slogans and banners of the black American struggle were taken up by West Indians and Africans in Britain and were used to expose the legendary 'British fairness' as a fraud. Britain, it was said, would go the way of the USA; ghettoes would form, and blacks would rise up against the system. Out of this constant linkage of the two countries, the oppressive legacies of each were crystallized into the present under one bold heading: white racism. No matter that the histories of these oppressive systems were different or that the people came from different social and cultural contexts; their experience here and now was the same: white hegemony, white racism.

By the 1970s the term 'black' had become the most acceptable description in British sociology for the 'non-white' groups. West Indians, Asians and Africans were viewed as one political entity – a black community – since all these groups suffered equally from white institutional racism. This model has proved largely satisfactory for the analysis of the way British racism works, but little thought has been given to how well it applies to the study of individual identity. The different ethnic groups may be similarly oppressed by racism, but how many 'black Britons' actually see themselves as members of a black community? And of those who do see themselves in these terms, how significant is the concept of blackness to the development of their self-esteem?

One of the first sociologists to recommend caution in pursuing the black/white theme too relentlessly in relation to British racial thought was Michael Banton. Although Banton was also among the first to see the applicability of US models of race relations to Britain, he apparently began to feel in the 1970s that the model was being used too uncritically. In 1979 he wrote: 'There has been a tendency to import into Britain the American terminology without, so far as I am aware, any serious public discussion of the circumstances and groups to which it is appropriate' (Banton, 1979). The term 'black', he argued, was adopted by research workers in deference to political activists within minority groups with whom they shared political sympathies. The activists believed that power for the new minorities in Britain could come only from unity and a common definition. If every 'non-white' person could be persuaded to identify as 'black' then a wide power base would be created which would prevent the 'divide-and-rule' tactics of the white majority. Yet Banton felt that for sociologists to adopt this tacit anticipation of a future collective black community was over-hasty in the light of the evidence. He suggested that observers of the British racial scene who expected a US-type racial polarity to develop in Britain were forgetting that, seen in a world perspective, the USA was a very special case. Banton warned: 'There is no more reason to expect Britain to take this course than for the society to develop a continuous scale of colour gradation like that in Brazil or parts of the Caribbean' (1979).

Banton has been concerned in recent years to urge sociologists to consider the implications and effects of the racial labels they use. To label all non-white people 'black' may challenge the white status quo, but it may not be an entirely accurate description of how people see themselves. Banton suggests a more circumspect approach:

When referring to youngsters of West Indian origin brought up in Britain it is often appropriate to refer to them as black . . . because the social and self-definition of them as black may be the main variable. This may not apply to their parents and it may not apply to Asian children. We should never reinforce the assumption that because individuals come from the same place or have similar complexions, they therefore think alike.

(Banton, 1979)

Comments in this vein have come not only from eminent sociologists but also from writers in the historical and political arenas. The Caribbean Marxist historian C. L. R. James, for example, made a similar point when writing about the report made by Lord Scarman in 1981 on the 'race riots' which had

28

occurred in Britain that summer. James criticized the parallels which were drawn in the report between Britain and the USA. Scarman had quoted an address by President Johnson to illustrate a point, and James countered: 'The report that President Johnson was introducing goes on to say that America is divided into two societies, one consisting of the white people and the other of the black. No such situation exists in Great Britain' (James, 1981). James argued that Lord Scarman, in taking the US model and applying it to Britain, was ignoring the sentiments of most white British people and their true reaction to the riots of summer 1981. He wrote:

They are disturbed and bewildered by what is happening but they are not in any way conscious that whites constitute one type of human being and blacks another in unalterable opposition to each other. If such a consciousness existed in Britain it would be obvious in Brixton. All evidence shows that it was not and is not.

(James, 1981)

In a rather different context from C. L. R. James, Robin White (1979) also argued that the British method of categorizing racial groups was radically different from the US system. He thought that the main difference was in the flexibility of racial divisions. In an article concerned with the problems of devising a question on ethnic origin for the 1981 census, White suggested that British racial categorization was in fact very confused and vague. Unlike the black/white division in the USA, which was governed by the 'one-drop' rule, British racial categorization drew on many different criteria. While categories such as 'black' and 'white' referred to 'race' and skin colour, other categories in current usage, such as 'West Indian', were strictly speaking territorial terms, and still others (such as 'Indian') denoted citizenship of a political state. When he analysed the various categories of response which had been suggested for the census, White discovered that at least six types of categorization criteria were being used: these were skin colour, territory, culture, nationality, religion and descent.

White (1979) suggested that the attempts of the census office to formalize British racial classification had exposed just how arbitrary and subjective the system was. Choice of ethnic criteria, said White, could be understood only in terms of the motive behind making the categorization in the first place. What the census question was actually trying to do was to count the population in accordance with the white British conception of 'us' and 'them'. The idea, in effect, was to establish how many 'thems' there were in the country; and yet, because the boundaries of this group were so ill defined, categorization proved extremely difficult. White's view of the essence of British racial classification was that it

divides the population into 'our group' (white), then tries to pin down as objective some swirling, inherently vague and contingent notions of groups distantly related to us and more or less distantly related to each other. Is the Turk really one of us? West Indians are all black aren't they? (Or, if not, they're our group, not West Indians.)

(White, 1979)

Yet in the US racial system the census question would not be hard to devise; theoretically, one would have only to ask, 'Have you any Negro ancestors?' in order to set the officially correct white/black, us/them boundaries.

Racial identity research appears to require a rather more flexible and complex view of British racial classification than the simple black-or-white choice. If a sociologist wishes to gain the fullest possible insight into racial identity, then he or she must be in tune with the wide variety of ways in which people experience their racial identity choice. The next section puts forward a modified version of the dualistic model of British thought – one which seems more appropriate to the study of racial identity. It must be stressed again that this is not a replacement for the black/white model of institutionalized racism, but a perspective which is complementary to it. In a study such as the present one of the identity of mixed race children, one is concerned with *the categories children use to express their ethnic loyalties*, rather than with the crude categories employed by whites to implement racial discrimination.

Racial Categorization in Britain

To be 'black' or 'coloured' in Britain means to be 'non-white'. Whether a person is Asian or West Indian, Negroid or Caucasian, light or dark-skinned, is irrelevant compared with the basic distinction between white and non-white; everyone acknowledges this to be meaningful and significant. This distinction is not however one which is 'agreed' in the sense that it was formulated and ratified by both groups equally. The white/non-white dichotomy stems from the *white* group and it represents the wish of white people to put social distance between themselves and groups which they perceive to be 'different' and 'inferior'. What makes non-whiteness more than just a description 'invented' by whites (no more or less valid than a label set up by any other group) is that whites in Britain have the economic and social means to *impose* their negatively charged racial classification on the consciousness of the non-white groups.

As Robin White (1979) pointed out, some degree of inconsistency and confusion surrounds the racial classification of certain ethnic groups, such as Arabs, Cypriots, Jews, Iranians and Chinese. None the less, the boundary between white and non-white is clear enough to allow institutional racial bias to be implemented. All Caucasian British are sure that they are 'white' and equally sure that people of Indian or African extraction are not. And because of the structure of economic and power relations in Britain, this definition is perceived as 'true' by these groups. They are *not* white; it is a 'fact of life'.

Here then are the crude and somewhat ill-defined parameters of exclusion set out by whites, reflected in a dichotomous view of the British racial structure, which forms a basic part of the racial thought of all members of British society. I think it is useful, in terms of the analysis of children's identity which is to follow, to call the white/non-white distinction the *primary racial categorization* of British society and the choice children make between black and white the primary racial identification. The distinction between white and non-white is the most important in terms of its effect on people's lives for it has behind it the concrete power of racist action. When the term 'black' or 'coloured' is used to describe the categories on which racism is based it has only one meaning: not white.

Yet common sense suggests that this is not the only racial distinction which is made by people in Britain. There are innumerable ethnic and racial labels, both derogatory and non-derogatory, which are in ordinary, everyday usage – terms such as 'West Indian', 'brown', 'Asian', 'Indian', 'fair-skinned', 'immigrant', and 'half-caste'. Even the labels used to describe the non-white group can be used to mean something different. 'Coloured' is used by some people to refer to only one section of the non-white group such as light-skinned people (see mother's comments in Chapter 6); and of course 'black' is employed as a statement of political and ethnic affiliation – a positive affirmation of what one *is*, rather than an acceptance of what one is *not*.

These categories (and alternative meanings of category labels) can be seen as part of the *secondary racial categorization* which develops, within the limits set by the white/non-white structure, to conceptualize, evaluate, or express racial diversity more

31

precisely. The distinction between these two types of category is not clear-cut (terms such as 'black' and 'coloured' span both types), but it is perhaps a more appropriate model through which to interpret British mixed race children's identity. For many of the children in this study being of mixed race had a reality and an importance which could not be seen purely in black/white terms. They saw themselves as part of a positively valued black/mixed race group, a view which was made possible by the ethnic pecking order in their area.

The criteria by which secondary categories are delineated are by no means fixed. Labels vary both in the meaning they have for the people who use them and in the extent to which they are understood by the rest of society. But because these labels are used in everyday thought and conversation about race, they often provide the most salient vehicles for the articulation of racial identity. In other words, although British society as a whole operates on the crude and slightly blurred distinction between white and non-white, for many people this is just the starting-point for the construction of more detailed, evaluative non-white classifications. These are employed in specific social situations towards the achievement of a particular end.

For white people, the motive to categorize further may be a desire to reject some non-white groups more than others. In racist invective, one often hears different groups being put forward as either more or less acceptable to whites than the non-white group as a whole. White people sometimes state that they 'don't mind the coloured but don't like black youths' or that they 'quite like West Indians, but don't like Pakistanis'. Other whites may continue to reject all non-white groups equally, but still recognize secondary categories to stress that the groups are unacceptable for different reasons. A stereotype which is often used to legitimate prejudice against West Indians is that they are 'noisy' or 'unruly'; whereas Asians are more likely to be rejected on the grounds of 'taking jobs' or because of 'strange' religious and cultural practices.

The oppressed groups use secondary categories for a variety of reasons. The use of the term 'black' as a challenge to the white-imposed primary categorization, and as a protector of self-esteem, has already been discussed. Another way of protecting self-esteem, which is the political antithesis of uniting under the term 'black', is to define *degrees of non-whiteness* within the black group. Some groups do this in order to declare that white rejection applies more to others than to themselves. For example, older West Indians who were brought up to think in terms of the

Caribbean colour class system often reject the idea that all 'coloured' people are 'black'; they see 'fair-skinned' people as closer to white than dark-skinned people and therefore to be placed on a higher status level. Some minority groups in Britain also adopt secondary category sets to demarcate boundaries between themselves and people towards whom they are traditionally, or newly, hostile. Asians tend to dissociate themselves from Afro-Caribbeans and vice versa; but the 'Asian' group is itself cross-cut by regional, cultural and religious divisions — ethnic legacies from the past — which are subjectively perceived as important descriptions of ethnicity.

The criteria by which secondary characteristics are distinguished depend upon the situation in which they are used and on the motives which prompted the categorization in the first place. 'Black' in its political sense refers to people who are oppressed by white because they have a darker shade of skin. The category is defined broadly because its purpose is to unite all dark-skinned oppressed groups, irrespective of their cultural and geographical origins. Other secondary categories (often fitted 'into' the category of black) may be defined more specifically. Their aim is to pin-point ethnic identity more precisely — to provide a more finely tuned set of self-descriptions which can be applied to each situation in which ethnicity is relevant.

Susan Benson provides a good illustration of this 'situational' character of ethnicity, in her study of interracial families in Brixton (1981). Benson analysed the secondary identities of a West Indian member of her sample — Mr Jimmy Brown, a Jamaican:

Take, for example, the individual case of Mr Jimmy Brown, born in the parish of Clarendon, Jamaica. Within his intimate circle of kin and friends, most of them also from Clarendon, ethnic identity was not a significant factor. As a customer in the local 'Caribbean' bakery, however, he was a Negro Jamaican buying bread from a 'babu man', an Asian Jamaican. In the West Indian-run drinking club where he spent a good deal of his leisure time he was a Jamaican amongst a circle of Guyanese, Trinidadians and Barbadians . . . At his workplace, a paper factory in outer south London, he was a West Indian in a workforce of Africans, English, Asians and Irish. Yet in speaking of the difficulties in finding a house, he chose to define himself differently again: 'It is hard for a coloured man to find somewhere to live in this country.'

(Benson, 1981)

The idea that ethnic categorization in Britain is not a fixed division between black and white, but is a circumspect manipulation of a variety of different criteria, can be found in the work of a number

33

of sociologists. Sandra Wallman (1979), for example, described ethnicity as a flexible shifting boundary between 'us' and 'them', where the boundary shifts because the criteria considered appropriate for distinguishing between 'us' and 'them' are not the same at all times and in all situations. Wallman emphasized that even within a dominant/subordinate structure, where the dominant group had the power to *define* the boundaries of all other groups, there were still two sides to an ethnic boundary and hence two perspectives from which to view ethnicity at work. Her aim in using this approach, she said, was to convey a sense of the *process* of racial categorization, to show that it was a dynamic negotiation between two groups, each of whom was trying to achieve its own ends through the social encounter. Ethnic boundaries can rise up and fade, bend, break and change: 'Depending on the perception of the actors and the constraints and opportunities of the context in which they act, ethnicity may be an essential resource, an utter irrelevance or a crippling liability' (Wallman, 1979).

Another point about secondary categorization is that it probably varies not just from situation to situation but also from place to place. Area may be an important factor in determining which racial categories are socially available for racial identification. In Banton's view: 'The categories commonly employed are likely to reflect whichever minority among the coloured immigrant population is most numerous or attracts the most attention' (Banton, 1979). But this, he warned, was not a matter on which safe assumptions could be made: 'The process by which racial categories are developing requires empirical investigation sensitive to local variations and is not a matter upon which it is safe to generalize from theoretical principles or American parallels' (Banton, 1979).

Finding and Keeping a Racial Identity

The idea that British racial categorization is more complex than a clear-cut, black/white dichotomy is relevant not just for the study of the identity of mixed race children but for that of all children in British society. It is not being suggested here that only mixed race children, because of the potential ambiguity of their position, have access to these secondary categories; all children and adults are faced with a range of categories and criteria from which they must construct a viable racial identity.

It would appear that those researchers who drew on marginality theory and on the 'problem' perspective to analyse the position of mixed race children in Britain did not use a full enough picture of the racial categorization system. They chose instead to see only those features which were like the United States system; in effect, they imposed a US framework on British racial thought. Because of this, the choices with which mixed race children were faced seemed more stark and seemed to have more potential for conflict and personality disorganization than perhaps they contained. Certainly, mixed race children *do* have to choose between black (non-white) and white, and this may cause more problems for them than for black children, because one of their parents is white. But beyond this, the child has access to secondary categories (only research can say how many and what they are) offering the means to salvage and protect their damaged self-esteem, which results from the negative, exclusively and residually defined primary categorization. Curiously, the post-Stonequist marginality theorists in the USA seemed to have realized this when trying to fit the marginality framework to the American Jews. Although these researchers agreed with Park and Stonequist (1937) that there was an intrinsic conflict between a black and a white identity, they were none the less puzzled by the ability of other ethnic groups to juggle successfully with apparently conflicting ethnic loyalties. Their conclusions about Jews in the USA are similar to those put forward here about black and mixed race people in Britain.

Aaron Antonovsky (1956), who made a study of the identity of a group of male second-generation Jews, found that individual responses to the marginal situation varied considerably. They appeared to lie on a continuum from active involvement in being Jewish, through ambivalent and dual identity to active participation in Gentile life. Only one of these – the ambivalent response – conformed to Stonequist's marginal reaction. Antonovsky concluded that it was possible for some individuals to construct for themselves a socially and psychologically viable solution to an apparently irreconcilable ethnic dilemma. His conclusion was that within the Jewish/Gentile dichotomy there are other identity choices expressing different levels of involvement with each culture. There are various *ways* of being Jewish, Gentile, or both which individuals find both satisfying and liveable.

Golovensky (1951–2) took this argument further by suggesting that Park (1937) had overestimated the extent to which the American/non-American division restricted people's identity. According to Park, the 'average American' had only *one* tradition to follow which embraced *one* loyalty, and this unassailable Americanism gave him a sense of certainty and belonging. But this, argued Golovensky, was 'an idealization of American culture, not a realistic picture or definition of it. Americanism is not a mono-lithic organism but rather a pluralistic mosaic, a congeries of conflicting and contradictory values' (Golovensky, 1951–2). Golovensky suggested that to see the American Jewish identity as a clear-cut choice between one category and the other was to underestimate both the complexity of US ethnic classification and the individual's capacity for dealing with it. Jews, he said, can be Jewish all the time and American all the time without encounter-ing any adverse effects.

It would be rather far-fetched to suggest that mixed race children in Britain can be 'black all the time and white all the time' without experiencing any identity conflict. But it may well be that black and white are both *elements* in their racial identity which can be played up or down according to context. Being of mixed race need not mean feeling torn between the black and white groups all the time; the concept of being of mixed race may provide a viable secondary identification in its own right which gives the child a sense of belonging and self-esteem. Other secondary identifications might also override the potential for black/white conflict in the child's sense of self. If identities such as 'brown', 'half West Indian', 'half black' are supported by people around the child, they may become adequate vehicles for the expression of a satisfactory racial identity.

So how does a British mixed race child develop a socially and psychologically viable racial identity? First, mixed race children, like all children in Britain, are faced with the question of whether they belong to the white or to the non-white group. In terms of how society views them, this question is not hard to answer. Unless they are extremely light and Caucasian in appearance, they will be viewed as a member of the non-white group. All the mothers who were interviewed in the study acknowledged this, regardless of which identity they saw as the 'true' one for their children. The white/non-white line is a heavily guarded social barrier, and having one white parent is not deemed a sufficient entitlement to cross it.

In psychological terms, this enforced negative identification (*not* white) presents problems to mixed race children just as it does to black children. Whiteness is linked indelibly with wealth, status and success, whereas non-whiteness is an exclusion from these things on the arbitrary grounds of 'race' and skin colour. Society's negative view of blackness becomes internalized as a negative view of self and can give rise to the well-documented symptoms of 'self-hate' (see Chapter 3). Some of the mixed race children who were tested in the study showed signs of being affected by this; they pointed to a lighter skin shade as their 'ideal' colour; they spontaneously expressed dissatisfaction with their appearance and endorsed negative stereotypes of the black group. Emotionally, it is a hard fact for mixed race children to grasp that their one white parent makes little difference to how they are treated in a racist system.

Secondly, however, mixed race children, like everyone else in British society, have a certain amount of *choice* about their racial identity. They have the power to construct a more detailed view of their ethnicity through negotiation with others in their immediate environment. Moreover, it is possible for them to juggle with any number of secondary identification categories – emphasizing some but not other aspects of their ethnicity, *without denying the enforced reality of their non-whiteness*. Provided such criteria are seen as legitimate by people in their social milieu (and, in particicular, by their parents) mixed race children's definitions of themselves may include ideas of 'mixture' or of being located between the black and the white group. In the present study, this was particularly true of children who lived in multiracial areas and whose parents and peers supported their 'mixed' identity.

The psychological viability of the secondary identification will depend on the extent to which each category is positively valued by the child. 'Non-white' may be transformed into 'black' with the help of an environment which promotes a strong, positive view of blackness. 'Being of mixed race' may also be seen as something good if the child sees other mixed race people taking pride in their unique dual heritage.

The various combinations and connotations of the categories which make up a child's identity can be discovered only by research. But if secondary identification is possible at all for mixed race children in Britain, their plight may be a far cry from the 'tortured misfit' image which emerges from US marginality theory.

Chapter Three

The 'Doll' Studies and the Present Study

The study with which this book is concerned belongs to a long line of research which started with an investigation of the racial identity of black American children by Kenneth and Mamie Clark in 1939. The Clarks used visual aids (black and white dolls) to elicit children's racial identification and preference. Today, their conclusions are well known; they suggested that many black children had a negative view of themselves and that they showed, through a consistent preference for the white over the black doll, a passionate desire to be white. Many studies of black children's identity have been conducted since the Clarks'. Some have confirmed their results, some have contradicted them and some have challenged aspects of their research methods. But each has added a small piece to the fragmented picture we have of the way black children see themselves. Studies since the Clarks have suggested several factors which can influence black children's identity, such as age, sex, skin colour and the area in which the child lives.

Readers who are familiar with the British and US doll studies and their findings may wish to skip this part of the chapter and to move on to the description of the research problem and method of the present study. Those who are not familiar with them will find this review of the literature a useful introduction to how the study of mixed race children was designed. Although the doll studies used the dichotomous black-or-white view of identity and so could not be applied to the present study without some modification, they provided a basic method for investigating the racial identity of young children and they also suggested various factors which might affect the racial identity of British mixed race children. For these reasons they are an essential part of the background to the study.

Black Children's Identity: the Doll Studies

In the early part of the twentieth century most people believed that children were oblivious to racial differences. Childhood was seen as a time of racial innocence, when infants chose their play-mates without any reference to the colour of their skin. However, in 1929, Bruno Lasker published the first study of children's racial attitudes, hoping to shed light on the process by which white people became prejudiced against Negroes and other minorities. Lasker elicited the opinions and observations of adults on preju-dice in children through the distribution of questionnaires to social and church discussion groups (Lasker, 1929) His results convinced him of two things: first, that racial prejudice *was* present in children to the extent of influencing their behaviour; secondly, that those around the child (and the parents in particu-lar) played a crucial role in *teaching* racial bias.

Although Lasker's conclusions are popular wisdom today, their impact at the time and their importance for understanding the social conditions in which prejudice develops should not be underestimated. Racial prejudice, which had hitherto been regar-ded as an abstract social evil, was suddenly exposed as a real-life process of persecution operating even at the level of young child-ren. For the first time it was recognized that, far from being inno-cent and insulated from such things, children reproduced the racial hatred and tension of adult society amongst themselves. Their games mirrored the manoeuvres of their parents, and their interracial relationships reflected those they saw in the commu-nity.

Not long after this pioneer piece of research, two further innovative steps were taken. Social scientists began to talk to the children themselves rather than to adults, and the field of interest was widened to include the development of racial attitudes and the self-image of *black* children. This first methodological shift came from a recognition that listening to what adults say about children is less reliable than listening to the children themselves, since an adult's knowledge of a particular child's attitude is often partial and distorted. The second move was strongly influenced by Cooley's 'looking-glass self' (1902) and by the concept of the 'significant mother' (Mead, 1934). Sociologists began to wonder how black children could develop a 'normal' (positive) self-image in a society where their race was undervalued. If white children were so quick to learn the prejudice of their parents then the 'looking-glass self' of black children would be negative. The key question was whether or not black children internalized the negative images held by white children, to become, in effect, 'prejudiced against themselves'.

The most influential research team studying black children's identity in the 1930s and 1940s was undoubtedly Kenneth and Mamie Clark (1939, 1947). Their researches are often referred to now as the classic studies of black children's identity, and their results have served as a reference-point for most of those that followed. However, the research method used by the Clarks was a technique devised earlier by the Horowitzes, another husband-and-wife team, who were interested in tracing the development of prejudice in white children towards 'Negroes'. For the purposes of their study of prejudice, the Horowitzes needed to design a method which could be used to tap the racial attitudes of children from kindergarten to early teens (E. L. Horowitz, 1936).

The three tests the Horowitzes devised – the 'ranks test', the 'show-me test' and the 'social situations test' – used pictures as aids to verbal communication and were suitable for use even with very young children. The basic idea was to ask white children to rank photographs of black and white children in order of preference, to provide a measure of the relative acceptability of 'Negroes' and whites as playmates to their subjects. In addition, they used photographs of posed situations (such as having lunch and choosing teams), in both all-white and mixed settings, in order to test their respondents' attitudes to the 'segregated' and the 'integrated' contexts. It was hoped that the children would respond to the photographs as if they were actual people and that they would treat each activity as if it were being offered as an immediate, real-life option.

In a later, smaller-scale study, the Horowitzes attempted to adapt the technique to the study of racial identity (Horowitz, 1939). They showed respondents portrait pictures of black and white children and asked them to choose the ones they thought they most resembled. Ruth Horowitz made explicit what she hoped to gain by using this picture technique rather than questioning the children directly. The study was designed, she said,

to get at children's ideas about themselves, at a phase of development when the children can communicate them, and when the ideas might still be conceived to be in the process of formation ... An attempt was made to get below the level of active language, to utilise the vast reservoir of understanding which comes before the organisation of verbal expression, the child's fund of passive language ... The child needed only to be able to understand the investigation, be willing to co-operate, able to make the choice requested, and point or nod. Most of the subjects fulfilled all the qualifications.

(R. Horowitz, 1939)

The contribution of the Horowitzes to the study of the young black identity was to introduce this simple technique, which provided an easy channel of communication with children on an extremely sensitive subject. It was simple to administer and quick, needed little specialised equipment and introduced racial issues to children in what appeared to be a non-threatening way. Moreover, it was a method which could be used to study almost every aspect of children's racial attitudes – including racial identity.

Kenneth and Mamie Clark (1939, 1947) adapted and developed the picture technique to focus more specifically on the racial identity of *black* children. The Clarks, themselves black Americans, were convinced that the US racist system provided an unhealthy environment for the development of the black child's self-image. White children, they argued, were surrounded by positive affirmations of the value of their whiteness; black children, on the other hand, were offered only negative images of blackness. According to the Clarks this could result only in a strong white bias which would be to the detriment of black children's identity.

The Clarks conceptualized racial identity as consisting of three separate but interrelated elements: racial awareness, racial preference and self-identification. Using a variation of the picture technique (employing dolls instead of photographs) the Clarks operationalized these variables into the form of a simple test. Each respondent was presented with four dolls, identical except for skin and hair colour (two had black skin/brown hair; two had white skin/fair hair). They were then asked eight questions. The first four questions were designed to reveal racial preferences by asking the children to attach value to the dolls' appearance and 'personality' – that is, which doll looked 'nice', 'naughty', 'pretty' and so on. The next three questions were attempts to test racial awareness; here the child was required to say which doll looked like 'a Negro', 'a coloured person' and 'a white person'. The final question asked the children to express self-identification through the dolls by pointing to the doll which looked 'most like' him- or herself.

In their 1947 study, the Clarks administered their doll test to a sample of 253 black American children. In their sampling, they controlled for the variables of age (3–7 years), skin colour (light, medium, or dark) and areas of residence (northern or southern

United States), since they considered all of these as likely to influence the racial identity of their respondents. The results from this test are well known and are still much quoted in sociological textbooks today. Although responses to the racial awareness section showed a high ability to distinguish between the races among these children, the racial preference measures indicated that the majority of respondents *preferred* the white doll and had a corresponding distaste for the brown doll. The racial self-identification question elicited a result which caused even more consternation among social observers of the time; a high proportion of the black children in the sample maintained that it was the white doll which they most closely resembled. The Clarks concluded that these black American children had internalized the negative view of their race which was actively promulgated by their society. The deprecation of Negroes in US life had led to a damaged racial identity and an undervaluation of self among black children. Moreover, according to the Clarks' findings, this was true of both the North and the South of the United States.

The racial awareness results of this study pushed back the age of 'racial innocence' even further, for even the 3-year-olds were able to distinguish between the white and the brown dolls. From the point of view of racial classification in the 1940s USA, it is interesting that the term 'coloured' elicited a more accurate response from the children than the label 'Negro'; 93 per cent of subjects chose the brown doll when the classification 'coloured' was offered in contrast to 72 per cent for the term 'Negro'. However, the Clarks explained the discrepancy in terms of age. 'Negro' was apparently a more complex concept to grasp, and understanding of it increased with age. The most rapid progression in racial awareness seemed to occur after the age of 5 years, when the child had entered school. The Clarks concluded that

These data indicate that a basic knowledge of 'racial differences' exists as part of the pattern of ideas of Negro children from the age of three through seven years in the northern and southern communities tested in this study – and that this knowledge develops more definitely from year to year to the point of absolute stability at the age of seven.

(Clark and Clark, 1947)

Response to the first four questions designed to measure racial preference showed that approximately two-thirds of the Clarks' sample preferred the white doll to the brown doll; this was the one they judged to be 'nice', 'a nice colour' and the one with which they would like to play. Correspondingly, two-thirds of the sample indicated that the brown doll 'looked bad'. At each age, from 3 to 7 years, the majority of children in the sample showed a preference for the white doll, although this bias did seem to decrease as the child got older.

The self-identification question ('Which doll looks like you?') elicited misidentification from one-third of the research sample – 33 per cent identified themselves with the white doll while 66 per cent said they looked like the 'coloured' doll. The Clarks also noted that this question brought some extreme emotional reactions among the children they tested. Subjects who were relaxed and cheerful at the beginning of the experiment became resistant and tearful when asked to make a self-identification choice. As with preference for the white doll, misidentification generally decreased with age; at age 7, only 15 per cent identified with the white doll, compared with 33 per cent in the sample as a whole.

No statistically significant differences were found between northern and southern children in awareness, preference, or identification. However, of particular interest were the results on skin shade, which showed that light children were less likely than darker children to identify with the brown doll. Whereas 81 per cent of the dark children chose the brown doll in response to the question 'Which doll looks like you?', 73 per cent of the medium and only 20 per cent of the lighter children made this choice (see Table 3.1). The main difference was between the light group and the combined medium and dark groups, leading the Clarks to conclude that 'some of the factors and dynamics involved in racial identification are substantially the same for the dark and medium children, in contrast to dynamics for the light children' (Clark and Clark, 1947). Skin colour was also found to influence racial *preference*; a greater proportion of lighter children favoured the white doll on the preference question.

Table 3.1 *'Which Doll Looks Like You?'*

| | Children | | |
	Light	Medium	Dark
Brown	20%	74%	81%
White	80%	26%	19%
Total	100%	100%	100%

Source: Clark and Clark, 1947.

The Clarks' conclusion from this study, accepted by many socio-logists today, was that the combination of awareness of racial differences (as indicated by doll choice), preference for the white doll and yet the inability or unwillingness to identify with the coloured doll, indicated a wish to be white on the part of these black children and a corresponding rejection of Negritude and self. In a later publication, Kenneth Clark was unequivocal in his interpretation of why this should be so:

The fact that young Negro children would prefer to be white reflects their knowledge that society prefers white people. White children are generally found to prefer their white skin – an indication that they too know that society likes whites better. It is clear, therefore, that the self-acceptance or self-rejection found so early in a child's developing complex of racial ideas reflects the awareness and acceptance of prevailing racial attitudes in his community.

(Clark, 1955)

Further Studies of Black Children's Identity

Over the last thirty years there have been many replications of the Clarks' investigations of black children's identity. Some quite recent reviewers of this vast literature, surveying the confusing array of studies using different methods, settings and samples, have concluded that black children still exhibit some tendency to prefer white dolls to black ones (Brand, Ruiz and Padilla, 1974; Simon, 1974; Teplin, 1977). None the less, many social scientists would argue that there has been a marked decrease in black children's out-group preference over the last ten to fifteen years, as a result of the Black Consciousness movement of the 1960s and 1970s.

What seems to have happened in the 1960s and 1970s is that black children's tendency to *identify themselves* as white has decreased rapidly, whereas their *preference* for the white race has been more slow to change. The Black Consciousness movement seems to have heightened children's awareness of their blackness and to have eliminated all shame in declaring 'who they are'; but it has not made them less conscious of the advantages of being white. The two major British studies completed in the last fifteen years tend to confirm the trend towards a greater degree of own-group identification among black children. David Milner's investigation, conducted in the late 1960s, obtained similar results to those of the Clarks (Milner, 1975), whereas the recent Davey and Norburn study (1980) underlined the changes noticed by researchers in the USA. Although black children now tend to identify with their own group at a relatively early age, they still show white orientation on the preference section of the test. Davey and Norburn interpreted the discrepancy between the identification and preferences responses as indicating that, although minority groups have been successful in developing a greater sense of black pride in their children, this has also sharpened their awareness of racial inequality: 'self-pride and self-enhancement necessitate comparison with the dominant group, which has led to a keener appreciation of the more favourable status of the white majority and the unequal competition for higher living standards and job opportunities (Davey and Norburn, 1980).

As well as showing the changes in black children's identity which have taken place over the last three decades, more recent studies have improved on those of the Clarks in two main ways. First, heavy criticism of the doll method has resulted in a number of changes in the way the identity test is conducted. The dolls, for instance, are now more carefully matched to the children so that each subject has an identity model of their own sex, skin shade and hair type. Secondly, a considerable amount of work has been done to establish how various factors influence the children's choice of dolls. Investigations since the Clarks have studied the subjects' socioeconomic level and their parents' attitudes as well as the influence of their age, sex and skin shade.

It is important to look more closely at these areas – methodology and variables related to identity – because they both contributed to the way the present investigation of mixed race children was devised. The method used in the present study benefited from improvements made since the Clarks, and many of the variables which have been found to influence black children's identity are likely to affect that of mixed race children in exactly the same way.

Methodology

Some of the most critical doubts which have been expressed about studies of ethnic identification and preference have been concerned with the nature of the materials used in the tests. The point at issue is the internal validity of the method – that is, whether studies which elicit children's attitudes to inanimate representations of different races are actually measuring their real-life racial attitudes.

Jones (1972) among others has put forward the very basic suggestion that children of both races are relatively unfamiliar with brown-skinned dolls. Even now (and certainly when the Clarks conducted their study) there are very few black dolls available commercially, and Jones suggested that a bias against the 'unusual toy', rather than a detection of racial difference, may partially account for the unpopularity of dark-skinned dolls in preference tests. However, this explanation cannot take us very far, since it rests on the somewhat shaky assumption that children recoil from unfamiliar toys. It also skates over the more serious problem of why black dolls are uncommon and what this fact may have already communicated to the children about the 'unattractiveness' of dark-skinned dolls.

A more penetrating criticism raises doubts about whether the young respondents in the studies were associating differences between the stimuli they were given with actual *racial* differences. The Clarks were aware of this difficulty but they made their position on it quite clear; the characteristics of skin, eye and hair colour between the two sets of dolls were being used as indicators of the totality of racial differences in real people. The attitudes expressed by the children towards a particular doll were therefore taken to be their attitudes *to people of the race that the doll represented*:

Our evidence that the responses of these children *do* indicate a knowledge of 'racial difference' comes from several sources: the results from other techniques used (a coloring test and a questionnaire) and from the qualitative data obtained (children's spontaneous remarks) strongly support a knowledge of 'racial differences'.

(Clark and Clark, 1947)

Yet it has been argued that the contrast between a yellow- and a brown-haired doll (regardless of skin colour) is enough to bring out a bias which bears little relation to prejudice commonly designated as 'racial'. Aesthetic beauty, in most Western countries, is associated with blond(e) hair and blue eyes – the 'Nordic look' – and this may help to explain why the white (blond(e)-haired) doll was consistently preferred.

This was one of the arguments put forward by Katz and Zalk (1974) in a study designed to test the salience of the single characteristic of skin colour in children's doll choices. Using brown-haired and brown-eyed dolls which were identical except for skin colour (one brown, one white) and asking the same questions as the Clarks, these researchers found that both black and white children's preferences departed little from chance and that both groups identified themselves accurately. They concluded that 'Children, like the proverbial "gentleman", may prefer blondes' and that earlier studies reflected this cultural bias rather than racial or skin colour preferences. However, this is certainly not the only conclusion which could be drawn from these results. One could interpret the children's evenly distributed identification as indicating that many of them thought the dolls were two white dolls, one of which had a (positively valued) 'tan'. If this was the case, respondents were reacting neither to permanent skin colour differences nor to the racial categories of 'Caucasian' and 'Negro'.

A more conclusive result came out of a study by Gitter, Mostofsky and Satow (1972), which used more realistic representations of people of different races. The dolls used in this study varied not only in skin colour, but also in other physical characteristics associated with race. The 'Negro' dolls had thick lips, a wide nose and tightly curled hair, whereas the 'Caucasian' dolls had thin lips, a narrow nose and straight hair. The results from this study entirely confirmed those of the Clarks; black children misidentified themselves significantly more than white ones. There seemed little doubt here about the children's understanding that it was racial differences, rather than variations in skin colour, which were being represented by the dolls.

One way of overcoming the problem of the test materials not being lifelike is to use photographs instead of dolls – and, indeed, many researchers working in the field in the last few years have done this. A lack of realism, however, is not the only criticism which has been levelled at the Clarks' test stimuli; it has also been argued that the brown/white doll choice did not provide an adequate range of identification models for children who varied by skin shade (light, medium, or dark) and, in the case of Britain, by ethnicity. This is a significant criticism because it is closely associated with the issue of categorization. The idea behind the doll/photo method is to present children with the *identification options with which they are confronted in real life* and then to compare their choice with the one *which has been prejudged as the most socially and psychologically viable for them*. The researcher, in designing the identification test, has to make prior assumptions about which are the most salient identification options available to the child and about which of these is the most feasible for him or her to adopt. The choice of test materials is crucial in this respect.

A number of studies have added a brown or 'mulatto' doll to the test in an effort to represent more closely the appearance of lighter-skinned Negro children. When Greenwald and Oppenheim (1968) repeated the Clarks' study using a white, a medium-brown and a dark-brown doll, they found that fewer of the dark-skinned children identified with the white doll and that all the children's choices were more evenly distributed. However, the results of this study are open to numerous interpretations, depending on how one has prejudged a viable racial identity for black American children. Milner (1975), for example, pointed out that on the racial-awareness section of the test most of the children agreed that it was the *darker* doll which most resembled a Negro; yet many of the darker-skinned children chose the 'mulatto' doll as the one which looked most like them. Milner's argument was that this, too, was misidentification to an extent; the darker children may have chosen the lighter figure to avoid the more obvious fiction of choosing white.

Later studies (like that of Gitter, Mostofsky and Satow, 1972, mentioned earlier) have compromised by including a range of skin colours in the identification test, but have judged misidentification as any choice which is lighter or more Caucasian-looking than the subject making the choice. These differences of interpretation come down to *which type of categorization* is being considered. Milner (1975) made his interpretation of the Greenwald and Oppenheim (1968) results in terms of the *primary* categories of 'Negro' and 'white', whereas Gitter, Mostofsky and Satow (1982) took account of the secondary categories of physiognomy, skin colour and hair type. In his own British study Milner incorporated *ethnicity* into the test rather than *skin colour*, since he judged this to be a more important ethnic division for children in the British context.

A similar problem stemming from the use of dolls in these tests has been the influence of the gender of the ethnic stimuli on preference and identification choices. It has been argued that since the Clarks used only female dolls it was difficult for male children to make an identification with any of the dolls. In more recent studies, then, it has become the usual practice to use female dolls for girls and male dolls for boys or to make both sex choices available to the children. Similarly, where photographs are used, the age of the respondent and of the child in the photograph must be taken into account.

Another suggestion of critics of the doll method is that certain characteristics of the researcher conducting the test (in particular, of course, their race) may influence the responses of the children. A white investigator may tend to elicit more choices for the white doll because the child is trying to please the adult; conversely, the

48

presence of a black examiner may cause more black choices to be made. Despite the fact that this idea seems good common sense, a number of studies have found no black/white experimenter effects – for example, those of Morland (1958) and Hraba and Grant (1970). Milner (1975) has argued that results are so contradictory on this point that it is impossible to draw any firm conclusions.

Even with incomplete evidence about the effects of the ethnicity of the examiner, the more general point remains that the investigator's manner, questions and prompts during the test should be carefully controlled so as to minimize any appearance of expecting a particular response. Lengthy instructions and a large number of questions should be avoided in order to allow the child to become involved with the ethnic stimuli being offered, rather than engaging primarily in a performance–reward relationship with the examiner. Research suggests that the test materials are involved again here; interesting and attractive test materials are essential for focusing the child's concentration and for encouraging a more spontaneous response.

Looking generally at the doll method, it would appear that many of the specific methodological problems raised by the Clarks' (1939, 1947) investigations have been overcome. None the less, lingering doubts remain about the validity of testing identity in this way. How can a child's expressed reaction to dolls in an artificial, 'experimental' setting be taken as a serious statement of his or her ethnic identification?

Some reassurance can be drawn from the *qualitative data* which has come out of these tests. Again and again in accounts of doll-type investigations researchers are able to cite examples of the children reacting to the test stimuli as if they were real people. Not only do respondents comply with instructions which invite them to engage in imaginary activities with the dolls or photographs, but they also display *emotional responses* when asked to put themselves into the fantasy. The Clarks were not the only researchers to encounter tears and resistance during the identification sections; more recent investigators such as Milner (1975) have noted a tendency for black children to withdraw their hands under the table when identifying themselves as white and to have difficulty in dealing emotionally with the identification part of the test. With some children at least, the doll method taps an aspect of their racial self-identification about which they feel very deeply.

However, the obvious shortcomings of the method force us back to Wallman's (1979) conclusion that it is extremely difficult to observe ethnicity 'in action'. This is even more true of the ethnic identity of children, which is still in its developmental stages. The ideal method of studying racial identity would be to observe and question the child in every situation where ethnicity was relevant and to gather information about the child's identity from all those who have a hand in shaping it. But this is clearly impractical; all the researchers can do is supplement the doll test material with as much real-life data as possible, such as information about the child's racial friendship pattern. The important thing is to see the child's reaction to the doll test not as a definite statement of his or her ethnic allegiance, but as a still photograph from the moving picture of racial identity formation. The identity test is just one of many situations in which the child is required to make an ethnic identification choice. If this can be viewed alongside some of the child's choices in other racial situations, results from the doll tests can be interpreted with greater confidence.

Variables Related to Racial Identity

The second way in which research initiated by the Clarks (1947) has advanced is in isolating the variables which affect a child's racial identity. Racial identification and preference do not develop in a vacuum; however similar the situations of black children appear, children in different countries, areas and schools – and, of course, in families with varying attitudes to racial socialization – will be exposed to different influences on their racial self-perceptions. Researchers have long realized that it is not enough to make general statements about the racial identity of 'black children'. These must be qualified with a description of the conditions under which particular types of identification are most likely to occur.

Some intervening variables in the relationship between the child's race and his or her racial identity were investigated by the Clarks (1939, 1947). They analysed their data by age, by skin colour and also by area of the United States (North or South). However, other variables have since been suggested, and more work has been done to assess the influence of the factors considered by the Clarks.

SEX, AGE, SKIN COLOUR AND SOCIOECONOMIC LEVEL OF SUBJECTS
In most studies of racial identity since the Clarks, sociologists have been concerned to find out whether boys and girls, older and younger, light and dark, and working-class and middle-class

chidren react differently in terms of racial preference and identification. There is considerable evidence that they do, although the nature of each relationship is still unclear.

Some investigators have offered evidence to suggest that males develop ethnic awareness earlier than females (Clark and Clark, 1939; Porter, 1971): in other words, that boys attain a conceptual knowledge of different racial categories earlier than girls. Another hypothesis about gender differences is that girls' *identification and preference* are more affected than those of boys by the white norm of physical beauty. A study by Asher and Allen (1969) found that black *males* showed a greater preference for the white puppet, but the majority of studies suggested that minority-group girls were more prone than boys to internalize a negative perception of their physical selves, through comparison with a positive white ideal. Conventional wisdom has it that girls are generally more aware of their appearance than boys, because they are encouraged to 'attract' rather than to be attracted; they may have, as a consequence of this, a heightened awareness of the contrast between how they actually look and what society dictates as an aesthetic ideal.

Evidence on the influence of the child's *skin colour* on racial misidentification is more contradictory. Clark and Clark found that light children misidentified more than dark children, and this finding was confirmed in Britain by Milner (1975). The argument used to explain this in both Britain and the USA was that lighter children were seen by many black people as 'better looking' – that is, closer to white – and so were encouraged to think of themselves as 'almost white'. The idea of light skin colour being highly prized was thought to be particularly true of the West Indian community in Britain, especially among the older immigrants in whose minds the Caribbean colour-class scheme was still firmly embedded. However, Gitter, Mostofsky and Satow (1972) made a contradictory finding; in their study it was the *darker* subjects who misidentified the most. There have also been a number of studies which have found no relation at all between skin colour and racial identity (for example, Hraba and Grant, 1970; Gregor and McPherson, 1966). The issue remains controversial.

Some clear relationships emerge, however, when the age of the subject is considered. In his pioneer study, Lasker (1929) conycuded that ethnic awareness developed around the age of 8 and that at every age level blacks were more aware of the difference than whites. More recent research has suggested that racial awareness emerges between ages 3 and 5 years (Goodman,

1952; Porter, 1971). Reviewing the literature on age and racial awareness, Brand, Ruiz and Padilla concluded that 'in general research has indicated that ethnic awareness emerges about age 4, with finer discrimination and conceptual skills developing thereafter' (Brand, Ruiz and Padilla, 1974). As the child's general cognitive awareness develops, so awareness of racial categories becomes more sophisticated; horizons widen, and knowledge of all aspects of society increases.

Age has also been found to affect misidentification and out-group preference in black children. Many studies have shown that, as children get older, identification with the white doll decreases and there is a greater tendency for the child to see him- or herself as a member of the black race (slight trend in Milner, 1975; Davey and Norburn, 1980). This has been taken to indicate a growing realism in the child's attitude, leading to a recognition that society defines him or her as black. This is in keeping with a general developmental trend for retreat into fantasy to decrease with age; 'normal' children come to terms with their environment at least by recognizing classifications imposed by society. One or two studies report contradictory results, finding no age differences in racial identification and preference (for example, Gitter, Mostofsky and Satow, 1972), but the majority have tended to show that sophistication in racial categorization and identification increases with age.

A complicating factor here is that age brings not only greater conceptual skills but also a wider social experience. Williams and Morland (1976) argued that it was not age *per se* which affected children's perceptions of race, but the entry to school, which brought into full force the reflection of adult patterns of ethnic relations within peer-group organization. Morland suggested that, within a year of entry to school, a child's whole outlook on race and its relation to self has undergone a radical change (Williams and Morland, 1976). School brought the knowledge not only of racial categories and evaluations, but also of where the child 'belonged' in the hierarchical system. In Morland's view many of the discrepant results between studies were due to comparisons between pre-school and in-school studies; studies of black children in school tended to find a higher incidence of *black* identification and preference.

Socioeconomic level was another variable which was found to influence racial identification and preference. The main finding here was that lower-class children tend to accept their racial group membership more than middle-class children; or, as Brand, Ruiz and Padilla (1974) put it: 'Consistently, lower class ethnic minority subjects exhibit higher ethnic identification than middle class respondents.' Asher and Allen (1969) found that middle-class black children showed significantly more preference for white dolls than did the lower-class black children; Porter (1971) obtained a similar result with a pre-school sample.

One explanation put forward for this relationship was the subculture theory, which suggested that lower-class minority group members developed a value system distinct, and to some extent separate, from that of society overall, and that this value system provided alternative criteria for success. McCarthy and Yancey put forward this view, arguing that 'There is some evidence indicating that Negroes generally and especially working- and lower-class Negroes, have developed life-styles that reflect relatively autonomous and cohesive subcultures' (McCarthy and Yancey, 1971). This view finds support among recent observers of the British situation who have noted that young black people now identify with a specifically black British culture and value system.

A complementary argument which comes from a more psychological perspective was offered by Battle and Rotter (1963), who gave evidence in support of the idea that class is generally related to the conceptualization of power and control. Whereas the middle class tends to see itself as responsible for any failure to achieve a given goal, the working class tends to attribute such failure to external sources – fate, or the exercise of power of some remote body. Where race was concerned, Battle and Rotter suggested that lower-class blacks were more 'externally oriented' than middle-class blacks and that this explained why they were less prone to a negative self-concept.

GEOGRAPHICAL AND SOCIAL ENVIRONMENT

Following the established line of thought which saw the development of the self as inextricably bound up with the attitude of others, sociologists have placed enormous emphasis on establishing causal links between children's racial identity and the racial attitudes of those around them. Every agent of socialization is thought to have an influence on the child's racial conception of self, beginning centrally with the intimate penetration of the consciousness by the parents and family, then moving to wider spheres of influence (school, peers, neighbours) and to the more insidious and diffuse persuasion of the media. No widely applicable generalizations have been formulated concerning any single factor, but studies have consistently found links between aspects of the child's environment and his or her racial identity. Kenneth Clark summarized these as follows:

The available studies... indicate that children get their racial attitudes from a number of interrelated social influences which begin to affect the child even before he enters school. This pattern of social and cultural forces from which the child learns how to evaluate himself and others may include his family, his playmates, his neighbors, his school, the socio-economic status of his family in the community, and the influence of the church and the mass media of communication. The impact of any single influence may vary according to the age of the child, and some of these influences are more direct than others.

(Clark, 1955)

Sociologists assessing US studies of racial identification and preference showed great concern with the area in which the study was carried out. Historical and social diferences between northern and southern black/white relations were considered to be important determinants of black children's images of them-selves. To some extent the North/South issue in the United States has been confounded by the debate about school desegregation and has produced heated arguments – as well as diametrically opposed results – among sociologists. While some studies have found that minority group children showed *greater out-group orientation* in an *integrated* setting (Horowitz, 1939), others have found greater *own-group* orientation (Clark and Clark, 1939; Porter, 1971).

British studies of white children also found that area affected racial attitudes. Children in areas of high racial tension tended to exhibit more prejudice than those in more harmonious areas. However, studies of *black* British children have found no clear relationship between racial identity and area, type of contact between the races, or the numbers of minority group children in the school. From their study, Davey and Norburn concluded that

Overall... the results suggest that although specific local experiences can enhance or depress the quality of life for the individual it is society's categorising system which determines in what manner his group membership will define his place in the community. It is being black in Britain, rather than in Brixton or Bognor Regis that appeared to be the dominant factor behind the children's responses.

(Davey and Norburn, 1980)

This finding contradicts the assertions made by sociologists such as Banton (Miles and Phizacklea, 1979) that area was bound to affect both categorization and identity; but this discrepancy can once again be understood in terms of the type of categorization which is being considered. Studies of identity which are concerned with the primary black/white division are likely to apply country-wide, whereas those which allow for local variations in racial classification will, by definition, be more area-specific. In most respects, the experience of being black in Brixton and Bognor Regis is similar. However, in Brixton a child can identify him- or herself meaningfully as 'dark-skinned', 'Jamaican' and 'Rasta' and gain self-esteem from such a self-definition, whereas this is unlikely to be possible in Bognor Regis. The *content* of a child's racial identity and the value placed on each secondary identification will depend upon the secondary categories which are available in the child's immediate environment.

The association between parents' and children's racial attitudes – and in particular between a mother and her child – is thought to be highly complex. Although the *origin* of racial attitudes may be with the parents, these attitudes are subject to constant modification and intervention from forces outside the home. A study by Goodman (1952) suggested that the mother's attitude to race was not as influential on children's racial preferences as was commonly supposed; none the less, Goodman was struck by the extent to which mothers were unaware of the strong *implicit* racial messages that they communicated to their children. In fact, many writers have since made the point that, in any study of parental influence on children's racial identity, it is crucial to consider *unconscious* as well as *conscious* racial socialization. Kenneth Clark, for instance, noted that 'Many parents... communicate the prevailing racial attitudes to their children in subtle and sometimes unconscious ways' (Clark, 1955).

In addition to the mother's racial *attitudes*, it has been suggested that *her own racial identity and self-conception* also affect her child's preference and identity responses. In a study of a small number of disturbed Negro boys and their mothers, Brody found that a mother would often consciously deny the importance of race to her son, while simultaneously conveying her own extreme sensitivity about it:

While it was possible to define a conscious message about color deliberately offered by mother to son, it was also possible to define another message transmitted through action, attitudes and feelings, rather than words. The most frequently transmitted conscious message was to the effect that 'People are all the same inside', or 'We are all human', or 'People are what they are and skin color is unimportant'. The implied, simultaneously transmitted, unconscious message, mediated through affective and behavioral cues was essentially: 'While I tell you that people are the same inside, I expect you to behave as though this is not true, and, in fact, I don't believe it myself. People are divided into classes; they are not the same; we are different.'

(Brody, 1963)

55

In Britain, Davey and Norburn (1980) found no strong link between parents' and children's racial attitudes, except at the extremes of their ethnocentrism scales. Pushkin (1967) similarly found only a direct relationship between mothers' and children's attitudes when the mothers' views had been particularly strongly expressed. However, as Brody (1963) pointed out, there have been very few studies explicitly concerned with relating parents' racial attitudes and racial identity to their children's responses on racial preference and identification tests. Studies have more usually been concerned with children's general racial attitudes. As a consequence, we are still at the stage of speculation.

A final aspect of the parents' attitude which has been considered important for children's racial identity is their cultural awareness. It has been the basic assumption of the Black Consciousness movement that an open, positive conception of blackness among parents, together with an honest representation to the child of both slave history and their African roots, reduces the likelihood of self-hatred developing. In Britain, an added issue is the homeland culture of the immigrant black parents. One of the main ideas behind the recent multicultural curriculum impetus has been that giving black children a sense of cultural pride increases their self-esteem. Of particular interest for the present study is Verma and Bagley's (1979) investigation of the racial identity of a small number of adopted black and mixed race British children. Relating the children's responses on an identity test to the cultural awareness of the adoptive parents (that is, whether or not they had black friends, and the extent of their commitment to teaching about the child's African and Caribbean heritage), they found that 'adopted mixed race children of racially unaware parents tend to identify themselves as white, prefer white figures, and have some negative stereotypes of black figures' (Verma and Bagley, 1979). High cultural awareness, then, appeared to heighten mixed race children's positive view of themselves.

To summarize: researchers since the Clarks (1947) have identified six main influences on black children's racial identity: the sex, age and skin colour of the child; the socioeconomic status of the family; the area in which the child lives; and the racial attitudes of the parents. The racial attitudes of the child's peers, school and neighbours were also held to be important, but few studies have investigated these influences systematically.

The most consistent result in the sex-identity correlation was that girls tended to misidentify more than boys. Age appeared both to decrease misidentification and to increase the sophistication of children's understanding of racial categories; and the influence of skin colour meant that the lighter the child, the more likely he or she was to identify as white. Working-class children had a more positive orientation to their blackness than did middle-class children, perhaps because they lived in a working-class subculture which had developed an alternative to the dominant white value system.

The influence of area in British studies was somewhat unclear but it was suggested that its main effect would be on secondary rather than on primary identification. The parents' attitudes were believed to be important in shaping children's identity; unconscious as well as conscious socialization was considered influential. The parents' cultural awareness was felt to have some effect on black British children's feelings about their race; a strongly positive attitude to the child's non-British heritage encouraged a black rather than a white identity.

The Present Investigation: Mixed Race Children in Britain

The present study of British mixed race children owed a lot to the doll studies tradition. Its method was a variation of the Clarks' type of identity test, and the influences on racial identity were assumed to be the same for mixed race as for black children. None the less, there were important differences between this and previous research; primarily, these differences stemmed from the fact that the study did not use the single, dichotomous model of identity as a choice between 'black' and 'white'.

THE STUDY

The subjects of the study were fifty-one children, aged between 6 and 9, who had one parent who was African or Afro-Caribbean and one parent who was white. The lower end of the age range was set at 6 years because previous research suggested that children's articulacy and racial awareness would be sufficiently developed at this stage to allow them to talk in detail about racial categorization; yet the scope of 6 to 9 years also kept the study within the age limits set by previous research on black children, so that comparisons could be made. Only the natural children of one black and one white parent who lived in their own families were considered eligible for the study. The position of adopted mixed race children in either white or black families seemed too different to be included in the study. Children of Asian/white marriages were also excluded on the grounds that cultural and religious differences wihin many Asian/white families introduced extra factors into the issue of the children's identity. It could be argued that these children would potentially experience as much *cultural* as *racial* conflict in the formation of their identity.

The aim of the study was to investigate the racial identity of mixed race children in the same way as the Clarks and others studied black children, but with the additional proviso that *secondary, as well as primary identification* would be considered. In terms of the basic black/white division, the problems being posed were identical to those posed by previous research — that is, first, how *aware* the children were of the white/non-white distinction; secondly, whether their *preference* choices showed an internalization of society's negative view of black people; and thirdly, whether the children *identified* themselves 'correctly' with the black rather than with the white group. The investigation also sought to trace some of the conditions which influenced whether or not the children adopted a realistic and viable racial identity.

However, the exploration of *secondary* identifications involved a departure from the well-trodden path of conventional identity research. The first concern here was to find out which everyday racial categories mixed race children recognized and by what criteria they delineated them. In other words, the study was trying to elicit the number and names of the racial categories known to the children so that a picture could be built up of how they viewed the racial structure. The second stage was again to ask the children to identify themselves, but this time to do so *within their subjectively defined system*. It was then possible to see mixed race children's identity in terms of both primary and secondary categorization.

The questions posed by the study can be summarized as follows:

(1) In terms of the basic, dichotomous structure of racial thought:

   (a) How conscious are mixed race children of the white/non-white division in British society? (Racial awareness.)
   (b) Have they internalized the value associations of race current in our society? (Racial preference.)
   (c) Have they accepted society's definition of them as non-white? (Self-identification.)

(2) At the level of identity construction:

   (a) Which secondary racial categories do mixed race

children recognize and by what criteria are these delineated? (Racial awareness.)

(b) Do mixed race children perceive themselves as 'mixed' or 'in-between', within their perceived system? (Self-identification.)

(3) Do the variables which are known to affect the racial identity of black children, and of marginal people generally, also influence the adoption of a viable racial identification by British mixed race children:

(a) Within the white/non-white dichotomy?
(b) In the context of secondary category sets?

Because of the limitations of time and resources, the investigation of variables influencing identity was limited to information which could be provided by the mother. Unsatisfactory as this might appear, the decision was guided by two main factors. First, even in these times of greater democracy in marriage, it is usually the mother who plays the larger role in child care and who, rather than the father, deals with everyday matters in a child's life. Whatever philosophy the father has on how the child should be brought up in terms of racial identity, the *identity content* is usually controlled by the mother. Secondly, it became clear early on in the fieldwork that many of the children who were to be included in the study were single- (female) parented so that they were, to an even greater extent, subject to the mother's influence.

Some of the children interviewed were siblings, so in all there were thirty-eight mothers – thirty white and eight black. The sample was obtained by 'snowball' effect. A small group of respondents was contacted through an organization for interracial families called Harmony, and these women were then asked if they knew of anyone else who would be willing to be interviewed. It cannot be claimed that this sample was random or in any way representative of the mothers of mixed race children in Britain. Membership of an organization which encouraged an awareness of racial issues and involved a certain willingness to talk openly about race must be regarded as an obvious source of bias. The sample covered a wide range of socioeconomic groups, but there were a large number of single mothers, and the percentage of black women in the group was regrettably small. However, the controversial nature of the inquiry made it essential that the interviews with both mother and child be carried out in an atmosphere of mutual trust. A 'snowball' sample, which begins with the endorsement of the researcher by a 'core group

Mixed Race Children

(indicating a degree of commitment rather than prurient curiosity) has certain advantages in this respect. Each respondent is approached through the personal recommendation of someone who is known to her; rapport established with one respondent is therefore halfway to establishing a similar rapport with the next. It would have been difficult to obtain a similarly co-operative sample by other, more anonymous means – such as doctors' lists, approach in the street, or through schools. (A description of how the sample was recruited is given in Appendix 3.)

METHOD: THE IDENTITY TEST AND THE MOTHERS' INTERVIEWS

Two methods of data collection were used in the study: a modified version of the Clarks' (1939, 1947) identity test for the children, and an in-depth, semi-structured interview for investigating the attitudes of the mothers.

The identity test

A test which would be suitable for this interview required two major modifications to the mainstream doll/picture tests. First, materials intended for use with mixed race children had to provide not only male and female, Asian and Caribbean identification stimuli, but also a clear and realistic representation of *mixed race* children themselves. Secondly, in order to answer the study's questions concerning secondary racial categorization, a new section, designed to elicit the children's racial classification system, had to be added to the usual identification test.

Colour photographs rather than dolls, puppets, or pictures were used as the identification stimuli, since it was important to show variations in skin tone, hair and facial features as accurately as possible. First of all, before introducing the notion of race, the child was asked to name his or her three best friends. He or she was then handed several large cards which carried photos of a couple (photographed together) and beneath them one boy and one girl (photographed separately) who were their children. There were seven families in all, giving the variety of 'mixtures' shown in Figure 3.1.

With all the cards visible on the floor, the usual real/ideal identity questions were put to the child: 'Which child looks most like you? ... If you could be one of these children, which one would you be? ...Which four children would you have to your party?' and so on. The children were also asked which photos most resembled their three best friends. After this, however, a categorization section was added, where the children were required to put the photos of the children in groups, according to

60

Black man/White woman	White man/Asian woman
Mixed boy/mixed girl	Mixed boy/mixed girl
Black woman/White man	Asian man/Asian woman
Mixed boy/Mixed girl	Asian boy/Asian girl
Black man/Black woman	White man/White woman
Black boy/Black girl	White boy/White girl
Asian man/White woman	
Mixed boy/Mixed girl	

Figure 3.1 The photographs

their 'race'. The exact instruction was, 'Put all the white children together, and so on...' or, 'Put all the white children together – now, what about the others?' When the groups had been constructed, the respondent was asked, 'Which group are *you* in?' to allow a second identity choice to be made on the basis of secondary categorization.

The children were then asked to imagine that a spaceman had just come through the window and he wanted to know *how they knew* the right group for each photo; how would they teach *him* to sort the photos properly? Talking about the categories in the context of 'teaching the spaceman' was intended as an exploration of the main criteria employed by the children in grouping the photographs and of the names by which they referred to each group. They were also asked, tentatively, about their identity choices – 'What is it about that photo which looks most like you?' – so that they could expand on similarities and differences if they wished. The test was concluded by a sounding out of any relatively neutral racial labels that the child had not mentioned – 'Are there any coloured children in the photos?... Are there any brown children?' – to see how these related to the 'spontaneously' constructed sets.

The mother's interviews
The idea of the semi-structured interview is to gain maximum insight into the subject's *own* view of the matter being investigated. The questions are therefore designed to give the respondent space to express her full opinion with all its myriad overtones, nuances and contradictions. The researcher uses questions and related probes to guide the interview through certain subject areas, but the response set is determined by the

respondents themselves, and attitude scales are constructed *after* the interviews, on the basis of the total range of replies obtained.

The interview schedule which was devised to investigate the variables relating to the mother was structured to the extent that every respondent was asked a set of identical questions in the same order, and in one section a collection of statements with which the respondent could agree or disagree was used as the focus for discussion. Within this format, however, the mother was encouraged to elaborate on any point she wished, to think aloud about the questions and to articulate her feelings at her own pace and in her own way. Primarily, the role of the investigator was to listen, although responses to the most complex items were checked and rechecked throughout the interview, and clarification of an attitude was sought when it seemed to be required. All this, of course, made the interviews quite long ($1\frac{1}{2}$ to 2 hours) and demanding for the respondent; but it also gave her the satisfaction of getting her views across in all their complexity, so the involvement was potentially rewarding.

After being given a short list of factual questions about the age and socioeconomic and ethnic background of herself and her spouse, the mother was asked about her own and her child's social contacts. Who did she see during the week? Where did she go? This section built up a picture of the mother's pattern of social relationships and of where her children fitted into it. Moving on to categorization and to racial attitudes, the interview schedule then required the mother to 'describe the racial situation in Britain'. This instruction was deliberately vague and unspecific so as to force the mother to introduce her own racial classifications without being influenced by those of the investigator. At this point, the mother's expression of her feelings about the different racial labels and about relationships between ethnic groups in Britain often formed the basis of a long and revealing discussion.

After this discussion, the questionnaire moved on to specific problems which might arise from bringing up mixed race children in Britain. The mother was given four 'critical situations' and asked how she would react to each of them. They were, briefly: a child expressing the desire to be white; anxieties over racial inequality; rejection of the white parent; and name-calling at school. The next section was even more structured: a series of statements with which the mother was asked to agree or disagree to various degrees. These statements concerned categorization, child-rearing and racial attitudes, so they provided a useful way of checking attitudes which the mother had expressed earlier on. At the end of the interview, the ethnicity of all the mother's and child's friends was recorded, and some short notes were made on the area in which the family lived.

Although information was sought from the women about the fathers of the children, this was sometimes difficult to obtain. The main problem was that a fair proportion of the women were either separated from their child(ren)'s father or were single parents; some had ongoing relationships with men or still saw the child(ren)'s father, while others did not. Where the mother was separated from her husband and where successive children had different fathers, it was often a complicated process to distinguish between current boyfriends, the former husband and each child's father. Since the idea of gathering information about the father was partly to assess the socioeconomic status of the family (if he was the main bread-winner) and partly to get an idea of his influence on the child's identity, I tried as far as possible to ask questions about any man seen currently and regularly, including (if applicable) the father of the child I was to interview.

A copy of both the mother's interview schedule and the children's identity test is included in Appendix 2. The next four chapters go on to discuss the results.

Chapter Four

Who Am I?
Categorization, Identification and Preference

This chapter is concerned with the central question of the British mixed race identity, namely: How do mixed race children view the racial structure and how do they place themselves within it? The next chapter will answer this in a more complex way by considering the influence of area and other external factors on racial identity; but here the aim is to concentrate totally on the children and to empathize with their position. If one were to follow the upward gaze of a mixed race child in his or her quest for a racial identity, how would the classification system appear? And what criteria would the child use to discern where he or she 'really' belongs?

The first part of the chapter looks separately at the three main components of identity: categorization, identification and preference. In other words, it explores how mixed race children *classify* the different groups, how they *locate* themselves in the racial structure and how they *feel* about the various racial groups. The final part of the chapter examines the responses of individual children rather than those of the sample as a whole. The degree of consistency shown by each child in categorizing the photographs, in identifying with a single photo and with a group, and in expressing racial preferences, gives some measure of his or her *identity conflicts*. A useful analytical step, then, is to consider the categorization, identification and preference choices of each child as a single *identity pattern*. These patterns can then be graded according to the amount of identity conflict they display.

Racial Categorization

The racial categorization section of the test was where the children were asked to arrange fourteen photographs into categories according to their 'race' and to label the groups (verbally) as they thought appropriate. No clue was given as to the number or names of groups expected, to allow the children space to express their own image of the racial structure. The photographs were numbered 1–14 and were arranged in seven brother-and-sister pairs as shown in Table 4.1. No. 4 was a particularly light-skinned boy with blue eyes.

Table 4.1 *The Numbered Photographs*

Girl	Boy	Parents
1	2	Both Asian
3	4	White mother, West Indian father
5	6	Both West Indian
7	8	Both white
9	10	Asian mother, white father
11	12	West Indian mother, white father
13	14	White mother, Asian father

THE YOUNGER CHILDREN: SIMPLE COLOUR CATEGORIZATION

Children under the age of 8 tended to group the test photographs according to their skin colour. Thirty children grouped the photographs in this way, of whom twenty-one were less than 8 years old. There were two different ways of organizing the photographs according to skin colour, but the most common was to divide them into three groups: black, white and brown (Figure 4.1).

The black group consisted of the two West Indian children; the white group was the white brother-and-sister pair *placed with any other child who was light skinned*; and the brown group was all the remaining children who were not 'black' or 'white'. Most often, it was just one extremely light-skinned mixed race boy (photograph no. 4) who was seen as white, although other mixed race children (Asian and West Indian) also appeared in this category occasionally.

The second way of grouping the photographs was to place them in a continuum from light to dark, making only a tentative distinction between black (or brown) and white (Figure 4.2).

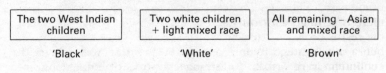

The two West Indian children	Two white children + light mixed race	All remaining – Asian and mixed race
'Black'	'White'	'Brown'

Figure 4.1   Simple colour categorizaton (1)

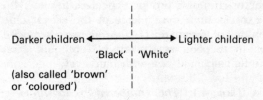

Darker children ←——————→ Lighter children
'Black' ┆ 'White'
(also called 'brown'
or 'coloured')

Figure 4.2   Simple colour categorization (2)

The first indication that these children were thinking along colour lines often came in the first few minutes of the test, in the form of spontaneous comments about the photographs. They were unable to tell whether or not some of the lighter children were white. Ella, for example, a medium-skinned girl with soft curly hair, puzzled over nos. 9 (mixed race Asian) and 12 (mixed race West Indian). 'These two are very pale', she said. 'I don't know where I should really put them.' Light-skinned Jane, like her darker brother Paul, pointed to no. 4 (the very light mixed race boy) and asked, 'Is that white or brown?' In all, nineteen out of the thirty children who used a simple colour categorization put at least one 'fair-skinned' child in a group with the two white children (compared with only six doing so in the rest of the sample).

When I posed the question of the spaceman – 'If a spaceman came through the window and asked you how you knew that was the right way to group the children, what would you tell him?' – the most common response was, 'I looked at the colour on the faces.' These children said that they did not look at the parents at all to classify the children, so that if they had not been able to see the photographs of whole 'families' they would still have grouped the children in exactly the same way. Skin colour dominated the scene and was treated in the most literal way. Each face was examined with the utmost care, and a number of children even noticed areas of the face which looked lighter or darker than others. In trying to decide where to put the light mixed race boy, Yvette (herself mid-brown with clearly Negroid features) mused,

66

'Some parts of his face look whiter than the others – like, that part there is getting a bit white. And that part there is white too – but the rest is brown... He's brownish like him [no. 12, mixed race] but a bit lighter.' 'White' appeared to be at one end of a continuum rather than a discrete category; photographs were described as 'a little bit white', 'a bit darker white' and 'whitish-brown'. Few children felt strongly about where the cut-off point should be between white, brown and black.

The type of facial features or hair of the children in the photographs did not seem to be as important as skin colour in classification. If the hair was taken into account at all it was according to its colour. Jessica was a mid-brown, curly-haired girl and one of the few children in the sample whose *mother* was black. I asked her whether her brown group was a group for children with curly hair *and* children with straight hair – and, if so, what 'brown' really meant. She explained, 'It means that all the brown people go together because they're all *brown* and they've got the same coloured hair, and because it doesn't matter if they've got curly hair or tangly hair or straight hair because they're all the same colour.'

Being less specific, I asked darker-skinned Akin if he looked at the hair at all. 'The colour,' he said firmly; 'if it was dark or light.'

Not all of the children understood skin colour to be a permanent characteristic. For some of them, it was associated with 'getting a tan'. The colour/suntan association (which has been noted in other studies) was by no means confined to the younger children, but it seemed to occur most frequently among them. Joanne, aged $6\frac{1}{2}$, explained that the light mixed race boy was white 'because he hasn't got any sun on him'. Ella went into more detail on this point: 'Black people has been in a hotter country longer. And the brown people haven't been there very long and they came back to England and so they didn't get any blackness because they weren't in a hot country any more.'

From the point of view of identity, there are considerable dangers in giving exposure to the sun as an 'explanation' of racial difference; for although it makes brown/dark skin a positive attribute, the child learns all too quickly that brown skin does not fade to white in winter and that racism does not extend to white people who have a tan. However, considering the number of mothers who emphasized the connection to their children, the idea appeared to find little favour. Only ten out of the total fifty-one children mentioned it during the categorization test.

A few of the children who used a simple colour categorization moved readily from a discussion of skin colour to talking about the parents in the photographs. Gemma, for example, who called her third group 'half caste' even though it contained two Indian children, said she noticed that some of the children in the photographs had 'a white mum and a black dad... or their mum was black and their dad was white'. However, when I asked her if she looked more at the parents or more at the colour when deciding how to group the children she said she looked more at the colour, because 'some half-caste children are more like blackish and some are more like white'. Akin gave 'having one brown parent' as the reason why he grouped photo no. 4 in the brown group even though the boy had very light skin. None the less, it was clear even among these respondents that skin colour was the primary criterion. Yvette seemed to speak for the majority of this group when she explained that she did not look at the parents because 'Like my mum – my dad's black and my mum's white, and the children are *brown*. So it's no use looking at the mum's face, 'cos you still don't know what colour the kid's face is. Could be a different colour... Sometimes they're white, sometimes they're brown and sometimes they're black.'

The final part of the categorization test – where the children were asked about racial labels other than those they had already mentioned – elicited only a limited response from these younger respondents. The best-known category apart from black, white and brown appeared to be 'Indian'. Several children were able to pick out the two Indian and four 'half Indian' photographs when presented with this label. Few children who were able to do this, however, could say clearly how they distinguished 'Indian' from other children, nor did they give any indication of what being 'Indian' actually meant. Terry said she could identify Indians because 'We see Indian people when we go to Southend sometimes'; yet when her older brother Leo attempted to describe Indian people, there seemed to be notions of both Chinese and 'red Indians' creeping in. (Later in the interview he said 'Chinese' when he meant 'Indian'.)

'Coloured' was the only other label besides 'Indian' which found some recognition among this group; its meaning, however, varied considerably. 'Coloured' was variously taken to mean 'black' (that is, describing photos no. 5 and 6), brown (describing people of intermediate skin colour), all non-white children, or else darker-skinned children. About a quarter of these children understood the term to mean one of these, but the remainder were unsure of its meaning (Figure 4.3).

The terms 'West Indian', 'African' and 'Jamaican' were similarly little known or understood; at least, few of the younger children

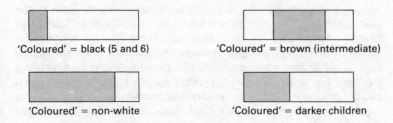

Figure 4.3   Meanings of the term 'coloured'

were willing to betray any familiarity with the terms. A notable exception in this respect was Leo, who seemed to be trying hard to remember when I asked him what West Indian children looked like before saying sheepishly, 'I *should* know that because my mum is!' Then he added, 'But she's black, so that's a little bit hard' – a remark which could be interpreted in a number of different ways. (The remark was uttered with puzzlement rather than with any deeper emotion. My view was that he had heard the term 'West Indian' but not really understood it or how it related to 'black'. His mother may have been a 'special case' of West Indianness for all he knew.) Among children using a simple colour categorization the term 'half black' was understood by about a quarter to mean 'very dark skinned'; the remainder did not understand the label at all.

To summarize: the simple colour categorization of the younger children either consisted of three categories labelled 'black', 'white' and 'brown' or else was a colour continuum from light to dark. The dividing line between white and non-white was blurred, allowing concepts such as 'darker white', 'almost white' and 'a bit white' to be applied to certain photographs, most commonly to no. 4. These children displayed little knowledge of racial labels other than the ones they used in their 'spontaneously' constructed set. Although 'Indian', 'coloured' and 'half black' were each recognised by about a quarter of the group of thirty children, the meanings they attached to the labels varied.

THE OLDER CHILDREN: COMPLEX, MULTI-CRITERIA SET

The over-8s tended to group the photographs according to ethnicity and parentage, although once again there were two variations in the groupings. Most of the older children (seventeen out of twenty-one) constructed a four-category set; all four mixed race West Indian children were placed together, the two black and two white children each formed separate categories, and then all the photographs of Asian or part-Asian children formed the fourth group. The categories were usually labelled 'half-caste', 'black', 'white' and 'Indian', although there were variations. A second way of organizing the photographs was to place the mixed race West Indian children with the two black children (calling this the 'black' or 'coloured' group) and to leave the white and Indian groups intact. Only four of the twenty-one older children chose to combine the 'black' and 'half-caste' groups in this way (Figure 4.4).

The racial classification of the older children involved considerably more knowledge of racial matters and a greater conceptual sophistication than the simple colour gradation of the younger respondents. These children had fewer problems understanding what was required of them in the categorization test and tended to complete their task quickly and with a minimum of hesitation and questions. (Two minutes was average for older respondents. Younger children took up to five minutes and needed repetitions of the original request.) When the 'spaceman' questions were put to this group they, like the under-8s, often mentioned colour first; but they progressed quickly to talking about the families of the children in the photographs, their hair, physiognomy and so on.

Sometimes without prompting and sometimes in answer to the question 'Did you look at the parents at all in grouping the children?' most respondents described the 'half-caste' group in terms of parentage. Martin, for example, whose own father was black and mother was white, bluntly and spontaneously noted, '*He's* black, *she's* white, so they're half-caste.' Michael, himself the darker-skinned son of a black father, more hesitatingly characterized them as 'the ones with white and ... other people families'. For about half the children using a complex multi-criteria set, the

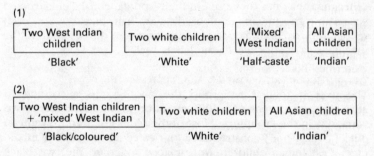

Figure 4.4   Complex multi-criteria set

parentage criteria were clearly paramount in their construction of their 'half-caste' group. Although colour of skin was acknowledged, it was looking at the family which finally decided the categories. However, parentage was not so much a factor where the Asian photographs were concerned; these were simply seen as 'Indian'.

Angela, an extremely light-skinned girl whose mother persisted in describing her as 'white', registered her main criteria by bursting out at the beginning of the test, 'These two people match! Them two and them two and them... [pointing to all the "mixed" marriages]... don't match!'

'Why don't they match?'

(Bursts into giggles). 'The lady's black and the man's white.'

All Angela's categories were explained in terms of the children's parents: ' 'cos of the colour of her mum', ' 'cos the mother's white and the dad's black', and so on. Skin colour was doubtless important to her too, but parentage was paramount.

The most articulate of these children for whom parentage criteria were obviously decisive was Esme, who carefully explained that she was able to group the 'half-caste' children because she had seen the parents: ' 'cos each of them either have a black father and a white mother or a black mother and a white father'. She had looked at the colour of the children's skin first, she said, but when asked why some children in *different* groups were the *same* colour, she replied unhesitatingly, 'Well, because afterwards I looked at the parents to see if it was right.'

Kieran, making some effort to remember what he had been told, said of the half-caste group, 'They're a bit coloured, they... [sigh]... they got some of their mum's genes and some of their dad's genes and they mix up.'

Other children using this set, while strongly aware of the parentage argument and agreeing that they took it into account, were apparently more, or equally, concerned with the colour of the children's skin and with their physiognomy and hair type. The four children who grouped the mixed race West Indian with the black children seemed to have done so on the basis of their facial features and their hair. Malcolm, who looked distinctly black, described his 'coloured' group as differing from the Indian group in that the former had 'flat noses' and the latter had 'pointed noses'. Karina, who also looked black, distinguished between the two according to hair type: 'The coloured group's is curly, and the white group's is straight, and the Indian's is straight but black and long as well.'

The remainder of the older children equated being 'half-caste' with a particular skin colour. As George said of his half-caste group, 'They're half white and half coloured. But together – they're brown.'

There seemed to be two main reasons why almost half the older children retained a strong interest in skin colour, even though they had grouped the photographs together according to the criteria of 'descent'. First, some children seemed to persist in the colour theme to avoid talking about the more sensitive subject of the parents. Although their initial grouping had been according to the mixed/not mixed criteria, an element of defensive resistance and/or denial came into play during the discussion. Secondly, some of the children seemed to be using *both* the black/white/brown *and* the mixed/Indian/black/white set, but had not quite worked out – or could not fully articulate – how 'half-caste' related to 'brown'. These children pitched their criteria to revolve upon the themes of hair type, colour of parents and skin colour, switching from one to the other in response to different questions.

When specifically asked what 'brown' meant, the most common response among those who recognized the label was to say that it was a medium colour and that a brown group would include all the children except the black (nos. 5 and 6) and the white (nos. 7 and 8). However, there were variations of meaning for the label, which may help explain why some of the children experienced difficulty in relating this to their other categories. Endorsed by one or two children each, other meanings for brown were 'non-white' (all children except nos. 7 and 8), Indian people, West Indian people (nos. 5 and 6) 'Negroid' people (all except white and Indians) and 'half-caste' people only. Esme, who used 'brown' to mean the latter ('half-caste only'), commented, 'When you said half black and half white, that's what I thought you meant by brown. 'Cos at school they call *them* brown. They call – *like me* – brown.'

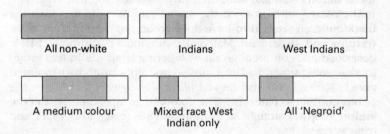

All non-white   Indians   West Indians

A medium colour   Mixed race West Indian only   All 'Negroid'

Figure 4.5 The meanings of 'brown'

72

Of some interest here is the fact that, when talking about the parents of various children in the photographs, many children corrected themselves after saying 'black', substituting 'brown'. If I asked them to repeat a phrase I had not heard, the tapes later showed that many who said 'black' in the first instance switched to 'brown' in the second. Clearly, these respondents felt more comfortable with the label 'brown' than with 'black'. Kieran, a very light skinned boy with wavy hair, drew attention to this fairly late on in the test in the following exchange; he had been asked which children were 'brown' and after naming all the mixed race West Indian children he suddenly pointed to the black children (nos. 5 and 6) and said, '*These* are supposed to be brown. They *are* brown 'cos they do look like brown.'

'Who is it that says they're brown, Kieran?'

' 'Cos there's no such thing really as black people.'

'Who said that to you?'

'Can't remember who told me that.' Puzzles for a moment.

'Do you think it's better to say "brown" than "black"?'

Warmly: 'Yes.'

Characteristic of all the older respondents, however, regardless of whether their classification was made on the basis of colour, physiognomy, or parentage, was their recognition of Indians as a separate group. Their criteria covered physical characteristics, a rudimentary knowledge of cultural forms and simple personal experience of 'knowing Indians'. Tina, for example, who lived in an area of West London where there was a large Asian community, stated simply, 'Sometimes I see children like that, and they *are* Indian.' More frequently, the colour and texture of the hair were picked out as a distinguishing feature. Martin said he knew 'the Pakis' because 'they got black hair, and their hair is straight'. Nancy noted that 'Black children have their hair round sometimes, and the Indian children have their hair down and plaited.' 'They speak Indian,' said Angela.

The comments of the other children got more complex as they tried to list as many criteria as they could. Nigel said he knew they were Indians by 'Their hair, eyes ... hair and teeth ... Their hair goes down, it's always neat, and you can get long hair, and for the teeth – well, nearly all the Indians I see they have, sort of, little ones.'

Tatum at first seemed to be trying to relate the concept of 'Indian' to skin colour: 'The Indian colours are slightly brown like half-caste and they've got a little bit of white in them and they're a little bit dark.' But then she remembered other features: 'They got soft hair and it's greasy, and they look like white people and they've sometimes got yellow spots on their hand when they've been to a wedding. And they can speak different languages.'

Esme mentioned skin colour, hair, eyebrows and eyelash colours and also cited her personal experience of 'seeing lots of different people so I can tell'. To underline the differences she mentioned, she pointed to a white man and an Indian man and said, '*That* face wouldn't really go with that colour skin, would it?' In addition, Esme thought that their religion may be different, though she wasn't sure: 'I don't think her [no. 1] mum's a Muslim. 'Cos Muslims usually wear some sort of mask or something. The father you can't tell by because I think if he's a Muslim he just does a Muslim prayer, he doesn't wear anything special. Except maybe a long thing like Arabs.'

Althea said it was 'the way they looked... if they were Asian, sometimes they would have a red spot there [pointing to the forehead]... or they wouldn't. And the same with the Indian people – you know, the people in India. Sometimes they have a red spot as well.'

It was generally agreed that although some of the children in this group were actually half-Indian, they were, in Nigel's terms 'mostly Indian'.

The term 'West Indian' ('African', 'Jamaican' and so on) was generally understood to refer to photographs nos. 5 and 6 (black) although several children said that their 'half-caste' group 'might be West Indian too'. Criteria for this label, however, were not as well understood (or perhaps as willingly articulated) as for the Indian group. Most children said that they did not know how they knew. Esme simply said she knew because 'My dad is West Indian.' Tatum and Sally, when asked if any of the children might speak a different language, pointed to the two black children with obvious delight: 'They can speak Rastafarian,' said Tatum, firmly. I asked her if *she* could speak it too, and she replied in a solemn voice, 'My dad can!' When asked if she could understand him when he spoke it she nodded proudly and said, 'Yes. *No one else can* in my family.

I inquired of Althea what 'Jamaican' sounded like: '[Sigh] Well, it's *very* difficult. I *can* speak a little bit Jamaican... a *little* bit.' She tried to imitate it but could not and collapsed in giggles.

George volunteered the information that in Jamaica 'they have coconuts. They have different sorts of houses; some have straw houses, and it's hot.'

Other than this, the label 'West Indian' could elicit few comments from the children. The remaining labels all evoked at least a list of photo numbers that belonged to them; 'half black' was understood by many children to mean mixed race; and 'coloured', though retaining the meanings given to it by the younger respondents, was also taken by some children to mean 'mixed race'. 'Pakistani' was generally believed to be the same as 'Indian'.

The complex, multi-criteria categorization, then, was essentially a four-category set, consisting of a black, a white, a mixed race and an Indian group. For almost half the children using this set, the black/white/half-caste classifications were close to the black/white/ brown grouping of the younger children, with careful note taken of which children had lighter skin and which were darker. The older children had a greater knowledge of racial labels than the younger ones and a more advanced awareness of how they related to each other, although they still seemed more able to talk about Indian than about West Indian or any other cultural label. And among all the children who used a complex multi-criteria set, the term 'brown' was still more popular than 'black', despite the fact that these children did not construct a separate 'brown' group in their initial categorization.

THE DEVELOPMENT OF RACIAL CATEGORIZATION

From the responses of the fifty-one mixed race children interviewed, it appeared that between the ages of 6 and 9 there was a progression from a simple colour classification to a multi-criteria system. How does this compare with the research on black children's racial identity that was discussed in the previous chapter?

Research on the development of black British children's identity touched on racial categorization only in general terms. Although it was suggested that a rudimentary knowledge of racial differences existed as early as age 3, and it was assumed that the complexity of the child's conceptual scheme increased with age, the development of children's knowledge of *specific* racial labels was not deemed to be problematic. However, one aspect of the age/categorization link among these mixed race children finds some confirmation from US identity research. Table 4.2, which gives the type of categorization endorsed by each age level, shows that the biggest jump in complexity is between the sixth and seventh years. This is entirely in keeping with Williams and Morland's (1976) findings, which suggested that the greatest single change in the development of racial categorization was brought about after the first year of school.

The simple colour and multi-criteria classifications can be seen as two stages in the development of racial categorization. The first

Table 4.2 *Racial Categorization by Age*

Set	Age				
	6 (72–83 months)	7 (80–95 months)	8 (96–107 months)	9 (108–119 months)	Total
Simple, colour	13	8	4	5	30
Complex, multi-criteria	1	5	7	8	21
Total	14	13	11	13	51

stage (lasting possibly from ages 3 to 6) is when the child learns to distinguish between different skin colours – the various tones from black to white. At this point, children see the racial structure as consisting of a series of skin colour gradations from white through brown to black. The cut-off point between each group is deemed to be relatively unimportant. Descriptive detail is supplied by such terms as 'lightish', 'blackish', 'beige' and 'pale'; each child seemed to have some favourite idiosyncratic term to pin-point what he or she sees as the finer points of difference between the various shades.

As the child gets older (say, 6 years onwards) the criteria of categorization become more complex, and the *boundaries* between groups become more rigidly defined. 'Half-caste' children are those who have one black and one white parent; 'white' children have two white parents and 'Indian' children are recognized by a clear set of physical and cultural criteria. Whereas the decision of where particular *skin colour* categories start and finish is a matter of some subjectivity (the child him- or herself controls when 'whitish' becomes 'brown' and at what point 'dark' merges into 'black'), the more complex categories take on an *objective reality* for the older children. Although the meanings attached to different racial terms differ among children, neither these nor the actual labels are idiosyncratically defined; they appear to be a fragmented reflection of the bewildering array of criteria used by British people to express ethnic difference.

An understanding of *cultural* differences also comes with age, yet it will be recalled that knowledge of the label 'Indian' seemed to be acquired *earlier* than that of 'West Indian' or 'African'. This could be for one of several reasons. First, the cultural forms of

Asians in Britain are rather more visible than those of people from Africa or the Caribbean; they involve modes of dress, worship and family organization which are markedly different from the British pattern. It is possible that, for this reason, younger children come to recognize what constitutes membership of the Indian group more quickly than that of any other. On the other hand, there may be more affective components at work in this process of learning. The earlier discrimination of Indians may be precipitated by the acquisition of negative stereotypes concerning the Asian groups. Or, conversely, the *tardy* appreciation of West Indian and African culture could be interpreted as evidence of a negative black bias and of mixed race children's resistance to the idea that a minority group culture is part of their own heritage.

Racial Identification

The children were asked two direct questions about their identity. When the photographs were first produced, they were asked, 'Which child looks most like you?' Later on, after they had organized the photographs into categories, the question 'Which group are you in?' was posed. If the responses to these questions are taken at face value, they show a remarkable degree of identification with the mixed race West Indian photographs and the brown/mixed race group. This suggests that the majority of children categorized the photographs in such a way as to give themselves an unambiguous place in the racial structure.

However, to establish a more accurate picture of the children's subjective racial identification it was necessary to combine these results with those from other sections of the test. Some children made comments during the categorization and preference tests which either confirmed or contradicted their racial identification choices, and some gave revealing reasons as to why particular choices had been made. In order to make maximum use of the information available, the relevant responses for each child also had to be considered as a whole – in the form of a single *identity pattern*.

Bearing this in mind, the responses to the direct questions about identification will be considered only briefly. This will be followed by a description of responses to the preference section, which also showed a strong orientation to the mixed race West Indian photographs. The rest of the chapter will be concerned with the combined qualitative and quantitative information about identification which was gleaned from all sections of the test.

77

These results show that a positive mixed race identity was not quite as widespread as the preference and identification results suggested. In fact the sample appeared to fall into two main identity patterns: those who were preoccupied with the black/ white dichotomy and seemed to be in conflict about where they belonged within it, and those who made more use of secondary racial categories and seemed to be content with a black/mixed race identity.

THE 'LOOK-ALIKE' AND 'GROUP IDENTITY' RESULTS
The majority (80 per cent) of the children in the sample chose a photograph of a mixed race West Indian child as the one which 'looked most like them'. The remainder chose either a West Indian, a white, or a mixed race Asian child. None of the respondents thought that the Asian children resembled them (Table 4.3).

It is, of course, difficult to compare these results with previous studies of *black* children for all the reasons outlined in Chapter 2. The definition of *mis*identification depends entirely on one's prior assumptions about what constitutes a socially and psychologically viable racial identity. However, if in this instance misidentification is defined as any choice which is not West Indian or mixed race West Indian, then the results are similar to those of the most recent study of black British children (Davey and Norburn, 1980). Unlike in Milner's 1975 study, when almost half the West Indian children misidentified, in the Davey and Norburn study only 8 per cent did so; the authors explain this decrease in misidentification in terms of the Black Consciousness movement, which has made the affirmation of blackness a more positive experience for black

Table 4.3 *Photograph Chosen as 'Look-Alike'*

	Number of times chosen	%
Mixed race West Indian	41	80
West Indian	7	14
White	1	2
Mixed race Asian	2	4
Asian	0	0
Total	51	100

British children. In the present study of mixed race children, 6 per cent of the sample misidentified. This suggests that there is less misidentification among these children than among black children ten years ago and a similar amount as among black children today.

There is, however, another way of looking at these results. Because mixed race children vary considerably in skin colour and physiognomy, and because one of the mixed race children in the photographs was much lighter skinned than the others, a useful additional measure of racial identification is to compare each child's look-alike choice with his or her appearance. Misidentification could then be defined as choosing a look-alike who has lighter skin or more Caucasian features than the respondent. (A further advantage of this measure is that it attempts to compensate for the fact that 'non-white' photographs outnumbered 'white' photographs by seven to one and that a mixed race West Indian or mixed Asian choice was doubly likely compared with a white, West Indian or Asian one.)

When this comparison is made, the misidentification figures rise; 17.5 per cent of the children made a 'lighter' look-alike choice compared with 82.5 per cent making a 'realistic' or 'darker' choice. The figures for the two definitions of misidentification are shown in Tables 4.4 and 4.5.

Table 4.4 *Misidentification Defined as Any Choice Which Is Not West Indian or Mixed Race West Indian*

West Indian or mixed race West Indian		Other		Total	
N	%	N	%	N	%
48	94	3	6	51	100

Table 4.5 *Misidentification Defined as Any Choice Lighter than Respondent's Own Appearance*

'Lighter'		'Realistic'		'Darker'		Total	
N	%	N	%	N	%	N	%
9	17.5	33	65	9	17.5	51	100

Table 4.6   *Identification in Context of Category Set*

Type of set	Brown/ half-caste	White	Black	Asian	Total
Simple, colour	25	4	1	0	30
Complex, multi-criteria	18	2	1	0	21
Total	43	6	2	0	51

Despite this rather higher misidentification figure one can still conclude that these mixed race children, like modern black children, are well aware that they do not resemble blond(e), blue-eyed figures and that the emotional content of this knowledge is not so great as to inhibit them from expressing it. However, it is also evident that they are not immune to the belief that 'light is better' – a belief that is perpetuated not only in the white population but also by some sections of the black.

The second direct question about racial identification – 'Which group are you in?' – came later in the test, after the children had arranged the photographs into categories. Responses to this question show evidence of slightly more identity conflict (or wishes to be white) than the look-alike results, but even so a large proportion of the sample (88 per cent) remained consistent with their look-alike choices and identified themselves as members of an intermediate 'mixed' or 'brown' group. The children's choice of group is shown in Table 4.6 in the context of the kind of category set they constructed.

The number of children who identified themselves as white increased from one to six (2 to 12 per cent). Once again, however, none of the sample said that they belonged to the Asian group. The children's interest seemed to centre on the white, black and mixed race West Indian groups when it came to expressing their identity, and the Asian group did not appear to be of relevance.

These results seem to lead to similar conclusions as the look-alike choices. The majority of these mixed race children seem to identify themselves as members of either a brown or a mixed race group. They have few or no illusions about resembling white children.

Racial Preference

There were three parts of the identity questionnaires which were meant to tap the children's *feelings* about the different racial groups. The first was the 'ideal' identification question, which asked the children to point to the photograph that they would most like to be. The second was the activities test, where they were asked to choose two children as imaginary companions for a range of activities; and the third was the section on stereotypes, where they assigned positive and negative attributes to the children depicted in the photographs.

The ideal identification question elicited more white and fewer mixed race West Indian choices than the more factual look-alike question. When the 'ideals' of individual children were compared with their actual appearance, it was found that about a third had chosen a photograph which was lighter than themselves. But the activities and stereotype responses continued the trend of the identification results in showing a strong bias towards the mixed race West Indian photographs. These were the most popular choices as companions for activities and were the *most* positively and *least* negatively stereotyped of all the photographs. Similarly evident in these two sections was the unpopularity of the Asian and mixed race Asian children. Indian children were hardly ever chosen to take part in the activities and they were allotted a disproportionately high number of negative stereotypes.

'IDEAL' IDENTIFICATION

The racial orientation measure which was most closely related to the earlier self-identification questions was that of asking the children to point out their 'ideal'. 'If you could be one of these children (as if by magic) which one would you rather be?' The responses are shown in Table 4.7, with the look-alike percentages given in brackets for the purpose of comparison.

The numbers of children selecting a mixed race West Indian figure on this question are much reduced compared with the look-alike figures, with more respondents choosing white or mixed race Asian photographs. Clearly, when asked for their ideal, many children were seduced by the appeal of a lighter-skinned, more Caucasian-looking figure. As with the results from the look-alike question, these choices were analysed in relation to the children's actual appearance and assessed as 'realistic', 'lighter', or 'darker' (Table 4.8).

81

Table 4.7   *'Ideal' Identification*

Photograph chosen as ideal	N	%	(Look-alike %)
Mixed race West Indian	25	49	(80)
West Indian	9	17.5	(14)
White	9	17.5	(2)
Mixed race Asian	7	14	(4)
Asian	1	2	(0)
Total	51	100	(100)

Table 4.8   *Ideal Identification in Relation to Appearance*

'Realistic'		'Lighter'		'Darker'		Total	
N	%	N	%	N	%	N	%
26	51	18	35	7	14	51	100

Although half the sample said they would *prefer* to be the child they most looked like, just over a third seemed to wish to be lighter.

In the Davey and Norburn (1980) study cited earlier, where few children misidentified on the factual look-alike question, half the sample made an out-group *ideal* identity choice. The authors concluded that, although their respondents knew that they were black, they were still acutely aware of the advantages of being white. The same may be said of these mixed race children; despite the realism shown by the majority of the sample in making their look-alike choice, a substantial majority would prefer to be lighter skinned or white.

THE ACTIVITIES TEST

For this test, each respondent was required to point to two photographs as companions for various activities. These involved both high and low-intimacy situations. The questions ranged from 'Which two children would you like to stay the night at your house?' to 'Which two children would you have in your team for a game?' In addition, each respondent was asked to pick four children to be their guests at a party.

A useful overview of the popularity of each of the pairs of photographs can be gained by comparing the number of times each pair was chosen with the number of times one would have expected it to be chosen by chance. If the figures for the party and other situations are combined, and if occasions where no photograph was chosen are eliminated, there was a total of 1,119 choices to be made. Spread over the seven pairs of photographs, each pair was likely to be chosen 159.8 times. The amount by which each pair departed from its chance expectancy is shown in Figure 4.6.

It is clear from this graphic representation of the children's choices that the least popular photographs of the set were the Asian and mixed race Asian children, the most popular group being mixed race West Indian. The photographs of the West Indian children were chosen slightly more times than the white (202 as opposed to 182). On high-intimacy activities there was a slight bias towards the white and the mixed race West Indian photographs, and there was a corresponding tendency to choose West Indian or Asian companions for low-intimacy activities. However, the preference was not marked, and it is possible that the level of intimacy was not sufficiently spelled out to elicit any distinguishable pattern of response.

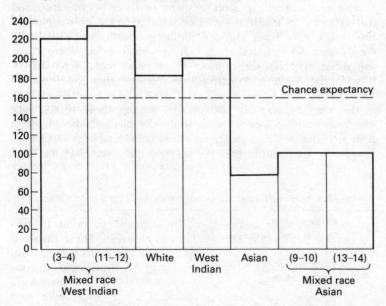

Figure 4.6 The activities test: popularity of photo pairs

Two features of these preference results are particularly striking. First, it would appear that the children tested preferred to imagine their playmates as either white, or West Indian, or mixed race West Indian. The sample as a whole showed little inclination to include children of Asian extraction in any of the suggested activities. Secondly, out of this trio of racial groups, it was the *mixed race* children who drew the most preference choices, with the West Indian and white children coming second and third respectively. The children appeared to be showing that, in their fantasy life at least, their playground activities involved only these three groups and that they found children like themselves the most attractive prospective companions for most leisure activities. This interpretation fits very well with the sociometric study of a British junior school carried out by Durojaiye (1970). It was noted in Chapter 1 that Durojaiye's results suggested that, although mixed race children were popular with both black and white children, they showed a strong preference for finding friends within their own, mixed race group.

This interpretation is also borne out when the preference patterns of individual children are examined. The bias towards the mixed race West Indian figures is not the result of just a few children choosing them exclusively. Most respondents tended to concentrate their choices on only two or three photographs, and the majority of children included a mixed race photograph in their top two or three choices. Similar proportions of the sample (less than half) included a white and/or West Indian figure in the top three, whereas the number of children including Asian or mixed race Asian photographs was considerably lower (Table 4.9).

The amount of white orientation among these mixed race children is low compared with studies of black British children. Although the white photographs enjoy considerable popularity as imaginary companions, they are no more favoured than the West

Table 4.9   *Inclusion of Photographs in 'Top Three' Choices*

Inclusion in 'top three' photo selection	% of children	N
Mixed race West Indian	67	34
West Indian	43	22
White	41	21
Asian or mixed race Asian	16	8

Indian children. The majority of children showed a bias towards their own, mixed race group.

STEREOTYPES

The strong positive orientation of these respondents towards the mixed race West Indian figures was carried through to the stereotype section where the children were presented with eight characteristics which are commonly attributed to one or other race (or to darkness or lightness generally) and asked to match them with a photograph. One of the mixed race pairs (not, incidentally, the one which contained the very light mixed race boy) received the most positive and least negative stereotype choices. However, the expected white bias in relation to the West Indian figures asserted itself in this section; white photographs were more positively stereotyped than black (West Indian) ones, and the *kind* of stereotype that each of these two groups was assigned followed the 'classic' pattern. On the other hand, the Asian children were once again universally stigmatized and rejected; they received fewer positive and more negative choices than any other group.

There were four positive stereotypes ('clean and neat', 'nice and friendly', 'good looking', 'never needs telling off') and four negative ('dirty', 'lazy', 'always picking fights', 'naughty'). The distribution of the total choices of the sample over the seven pairs of photographs is shown in Figure 4.7. The total number of times a pair was chosen for a positive stereotype is shown above the horizontal axis; the total number of times it was chosen for a negative stereotype is shown below the axis.

As with the distribution of preference choices, perhaps the most notable thing about these results is the negative view of the Asian photographs held by many of these children. The two Asian photographs were attributed wtih positive characteristics only six times compared with being chosen thirty-six times (more than another pair) for a negative stereotype. The negative view of Asians held by these mixed race children is in keeping with black (West Indian) children's attitudes according to the recent Davey and Norburn (1980) study. Writing of the relationship between West Indian and Asian children, as indicated by their sample's responses, they commented: 'In our study ... despite the fact that both minority groups might be thought to have problems in common in their relationship with the dominant group, their feelings of dislike were directed not towards the host community but towards each other' (Davey and Norburn, 1980).

It is interesting to note a trend in the *kind of stereotype* these

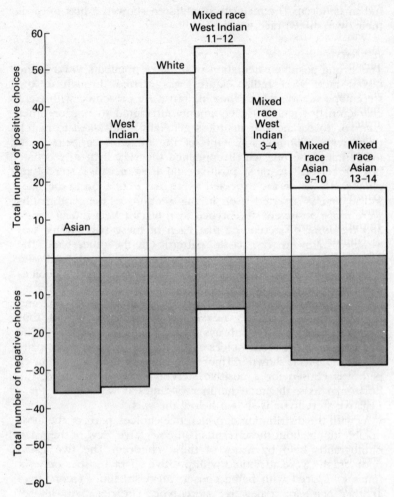

Figure 4.7 Stereotypes: distribution of choices

children assigned to the different groups. Positive personal attributes ('clean and neat' and 'good looking' as opposed to 'dirty') were frequently assigned to mixed race West Indian and to white children; however, West Indian children did better than white children on the positive *social* attributes ('nice and friendly' and not 'naughty'). This may suggest that although the clean, aesthetic assocations of whiteness are held up as an ideal, these mixed race children have experienced greater warmth and acceptance from black West Indian children.

Only one stereotypical comment was made spontaneously by any child during the test, but it is perhaps worth mentioning because of its starkness and the intensity with which it was uttered. When Victor, aged 6, was asked during the categorization whether black was the same as brown, he answered vehemently that it was not.

'Black is like dirt,' he said, 'but brown is like mud.'

'What is white like?' I asked him.

'Water,' he whispered, almost inaudibly. 'White is like water.'

Identity Patterns

The information which has been yielded so far from an analysis of the children's responses is fragmented and superficial. It is also subject to numerous interpretations. For example, the fact that most children chose a mixed race West Indian look-alike could be interpreted in the same way as the results of a study by Greenwald and Oppenheim (1968) where the researchers introduced a medium-skinned doll into the identity test; namely, that if 'non-white' children are given the choice between identifying with a white, a black, or a brown figure, invariably they will choose the brown. The argument is that children who live in a white-dominated society see this as the best compromise between what they wish to be (white) and what they 'know they are' (black).

In order to find out more about what these responses meant to the children who made them, it was necessary to examine each child's comments, inconsistencies and reactions in context. In particular, inconsistent responses on different sections of the test were felt to be important. Was it *the same children* who identified as mixed race on the look-alike, group identity *and* ideal identity sections? Or did some of the children who chose a mixed race look-alike betray a white orientation on a different section of the test?

When the individual response patterns were examined, it was clear that there was a greater degree of white bias (or identity conflict) than the results from the single measures suggested. A number of children were inconsistent in the way they answered different sections of the test and so betrayed ambiguous feelings about their own identity. Robert, for example, chose a mixed race West Indian look-alike but classified it as 'white' in the categorization test; he then went on to identify himself as a member of the 'brown' group (which did not include his look-alike). On some level, then, he was unsure whether he was 'really' white or brown. Angela chose in an even more complex fashion: a mixed race look-alike (classified as mixed race), a West Indian ideal identity and a white group identity choice. In this response pattern, Angela seemed to be displaying the classic mixed race conflict; she longed to be white, knew that she was not and felt guilty about her wish to abandon the black group (hence her 'appeasement measure' in setting it up as her ideal). Confirmation of this interpretation came in her response to the categorization test. When discussing how the white, black, Indian and mixed race groups spoke, she showed the same pattern of feelings. The Indian group was dismissed without hesitation: 'They speak Indian.' The mixed race group, approved of but not identified with, spoke 'normally – just like we speak'. Her description of the black group was less confident. After a pause, she said quietly, 'They speak . . . nice . . .' And the white group? She whispered, almost inaudibly, 'They speak how *I* speak.'

Other children gave more direct indication of identity conflict. In explaining why they had chosen a *white ideal identity*, Carlton and Simeon were both quite open in their admiration of the blond, Caucasian look. Carlton said simply that he liked the white boy 'because he's got yellow hair and a white face'; Simeon preferred the white group because 'white is my best colour'. A number of respondents expressed a mild dissatisfaction with their appearance – in particular their hair – when they compared themselves with some of the children in the photographs. Tatum described her hair as 'messy'. Ella, contrasting her own tumbling 'corkscrew' curls with the straight-haired white and Indian children, said, 'I don't like my hair. I'd like it to grow down my back.' Kieran was impressed by the straight black hair of the mixed race Asian boys; he sighed wistfully over one of these photographs and said, 'I look scruffy – my hair I mean.' Comments such as these were relatively common among children who had chosen an ideal identity which had a more Caucasian appearance than their look-alike. Their dissatisfaction seemed to be related to the 'white is beautiful' idea – hardly surprising in view of its pervasive presence in their environment.

The children who took the test also varied in their reactions to it, some being candid and talkative about the subject of race and others being more resistant. Children with different temperaments inevitably react in different ways when asked to talk about their feelings, but some of those who were chatty and open before the test became more and more defensive as it progressed. Others, who answered most of the questions with smiling confidence, suddenly resisted when a particular topic came up. One general finding was that children who had chosen a realistic look-alike were able to explain quite easily why they had selected a particular photograph and were happy to talk about it at length; on the other hand, children who had chosen either a lighter or a darker look-alike were more reticent on this point and occasionally retracted their original decision. This suggested that some degree of identity conflict was involved in both a lighter and a darker look-alike choice. The one child who said that a white photograph looked most like her was in fact very light in appearance, yet her response to the question asking for elaboration showed that she had not made the choice with ease. She whispered, 'Hair ... eyes', with her own eyes cast down, and became silent for much of the test. Only a moment before, she had been smiling and chatting freely.

Conflict Assessment

The extent of each child's racial identity conflict was assessed by comparison with the model of a 'viable mixed race identity' set out in Chapter 2. Whereas the tacit model of 'well-adjusted' black children was that they should see themselves as totally black and that they should overcome, with the support of the black community, the negative view of black people held by society at large, the literature on mixed race children suggested that a black *and* mixed race identity would be the most workable, provided that it had the support of the child's significant others. From a social and a psychological viewpoint, the most satisfactory racial identity for these children seemed to be one which embraced the uniqueness of a dual cultural heritage, but still retained a positive perception of the self as black.

How would children respond to the identity test if they were attempting to express a positive identity of this kind? One might expect a pattern to emerge as follows:

- a look-alike which is realistic in relation to the child's appearance (usually mixed race West Indian);
- a mixed race West Indian ideal identity, or one chosen from the darker-skinned photographs;
- preference choices which show a positive orientation to the mixed race and darker-skinned children;
- no pro-white or anti-black stereotypes;

89

- no apparently resistant or defensive test reaction;
- a willingness to talk about race and being of mixed race;
- a clear knowledge that he or she is not white; for example, look-alike classified as non-white on the categorization test;
- no obvious dissatisfaction with appearance;
- a clear knowledge that the mixed race *group* is not white.

A child who responded in exactly this way would constitute a paragon of positive adjustment. In a society such as Britain, where an anti-black bias exists, they would also be unusually impervious to the influence of racism. None the less, like Milner's (1975) 'positive black identity' this was a useful ideal type against which to compare the children's responses and to assess how much ambivalence and identity conflict they displayed. Using this ideal as a yardstick, the sample was divided into five groups according to their identity pattern.

Three of these groups were composed of children whose identity was entirely bound up with the black/white dichotomy. They said either that they were white, or that they were black, or they were in open conflict between the two. The other two groups consisted of children who made use of secondary racial categorization and saw themselves as members of an intermediate brown or mixed race group which was also black. However, one of these groups showed more white bias than the other in its preference choices. I have labelled these five identity patterns 'white', 'black', 'contrary', 'mixed race (light bias)' and 'black mixed race', although these names have been adopted for ease of reference only and they refer to patterns which are more subtle than the terminology suggests.

Within each of these five groups was a core of children who seemed to typify that particular identity response and a periphery of respondents who more or less conformed to the pattern. Some examples of core and periphery children now follow to illustrate how the classification was made.

GROUP (1): THE 'WHITE' PATTERN (SEVEN CHILDREN)
The first group consisted of those children who, far from having a positive orientation to themselves as mixed race or black, appeared to see themselves as belonging to a highly valued white or 'almost white' group. More than any other children in the sample, these seven respondents seemed to approximate to the 'white' end of Milner's (1975) continuum. They were apparently prone to taking refuge in the fantasy notion that they were white. All but one chose a look-alike lighter than themselves, all chose a

white or a light-skinned child as an ideal identity and all showed resistance to talking about race. In addition, several of these children showed a heavy white or light orientation in their preference choices and concentrated positive stereotypes on to the white pair.

Zara, a very light-skinned child, was the most extreme of this group and has already been mentioned as the only child to choose a white look-alike. Zara's group identity, her ideal identity and her preference choices were all consistent with the look-alike choice; she placed herself in the white group, indicated white as her preferred identity and chose mainly the two white children as her playmates. During the test she was silent and resisting and made no unsolicited comments at all. Yet her behaviour before and after did not suggest an unusually shy child.

No other respondent in this group maintained white choices so consistently. Simeon, for example, said he belonged in the white group, white was his 'best colour' and he would prefer to be white, yet he chose a mixed race West Indian boy as his look-alike and he polarized his preferences towards the black and the white children. Peter, however, was an example of a child who only just fits into this group; though choosing a look-alike and an ideal identity both lighter than himself and showing preferences for the lighter children, Peter said that he belonged in the brown group. None the less, the core characteristic of this group was *evidence of wishes to be white*, combined with a view of self *lighter than reality would allow*.

GROUP (2): THE 'BLACK' PATTERN (FOUR CHILDREN)
The four children in this second group maintained a consistent view of themselves as *black* and a preference for a black identity; they gave little sign of wishing to be white or lighter skinned, or of valuing a mixed race identity. John, for example, chose a black look-alike (darker than himself) and a black ideal identity and preferred the two West Indian children as playmates. In addition, he grouped the photographs into a dichotomous 'coloured'/'white' set and placed himself in the 'coloured' group. Mona and Joseph were similar to John in their responses, although Mona chose a mixed race West Indian girl as her ideal, because she preferred her hair. Noreen, the fourth child in this group, had a slightly different response pattern; although she chose a West Indian lookalike, she placed herself in a group which contained black *and* mixed race children and she showed more interest in herself as mixed race than the other three children in the group.

GROUP (3): THE 'CONTRARY' PATTERN (TEN CHILDREN:
FOUR BLACK REAL/WHITE IDEAL; SIX WHITE REAL/BLACK IDEAL)

The ten children in this group responded inconsistently on
different measures in the test and appeared to be unable to choose
between black and white, light and dark. There seemed to be two
forms of conflict at work here. On the one hand, there were four
children whose look-alike was unrealistically darker and whose
ideal identity was unrealistically lighter than themselves. On the
other hand, six children responded in exactly the opposite way;
their look-alike was lighter and their ideal identity was darker than
they were.

Patrick was a good example of the first group. His look-alike and
group identity were West Indian, whereas his ideal identity was
white. He also showed a heavy white orientation on the
preference choices and made positive comments about the white
boy's appearance. Similarly, Alison chose a West Indian look-alike
and a white ideal identity and in addition held negative
stereotypes of the black group; she chose the one black girl in the
photographs as 'lazy', 'dirty', 'naughty' and 'always picking fights'.
These four children appeared to have a basic conception of
themselves as black and yet displayed a strongly positive view of
the white and a negative view of the black group.

The second section of this group is typified by Kieran, who
chose a look-alike lighter than himself and yet a West Indian ideal
identity. Four out of the six children in this section chose a West
Indian ideal identity. The two children who did not were none the
less included in this section because their generally light
orientation was juxtaposed by a strong preference for the West
Indian photographs on the activity and positive stereotype
questions.

Typically, the children in both sections of this third group were
preoccupied with the black/white dichotomy, showed little
interest in the categories of 'mixed' and 'brown' and tended to
show conflict and uncertainty on the group identity question (by
moving their hand towards and away from the white group).

GROUP (4): THE 'MIXED RACE (WHITE BIAS)' PATTERN
(EIGHTEEN CHILDREN)

In the fourth group were the children whose self-identification
responses suggested that they saw themselves as members of
either an intermediate colour or an intermediate 'racial' category,
which was black, yet who also showed some evidence of white
bias. Their look-alike and group identity showed consistency and

realism in relation to their appearance, yet on the preference measures (including ideal identity) they were prone to seeing whiteness more positively than blackness.

A child who showed extreme white preference combined with a brown self-identification was Carlton, who clearly and openly expressed wishes to be white. More typical of this group, however, was Ella; despite choosing a mixed race West Indian look-alike, a brown group identity and even a mixed race ideal, she still succumbed to the traditional negative black stereotypes. These children appeared to have a basic conception of themselves as occupying a position on or around the mid-point of a continuum between light and dark – or in a clear-cut intermediate group which was black – yet they also seemed to be highly conscious of the fact that, in the eyes of society, white was more positive than black.

GROUP (5): THE 'BLACK MIXED RACE' PATTERN (TWELVE CHILDREN)
The fifth and last group consisted of those children who maintained a consistent view of themselves as black mixed race, not only in reality but also as an ideal. The preferences of these children leaned towards the darker end of the colour continuum.

Typical is Leo, who chose a realistic mixed race look-alike, a brown group identity, an ideal identity the same as his look-alike and a preference for the darker children on the activities test. Leo was open and chatty throughout the interview and appeared to feel comfortable talking about the interracial aspects of his family. The twelve children in this group appeared to be most like the ideal described earlier. They seemed to be able to ignore and tolerate – perhaps even to enjoy – their potentially ambiguous position between black and white, while retaining a knowledge of their blackness for self-defence and support (Table 4.10)

Table 4.10   *The Racial Identity of the Sample*

Group		N	%
(1) White ⎫		7	14
(2) Black ⎬ Dichotomy related		4	8
(3) Contrary ⎭		10	19.5
(4) Mixed race (white bias) ⎫ Intermediate		18	35
(5) Black mixed race ⎭		12	23.5
Total		51	100

To summarize: five groups of children displayed different patterns of response on the identity test. Three of these groups consisted of children who seemed primarily concerned with their position in the black/white dichotomy (41.5 per cent), tending either to see themselves as white (14 per cent), or as totally black (8%), or expressing the conflict openly (19.5 per cent). The remaining two groups of respondents seemed to have a central conception of themselves as mixed race (58.5 per cent), the first combining this with some white orientation (35 per cent) and the second with a dark orientation (23.5 per cent). The last group corresponded most closely to the 'ideal' of a positive black/mixed race identity.

Chapter Five

Identity Patterns:
Multiracial Area versus White Area

The children who took the identity test were divided in the way they saw themselves. Some of them were concerned only with the white/non-white dichotomy and with the problem of whether they were black or white (white, black and contrary patterns) whereas the others saw themselves as members of a mixed race group which was also non-white.

The results of the identity test, viewed in isolation, tell us little more than this. What is needed now is to look at the five identity patterns in context to see if they show any association with the factors which are known to influence *black* children's identity. What is being sought here, ultimately, is to explain why the children in the sample fell into one identification group rather than another; but the analysis is trying in particular to discover under what conditions a positive black/mixed race identity is most likely to flourish.

This chapter deals briefly with the influence of age, sex and skin colour on the children's identity patterns and then goes on to look at their association with geographical area. The area in which mixed race children lived appeared to be a powerful determinant of their racial categorization and identity. Whereas respondents in multiracial areas tended to see the racial structure as a complex pattern of many diverse groups, those in white areas seemed to have a more static picture which saw the structure as consisting of just two groups: black and white. The more cosmopolitan children were able to see their mixed race identity as one of a whole range of identities within the black group; but the children in white areas were forced to see themselves as either white or, if they were not white, then black. Secondary identifications in terms of categories such as 'brown' and 'mixed race' had no meaning in the context of a white social world.

Age, Sex and Racial Identity

Previous research on black children found that age exerted two kinds of influence on children's racial identity. The complexity of racial categorization and labelling increased with age, and older children showed a greater tendency than younger children to identify with their own, black group. The connection between age and racial categorization was also found in the present study; whereas the under-8s tended to see the racial structure as a set of simple, colour categories, respondents over 8 took a complex, multi-criteria view of racial classification. But the expected association between age and racial identity did not appear in the study. The five identity patterns outlined in the previous chapter were not related to age; however, the number of children in each cell of the table was small (Table 5.1).

One has to be to be hesitant about drawing conclusions from such small numbers. Like black children, increasing numbers of mixed race children may come to see themselves as members of the black group as they get older, but the relationship has failed to show up in such a small sample.

However, it would not be surprising if the 'realism' of mixed race children's identity (that is, the acceptance of the fact that they are black) stabilized slightly earlier than that of black children. The potential ambiguity of their position may force mixed race children into an earlier confrontation with the realities of the racial system. Many of the parents I spoke to tried to pre-

Table 5.1   *Identity Group by Age*

Identity group	Age		
	Under 8 years	Over 8 years	Total
(1) White	4	3	7
(2) Black	2	2	4
(3) Black/white conflict	3	7	10
(4) Mixed race (lighter orient.)	9	9	18
(5) Mixed race (darker orient.)	8	4	12
Total	26	25	51

Identity Patterns

empt their mixed race children's identity conflict by taking up racial issues when the child was very young – more so, perhaps, than black parents, who would assume that their child automatically 'knew' that he or she was black. Mixed race children's knowledge of the primary racial structure may be well established before the sixth year, at a rather earlier age than that of black children. More research is needed to confirm this idea.

The influence of sex on mixed race children's identity also ran contrary to previous research on black children. In most of these studies, black girls showed a greater degree of white orientation than black boys, being, it was said, more influenced by white standards of beauty and attractiveness. But among this group of mixed race children the reverse seemed to be true; the girls were *less* likely to be found among the children who were in conflict over their identity and more likely to see themselves as belonging to a positive, mixed race group (Table 5.2).

The contrast between these results and those from studies of black children may be connected to methodological differences – in particular, the use of photographs rather than dolls and the more active nature of the test. A choice between two dolls may elicit a specifically female identification in girls and recall the cultural link between whiteness, beauty and femininity. The use of photographs which are not passively chosen but must be actively grouped may forestall or bypass this association and give girls more freedom to express their cognitive perception of the racial structure and their own position within it – which, at this age, may be more positive than that of boys. On the other hand, the association between sex and racial identity may be a spurious one caused by the fact that there were more girls than boys who lived in a multiracial area and who were consequently more likely to see themselves as black/mixed race.

Table 5.2 *Identity Group by Sex*

Identity Group	Female	Male	Total
(1)–(3) (dichotomy)	8	13	21
(4) or (5) (mixed race)	19	11	30
Total	27	24	51

97

Skin colour

Results from previous studies of black children's identity were
equivocal on the subject of whether light- or dark-skinned
children were more in conflict over their identity. On the whole,
the responses of these mixed race children throw little light on
the controversy. There was some evidence to suggest that dark
children tend to be in conflict over their identity rather than
having an intermediate identity; but, again, the number of dark-
skinned children in the sample was so small that very little can be
deduced from this result.

The sample contained many more light and medium children
than dark children. I tested 19 light-skinned, 23 medium and 9
darker children. My impression while conducting the fieldwork
was that there was no consistent pattern of behaviour or of racial
identification among the respondents in terms of their appearance;
and, certainly, when one looks at the first three identity groups
(black, white and contrary) this impression is borne out. The
children in the 'white' group were evenly spread out over light,
medium and dark; of the four children in the 'black' group, two
were medium skinned and two were dark; and light, medium and
dark were equally represented in the 'contrary' group (Table 5.3).

However, spanning all the identity groups, there did seem to be
a tendency for light and medium children to be concentrated in
the two groups which chose an intermediate identification and for
the darker children to be in the three groups which were

Table 5.3 *Identity Group by Skin Colour*

Group	Skin colour			Total
	Light	Medium	Dark	
(1) White	2	3	2	7
(2) Black	0	2	2	4
(3) Contrary	4	3	3	10
(4) Mixed race (white bias)	9	8	1	18
(5) Black mixed race	4	7	1	12
Total	19	23	9	51

Table 5.4   *Identity Groups (Combined) by Skin Colour*

Identity group	Skin colour			
	Light	Medium	Dark	Total
Black/white/contrary	6	8	7	21
Mixed race (white bias)/ black mixed race	13	15	2	30
Total	19	23	9	51

preoccupied with the dichotomy. This difference is significant at the 5 per cent level (Table 5.4).

The numbers of dark children were very small, and it would go beyond the data to extrapolate too much from them. One could tentatively argue that for darker mixed race children an intermediate identity is not as socially viable as for children who look like they are of mixed race, since they are more likely than the latter to be regarded simply as 'black'. If total membership of the black group is hampered by black peer rejection or by a lack of family encouragement, it is possible that darker mixed race children may be more prone to identity conflict than light- or medium-skinned children. However, it must be reiterated that there was no additional qualitative data to support this.

One might be tempted, on the basis of the connection between lighter skin and intermediate identity, to revert to the argument that these middle-of-the road categories were simply expressions of white/light bias or else were the prerogative of 'fair' children who were conscious of occupying a favoured position in both the West Indian and the British racial structure. However, this interpretation is not supported when the children's responses are considered in further detail.

Within the two 'mixed race' groups, there were four different combinations of racial identification and preference: children who described themselves as 'brown' who showed a white bias; those who saw themselves as 'brown' with no white bias; those who described themselves as 'mixed race' with a white bias; and those who identified themselves as 'mixed race' with no white bias. I noted in the previous chapter that the label 'brown' appeared to refer to skin colour more than did the labels 'half-caste' or 'mixed race', which would make it a more obvious choice for the lighter-skinned children who wished to emphasize their 'better colour'. Yet these four divisions within the 'black mixed race' and the 'mixed race (white bias)' groups were not related to skin colour. Children who had a lighter skin were no more likely to stress the importance of skin colour in their racial categorization and preference responses than were children who had a darker skin.

Area and Racial Identity

WHERE THE CHILDREN LIVED

I divided the areas from which the children came into three types: totally white areas (which were all outside London); in-between areas (once again, outside London); and multiracial areas (which were in London). The number of families and children in each type of area is given below in Table 5.5.

Of the ten families who lived in white areas, six had made their homes in quiet seaside towns on the south or east coast of Britain. Predominantly, these areas were middle class as well as white, with a high proportion of owner-occupied houses. Although two of these families lived only a few miles from a port, where a few black faces could be seen, the immediate neighbourhoods of all ten families (and a radius of several miles for most) was exclusively white. The child I interviewed was usually either the only black child in the school or one of a tiny minority, and the black parent (present in five of the ten families) was often the only black adult in the area. This meant that all the child's potential friends were white – as were the relatives, friends and neighbours he or she saw on a day-to-day basis. This did not mean that the children never saw black relatives and friends or other mixed race children, but it did mean that such contact was infrequent and limited by time and distance. Visits to black relatives and friends were usually confined to holidays.

An in-between area was defined as one which had a small West Indian or Asian presence in the immediate area, but was near a town or city where there was a much larger black community.

Table 5.5 *Where the Children Lived*

Type of area	Number of families	Number of children
White	10	12
In between	4	6
Multiracial	25	33
Total	39	51

These areas could not be classified as totally white, since the child's experience was, in some small measure, multiracial; none the less, these children were still part of only a very small minority of black children in their school. Although some of their everyday contact was multiracial, their experience of a *black community* was limited to visits to the nearby town. Of the four families who lived in in-between areas, three lived in lower-middle-class suburban districts and one lived on a predominantly working-class council estate.

Twenty-five families lived in cosmopolitan communities in London. A multiracial area of London was defined as one where the percentage of either Asians or West Indians in the ward of residence exceeded 2 per cent of the total ward population and where the borough of residence was classified as 'concentrated' in *The Social Atlas of London* (Shepherd, Westway and Lee, 1974). (Where I had reason to believe an area had changed significantly in its racial composition, I checked with the local council.) The surroundings of these children, in terms of the visibility of the different ethnic groups, were in marked contrast to those of the children in white areas. Whereas the children of coastal and country towns saw one-colour, one-culture uniformity in their streets, shops and schools, the children in multiracial areas were surrounded by people and products from all parts of the world. Their schools often had to cater for several different languages and to make provision for a variety of religious practices.

The poorer families in this group tended to live either on crowded, 'concrete' housing estates several miles from the city centre or in run-down properties in the inner city. Sixteen of the families lived in one of these two types of housing. The remaining nine families lived either in lower-middle-class suburban districts (seven families) or in streets which had been 'gentrified' to suit middle-class owner-occupiers (two families). But these children had one thing in common, regardless of their family's standard of living; their everyday social contacts included black, white and brown people, and their neighbourhood reflected the multiplicity of cultures which coexist in multiracial Britain.

RACIAL TENSION IN THE DIFFERENT AREAS

The degree of racial tension and hostility in these areas was very difficult to judge. None the less, an attempt was made to reach a broad assessment of the 'racial temperature' of the different types of area, since this was likely to have some influence on the children's feelings and beliefs about race. Considerable care had to be taken in interpreting the mother's view of the amount of racial tension around her, for in many cases this turned out to be as much an indicator of her general beliefs about the state of race relations as an objective judgement about the area.

The women in white areas believed that racial prejudice was a phenomenon of the city. Pat Ward, for instance, a white mother who lived in a white area of Essex, said, 'If you go to an area of high population of immigrants such as Southall or Forest Gate, then, yes, you'll meet prejudice. If you move away – very little.'

Elaine Houghton, also a white mother, but from an 'in-between' area in the North of England, agreed that 'The problem is worse when there's a *lot* of coloured people in one area. In Liverpool... well, I feel the tension there.'

This view was to some extent borne out by the reports of the women in the cities. Although many of the mothers in multiracial areas claimed that they had never encountered prejudice ('Personally, I've never come across it'), several went on to relate incidents of racial harassment which ranged from verbal abuse to physical violence. Their initial statement that they had never come across prejudice seemed to come from a reluctance to sound militant or radical. These women took great pains to show that they held an optimistic view of race relations in Britain as a whole. Yet, for a number of women, the reality was a far cry from the rosy picture of racial harmony they had painted earlier.

Sybil Finlay (white, from a multiracial area) thought that race relations in Britain were 'pretty much all right', but she later recounted a story which showed that for the mothers of mixed race children on her estate things were not 'all right' at all:

When I walk up the street with Zeta, there's all these bloody skin'eads. There's a whole big gang of them gets in a bloody line. I grabs Zeta's hand tight and says, 'Just walk on', but I always think, 'Fuck me, we're gonna get beaten up.' I was telling my friend Michael that I'm scared of this British Movement – there's a lot of that going on around here. But Michael says it's not them you gotta watch, it's the skin'eads. So half the time I don't know whether to walk down the road or what.

Nora Ballini, who lived on a different West London estate, had been stoned and verbally abused by a gang of white youths. Two other women reported that, when they first moved into their council flats, neighbours had petitioned to have them evicted. Undoubtedly, mothers in multiracial areas were more likely to have experienced open racial hostility than women in white areas, and it is perhaps not too rash to assume that this was reflected in the experiences of their children.

One should nevertheless bear in mind the qualification which several women in white areas added to the statement that their neighbourhoods were tolerant of small numbers of black people. Although there was no *overt* prejudice, they said, it was possible that the hostile feelings were expressed out of the hearing of interracial families. In white areas, you never knew what people really thought. Pat Ward, who said that it was areas like Southall which were most racially tense, belived that in white areas 'they'll accept you for what you are'. But she added, more hesitantly, 'Whether they feel the prejudice in theirselves and they don't show it — it don't come out ... I don't know.'

Ruth McCarthy, a white single mother who lived in a small seaside town, contrasted the open racial violence in the cities with the 'muffled, middle-class, patronizing attitude' she encountered in her day-to-day dealings with white people:

In areas where there are large numbers of coloured people, you get resentment, but you also get a mixed society. In backwaters like this you don't get a lot of in-built antagonistic prejudice, but you do get this sort of reluctance to mix. If someone coloured was coming here I'd reassure them that *on the surface* it's not bad. But under the surface — well, they may meet with a few blank walls.

Mothers in white areas emphasized the uncertainty of their position *vis-à-vis* their white neighbours. They were never quite sure where they and their children stood. There seemed to be an underlying fear that, if relations between black and white deteriorated in the country as a whole, it would be *they*, rather than the interracial families in the cities, who would be most at risk from white hostility.

There were evidently class elements in the difference between multiracial and white areas. The white areas tended to be characterized by middle-class reserve rather than by working-class directness. But it still remained true that there was a feeling of safety in numbers. Living in a black community, among a wide variety of ethnic groups, the interracial family felt a greater sense of belonging. Gwen Smith, a white middle-class mother who lived in a multiracial area, tried to separate the influence of these two factors — class and racial diversity:

The friction that does seem to exist ... is more friction being a reflection ... of class and financial status, really. Everybody's jostling at the lower end for jobs and housing, and they tend to turn and back-stab the people who are neighbours, who, if they lived in a more prosperous situation, would quite happily rub along together. But then I've only lived in London, and it's quite a multiracial place. I know that in more isolated places in Britain mixed marriages would be regarded as sort of scandalous. But here you have only to go round the shops to see loads of mixed relationships and English women out shopping with mixed race children. You don't feel threatened.

She concluded that, although class played a part in fomenting racial tension among certain groups of people, such as the young and the very poor, interracial families felt safer in a multiracial area, whatever the class mix.

AREA AND RACIAL CATEGORIZATION (CONTROLLING FOR AGE)

One strong impression that was gained from the fieldwork, and was supported by some previous research, was that the children in multiracial areas were altogether more knowledgeable in their approach to race than the children in white areas. Their attitude bespoke familiarity, suggesting that racial classification, in one form or another, was a feature of everyday conversation. It seemed that even *young* children in poor, multiracial areas acquired a precise and complicated categorization system quite unlike their white area counterparts. This impression was borne out when the responses of the children who did not fit into the age/categorization pattern were examined; that is, *children of less than 95 months with a complex category set and children of more than 95 months with a simple colour-scheme set.*

Nine children over 8 years old had a simple 'black/white/brown' set, and five of these nine lived in an exclusively white area. With the under-8s who had a complex set, the association was even clearer; all of the six younger children who constructed complex, multi-criteria sets lived in multiracial areas. *Whereas in general it was the older children who were knowledgeable about inter-related racial categories which used the criteria of mixture and colour, the younger respondents in working-class, multiracial areas also showed this kind of sophistication.*

A good example of the relationship between area and racial categorization, with age controlled, was provided by the contrast between two children, Esme and Akin. Esme lived in a multiracial area and was probably the most precise and complex of all the respondents in the way she handled the categorization test. She grouped the photographs into a 'white/black/mixed race/Indian' set and she was familiar with a variety of ethnic criteria including colour, culture and religion. Esme was also the child who was quoted earlier as saying that a white mother and a black father were the usual combination for mixed race children at her school. In her neighbourhood, she said, there were 'lots of mixtures – like half-caste and half-Indian'. Esme was only $7\frac{1}{2}$. Akin, on the other hand, lived in a white area and he constructed a 'black/white/ brown' set on the categorization test. Although he was aware of some racial and cultural criteria, his rudimentary knowledge was a far cry from Esme's casual sophistication; yet Akin, at 9 years and 11 months, was the oldest child in the sample. Akin went to a school which was almost totally white and he saw other mixed race children 'about once a year at Harmony functions', according to his mother.

The youngest child to have a complex category set was Nancy, aged 6 years and 1 month, who lived with her mother, and her mother's black boyfriend, on a tough council estate in West London. They had previously lived on another estate, but had moved because of severe racial harassment. Unlike the 6-year-olds in white areas, Nancy was fully aware of the intricacies of racial classification. She labelled her groups of photos 'black', 'white', 'Indian', and 'half-caste' and explained the latter term by saying that their colour was 'made of white and black'. Nancy saw mixed race children every day and school and she lived in an area where a large proportion of her playmates were either mixed race or black.

It is not difficult to offer hypotheses about why even young children develop clear and complex category sets in the context of poverty, racial tension and racial diversity. Where there is a wide range of skin colours and cultures and where the child's everyday linguistic experience is not sheltered by euphemism, racial categorization is likely to be open and to the point. Many mothers found that name-calling motivated their child to demand an explanation of derogatory racial terms. To explain them, the mother translates them back into neutral or positive epithets, which the child then assimilates into his or her total knowledge of the racial structure.

In a more middle-class, white setting, racial slurs are often more subtle or concealed, and the range of terms used is more limited. A white child's loudly expressed curiosity about why the mixed race child is 'different' may be quickly quelled by an embarrassed white mother with a comment about 'coloured people' having a 'nice sun-tan', but the young mixed race child probably fails to connect the incident to information about race which has been given by his or her parents. Messages which have been concealed by euphemism are understood only as the child gets older. Mixed race children learn that the connection between having a sun-tan and being black is misleading and, more importantly, they come to see the adult's embarrassment as derogatory and to internalize the shame about being black which it implies.

AREA AND RACIAL IDENTITY

Children in multiracial areas not only acquired a detailed knowledge of racial classification at an earlier age than children in white or in-between areas, they also appeared to be more likely to identify with an intermediate group (Table 5.6).

The table shows that 76 per cent (23/30) of the children in the two mixed race identity groups lived in a multiracial area; 69 per cent of the children in white areas were in the three identity groups which were preoccupied with primary racial categorization. In other words, *there appeared to be something about living in a multiracial area which encouraged an intermediate identity.* However, this was apparently not a *sufficient* condition for such an identity to be adopted, for there remained ten children who both lived in a multiracial area and were in the white, black, or contrary groups.

Although the number of children living in white areas was small, the apparent vulnerability of this group to racial identity conflict was borne out by additional impressionistic data. The children who lived in white areas but who had a black mixed race identity were exceptions in several important respects. One was a girl whose mother worked at a nearby United States airbase, which made her potential playmates multiracial, according to the mother. This child had also spent a considerable part of her life on a US-influenced Caribbean island, so that her racial categorization and identity may have been as much influenced by US and Caribbean classification as by British. The other two children were siblings and were the children of the *only black woman in the sample who lived in a white area.* This woman also happened to have a very positive view of her own racial identity – a connection which will be discussed in a later chapter.

Table 5.6   *Racial Identity by Area*

Identity group	Type of area			
	Multiracial	In between	White	Total
White/black/contrary	10	2	9	21
Mixed race (white bias)/ black mixed race	23	3	4	30
Total	33	5	13	51

Chi^2 = 7.22, significant at the 5% level[1].

MIXED RACE FRIENDS

One factor which may explain why mixed race children who lived in multiracial areas were more likely to have a strong mixed race identity is the greater degree of contact they had with other interracial families. It will be recalled that the mother's interview schedule contained a question on how often her children saw or played with other mixed race children. An analysis of the responses to this question by area revealed not only that children in multiracial areas were more likely than children in white areas to meet other mixed race children, but also that most children in multiracial areas played with other mixed race children *at least once a week* and/or went to school with children of interracial parents. Children in white areas played with other children at most 'every few weeks' and at least 'hardly ever' (Table 5.7).

The tabulation of frequency of contact with racial identity group is shown in the table. If the figures for low and medium frequencies are combined – on the grounds that to see other mixed race children even every few weeks would not offer the kind of support that day-to-day contact could provide – these results are highly statistically significant ($chi^2 = 12.1$, significant at the 1 per cent level).

More than one mother in a multiracial area laughed aloud when I asked her if her child ever met other mixed race children. 'The estate is full of them!' exclaimed one mother. 'There are four just in this street,' said another. Clearly, to some of the children in my sample, having one black and one white parent was not an unusual situation.

In many cases, the children's contacts were reinforced by those of the mother, since a considerable number of the women in multiracial areas moved in friendship networks which consisted

Table 5.7 *Frequency of Contact with Other Mixed Race Children*

Identity group	Low/medium ('hardly ever'/ 'every few weeks')	High ('at least once a week')
White/black/contrary	14	7
Mixed race (white bias)/ black mixed race	6	24
Total	20	31

almost exclusively of interracial relationships. I came across several such networks in my search for women and children eligible to be interviewed. Joan Anderson, for example, was one of a group of three white women who lived near each other, were very close friends and helped each other out; all of them had black husbands and mixed race children. An even more dependent bond seemed to exist between a group of young single mothers on an estate, who cared for each other's children and supported each other through various crises.[2] This network involved several women, all but one of whom were white and all with young mixed race children. Another group of friends (of whom I was able to interview only one woman) linked some ten interracial families living on two run-down areas which were relatively close and an estate which was some distance away; despite the distance, the contact was considered sufficiently important by the respondent for her to make the journey whenever she could afford the bus fare for herself and her children.

Out of the twenty-six mothers in multiracial areas, eighteen mentioned at least one woman with a 'mixed' relationship as among their closest friends. Yet even this figure does not do justice to the extent of some women's friendships with other mothers of mixed race children. For example, Maggie Muir named all three of her closest friends as white women with black boyfriends and she knew others, with whom she was not so close. Liz Sanders knew four, of whom two were among her three best friends; and Linda Weaver numbered among her friends no less than nine white women with black partners. She commented:

Well, really, I find that the closest friendships I make are with other mixed couples . . . or girls with mixed children. The white friends are very nice, some of them, but they just don't understand a lot of the things you do if you've got a mixed – you know – mixed family and black husband or boyfriend.[3]

Women in white areas also tended to know other interracial couples, but saw them less often. There were no local networks of interracial families providing everyday support and companionship. Anticipating the next chapter a little, one could characterize the difference between families in the two types of area by saying that in multiracial areas being of mixed race was a visible numerical quality rather than a *concept*; whereas in white areas this was reversed – being of mixed race was a concept which was presented to the child by the parents in the context of a particular world view, but it was not a taken-for-granted part of everyday life. Although multiraciality was often forcefully stressed inside the home and extended to certain select friends, it was not part of the child's school or neighbourhood experience.

The families who lived in white or in-between areas could be divided into two groups in terms of their involvement with other interracial families. The first consisted of eight families where both mother and father were present and where the family did not have many close contacts outside the home. These were privatized middle-class families who were not caught up in neighbourhood mutual support systems which operated on a day-to-day basis. All eight families belonged to the Harmony organization or else knew other interracial couples, and many reported these relationships as being important to them. But apart from one or two exceptions, they could be seen only at intervals of a few weeks, and it was white friends who were seen most often. Mary Ogundele, for example, numbered several interracial families among her friends, but they all lived a considerable distance away, and she named three white women as her closest friends. Like several of these mothers in white areas, Diana Cambe named a white woman with a black husband as a friend who had greatly supported her through early problems of prejudice against her marriage and with whom she was consequently close, but again there was an interval of weeks – sometimes months – between visits.

The second group consisted of five mothers who were either single or divorced and who were consequently less privatized and more reliant on the help of people in the immediate vicinity. Yet because all their day-to-day help came from white people, the children of these mothers tended to be even more isolated in terms of multiracial experience. One of these mothers knew a black woman locally; and another had a black boyfriend who came to stay occasionally; but the women themselves were all white, and their everyday contacts tended to be all white too. Economically, these women were worse off than families where the father was present, so less money was available for travelling to see friends who lived some distance away.

BLACK AND WHITE RELATIVES

Another factor which may help explain why the children in multiracial areas tended to have a black/mixed race identity is that they had more contact with their black relatives. On the whole, the families in the sample saw white relatives more often than black relatives. This is hardly surprising in view of the fact that the majority of the mothers were white, and a large proportion were single or separated. The only children who saw their black as frequently as their white relatives lived in a multiracial area.

Forty-two of the fifty-one children in the sample saw their relatives on a regular basis, with either high or medium frequency. ('High' frequency was rated as at least once a fortnight; 'medium' once every six to eight weeks. In the latter category were most of the middle-class families, who tended to keep in touch by phone between visits.) The remaining children either had no relatives at all outside their immediate family (two children) or saw their relatives only very rarely (seven children). Among the children who did see their relatives, there appeared to be a slight tendency for the children who saw either *black relatives only* or *both sets of relatives* to be in the two 'mixed race' identity groups, while those who saw *white relatives only* tended to be in the white, black, or contrary groups. The difference between these two sets of figures is significant at the 5 per cent level (Table 5.8).

The children who saw only their black relatives were not all the children of black mothers; on the contrary, six out of the eight had a white mother. These white mothers were not, as a rule, close to their black relatives, but their own parents and siblings lived a long distance away (in Ireland, Scotland, or, in one case, Norway), so visits were infrequent. 'Seeing relations' was presented either as something which the children did on their own or as a contact which was kept up for their or their husband's benefit. As one white mother put it:

Well, my relatives are all in Scotland, so obviously it's his relatives, really, you know. He's got two sisters ... His mum lives just in Hammersmith, so the children go there quite a lot to see his young sister who lives there. So they see mostly – well, they've never seen my – well, they seldom see my family unless they come here [Q.: 'How often do they see his mum and sisters?'] Oh, about once a week if they go up on their bicycle, you know. They go up and see her.

Table 5.8   *Identity Group by Frequency of Contact with Relatives*

Identity Group	Relatives seen with high or medium frequency		
	Black only/both sets	*White only*	Total
White/black/contrary	7	12	19
Mixed race (white bias)/ black mixed race	14	9	23
Total	21	21	42

Among the families who saw *both* sets of relatives, there seemed to be more involvement on the white mother's part and a tendency for both white and black mothers to hint that the children were rather closer to *their* family than to their husband's. For example, Beatrice Turner, a black mother, lived very close to both her own and her husband's family. She reported:

'We go to my mother's at least once a week – at weekends mainly.'

'And the children go with you?'

'Oh, *yes* [warmly]. They probably go twice at the weekend.'

'How often do you see your husband's parents?'

Oh, they would come over to us, oh, I'd say – well, we might be over Mum's way, we drop in ... you know you can't – once a month. We might see each other twice, three times in a month. Another time we might go a couple of months without, sort of, seeing each other ... They travel all over to see the others or they go on holiday or something, so I don't see them as often as I do my mother.

Similarly, one of the white mothers in this group, when asked how often her daughter saw her black husband's relatives, replied, 'Oh, she sees them often. Nearly every weekend.' But when asked later about her own family she exclaimed, 'Oh! I see *them* every day!'

The children who saw only white relatives included families whose black relatives were still in the black parent's country of origin as well as children of single white mothers whose children saw neither their father nor his family. There was a distinct impression that many of the middle-class white mothers who saw *only* their own family expressed a certain coolness towards them. This hint of tension applied to some ten middle-class white women, and it was not necessarily concerned with prejudice against their husband (although in some cases this was mentioned as a factor). For these women, a somewhat fraught relationship with their family – in particular with their mother – seemed to pre-date (and may even have been a factor in motivating) their interracial relationship.[4] So although these families saw their white extended family at regular intervals, the relationship was not reported by the mother to be a close one.

The amount of contact the children of single or separated women had with their black relations was usually very difficult to unravel, since the family of both current and previous boyfriends was sometimes counted as 'family'. One might suggest that where there is extreme hostility between divorced parents, where one parent is black and the other is white, the child's racial identity is bound to be affected – but I have too little clear information on the quality and frequency of relations with the father to examine this idea.

One or two of the married women living with their husband also expressed hostility to both their husband and his family. Three women are worth mentioning here for the strength of their anti-black feeling, which was not counterbalanced by any positive relationship with black people acting as 'substitute relations'. Vera Kano, the mother of Angela, expostulated when asked about her husband's relatives, 'Well, we have nothing to do with my husband's family at all. I haven't spoken to them in eleven years. And I won't let the children go there or have anything to do with them.'

Less extreme, but in an equally disgusted tone, Ilona Gould said of her husband's mother, 'Oh, she *never* writes. Kevin has a birthday card from her once a year, a Christmas card, and that's it. OK, she phones now and again, but not often. She's not that kind of grandmother, you know. Not what *I* think of as a grandmother.' Both these women were living with their husband; the latter, however, was particularly scathing about him and about West Indians generally: 'Some of them – and I know this from experience – think they're doing everyone a favour by being here... My own husband is Jamaican and he thinks he's God almighty. He thinks he's the smartest, cleverest black person that was ever born. And a lot of his friends are like that.'

A white single mother commented, when asked about her children's cultural identity 'I suppose I would like them to feel they were partly Nigerian; but I don't press that point at the moment because I don't think my husband will have much more contact with us. So I'd rather they try to forget him.'

All four of the children of these three mothers were in the identity groups which were preoccupied with the black/white dichotomy and unable to choose between black and white.

So the relationship between contact with black relatives and the children's racial identity existed in the expected direction, but the association was not a strong one. Links with the extended family are, of course, just one element in a much wider process of identity formation. If seeing black relatives is to be effective in fostering a black/mixed race identity, presumably it has to be supported by the child's school, peers and other spheres of influence. None the less, it is possible that, for some of the mixed race children in the sample, feeling that they belonged to a black and a white family, or having contact with black relatives in an otherwise white-dominated social world, may have played a role in shaping their conception of themselves as members of a brown or mixed race group. Conversely, a lack of family ties with black people or hostility on the part of the mother towards black relatives may have caused some children to be in conflict over their racial identity.

Racial Identity in Context

It seemed, then, that some clue as to the meaning and origin of mixed race children's identification with an intermediate group could be found in the social diversity of their area, in a high level of overt racial tension, in the frequency of their contact with other black or mixed race people or in some combination of all of these. But how exactly did these factors influence children to see themselves as black/mixed race? What was the *meaning* of this identification, in the context of the children's social surroundings? There were several equally feasible hypotheses which could provide answers to these questions.

One explanation might be that identification with an inter-mediate group – despite appearing to be part of a positive black/mixed race identity – still contained an element of dissociation from the black group. In other words, the terms 'brown' and 'mixed race' were not positive expressions of a secondary identification, but were ways of qualifying the nega-tively viewed primary identification, 'black'. The open hostility which existed in some of the multiracial areas I visited may have led mixed race children to search for ways of avoiding being labelled as black and hence being able to escape the rejection of white children. *The presence of other mixed race children in the area gave legitimacy to an intermediate identity which was viewed as more socially acceptable than the despised category of black.*

This agument is supported by certain comments made by some of the mothers and children I interviewed, particularly in relation to the self-identification label of 'brown'. It was noted earlier that several children preferred the term 'brown' to 'black' and that one child took the euphemistic possibilities of 'brown' even further by claiming that 'there's no such thing really as black people'. Two of the mothers in the sample, who were friends but lived on different multiracial estates, took up this point during the interview. I had asked Chris Hastings if she ever used the term 'brown' to describe people racially; she said she did not, but commented, 'Well, kids say that a lot ... They know they're not black, they know they're

113

not white, you know? They'll say, "I'm brown, I'm brown." ' When I asked her what she thought was behind the classification, she said that it seemed to be the children's own word for 'half-caste', phrased in terms of a colour which could be set against black:

When kids or other people are taunting them, it's always, 'Oh, you *black* this', or, 'You *black* that', so they felt that they don't want – it's always about *colour* specifically, it's not about 'you *half*-Jamaican', or, 'you half-African', it's about colour. So, you know, they're sort of saying, 'Well, I'm not *black*, I'm *half*.'

Her friend, Liz Sanders, also commented that her daughter had started calling herself 'brown', rather to the annoyance of the father, who was black: 'My husband tells the child she's black, but she won't have it. She says she's not black. She says, "I'm not, I'm brown." But he says you'll be classed as black anyway, which is true.' Several other women were conscious of their children using 'brown' as a more acceptable term than 'black' and of the fact that this appeared to stem from peer-group norms.

On the other hand, a second explanation would be that the identification of 'brown' and 'half-caste' were simply *viable identification categories of the non-white group, within the local setting*. Two arguments might be feasible here, either separately or in combination. First, there was perhaps sufficient contact between mixed race children (and between interracial families) in the area to form a *marginal culture*, which provided the means for mixed race children to support each other in their individuality. Secondly, 'half-caste' and 'brown' may have been labels which were recognized by all children in the area to classify racially particular 'types' of children. Once again, there is some evidence to support both these views.

The first argument would be in keeping with the friendship patterns of both the mothers and the children in multiracial areas, which showed warmth and mutual support between the mothers and frequent contact between the children. Although numerically a mixed race marginal culture seems unlikely in Britain, on a local level there appear to exist networks of interracial families, which could act as subsystems for the formation of racial identity. (However, it should be remembered that my sample was obtained almost exclusively among people belonging to such a network.) Mixed race children whose daily life is carried out with other mixed race children close at hand are protected to some extent from black and white rejection, and they have the opportunity to develop racial self-esteem through a sense of belonging to their own ethnic group.

The second argument was supported by the casual, matter-of-fact way in which many mixed race children in multiracial areas grouped the mixed race photographs together. To use Esme as an example once again, it was clear that her understanding of the terms 'mixed race' and 'brown' had come partly from the categorization current at her school. This suggested that, within her peer group at least, there was an agreed system of racial classification in which mixed race children were *unambiguously* included: 'When you said half black and half white, that's what I thought you meant by brown. 'Cos at school they call *them* brown. They call *like me* brown.' Some of the *mothers* in multiracial areas also linked the dawning of an intermediate identification with starting school. Maggie Muir, when asked about her children's racial identity, said simply, 'They sort of accept it and they say, "We're brown" ... When they start school they say, "I'm half-caste" – things like that.'

If the situational model of ethnicity, set out in Chapter 2, is recalled, all of these arguments can be incorporated into a single picture of intermediate identification in a multiracial setting. Whatever meanings these labels have for mixed race children, it seems that both 'brown' and 'half-caste' were secondary categories whose reality was endorsed by people in the child's immediate environment. Whether 'brown' was a dissociation from black, an expression of membership of a marginal culture, or simply a technical classification for mixed race or medium-coloured children, there was sufficient evidence to suggest that it was a *socially legitimate* category for self-identification.

The literature on the situational aspects of ethnicity suggested that, where this was the case, such categories would not be subjectively related to primary racial categorization at all times or in all situations. In other words, a brown or a mixed-race identity need not necessarily be expressed in the child's mind as 'I am *more white* than black children'. For in the kind of multiracial, interracial environment I have described, it would be sufficient for the child to conceptualize being of mixed race as 'I am like other children who have parents like mine' and to view being brown as simply 'belonging with the other brown children in my class'. One seems justified in suggesting that this self-categorization as a member of a mixed or intermediate colour group was the child's conception of him- or herself in terms of *a secondary category which made sense in the context of his or her experience.*

None the less, it was argued earlier that at certain times and in certain situations the child would be forced to recognize the reality of primary racial classification and to squeeze these

115

identification categories into the constraints which it imposed: to decide whether 'brown' was black or white. Although only one answer to this – black – was socially viable, making this choice would seem harder to the child at some times than at others, depending on what gains or losses were at stake. As Sandra Wallman (1979), among others, argued, participant actors in ethnic situations are attempting at all times to negotiate the ethnic boundary to suit their own social ends.

If the subjective meaning of racial labels *does* vary according to the situation, then it is possible that *all three* hypothetical explanations of intermediate identity given above could be correct; for it would simply be a question of how membership of an intermediate group was being *used* by the child at any given time. It seems likely that all mixed race children who have an intermediate identity would use it, at some time or another, to escape white rejection and to intimate that 'brown' is more acceptable than 'black'. But an intermediate identity can also be used to enter other friendship groups. If the child is trying to become accepted by a black peer group, the *blackness* of brown may be played up ('Of course, I'm *really* black'); a light skin colour could be used to gain prestige among black friends ('I am black but I am fair-skinned'); or the ambiguity of brown may be presented as a social passe-partout ('Brown children fit in anywhere').

Rather than suggesting that in real life the children in the 'black mixed race' group had a positive view of being mixed race but that those in the 'mixed race (white bias)' group were always more white oriented, it would perhaps be closer to the truth to say that the children in both these groups were all capable of feeling at ease with being of mixed race – in certain groups, in certain situations, or in phases. One could argue for these mixed race children, as Milner (1975) argued for black children, that in practice the extent of their white orientation varies. At times, as they watch the world through white-dominated media, they realize that it is an indisputably white world and they feel acutely the material disadvantages of being black. In these periods it may seem necessary to use their intermediate identity to show that they belong to a 'nearly white' group and to tell the world that being of mixed race means being more white than black. This does not mean that their basic conception of self as black/mixed race is threatened; it simply means that the secondary category of mixed race is being used to express the conflict that all black children feel in a society such as ours, where white is the predominantly valued category. At other times, mixed race children who have an intermediate identity find the crisis of black/white conflict easier to resolve. Secondary categories can then be put to more flexible use once again, so that the child can align and realign in the ever-changing friendship pattern of the multiracial school.

What of the children in white areas? How should one interpret the responses of the children in the 'white', 'black' and 'contrary' groups, in the context of their day-to-day experience? In contrast to the children in multiracial neighbourhoods, who are able to locate themselves racially within a local subculture, children in white areas are more vulnerable to the white hegemony of British racial classification. They are also more dependent on the efforts of their families to create an environment in which a positive view of self can flourish. Unless the child is in a particularly sensitive school which has an unusually cosmopolitan outlook, the children in white areas are likely to be forced more often to confront the *non-whiteness* of their racial identity. Whereas secondary racial categories have meaning and significance in an area where people of many different cultures live, in a white area the most salient ethnic reality is the white/non-white dichotomy. The mixed race child must either come to terms with being considered 'coloured' or else deal with the subtle vagaries of honorary white status.

It is understandable that children in white areas – in particular children who have little contact with other mixed race or 'brown' peers – would react to the identity test similarly to other black British children, except that the fact of having one white parent may have pushed more children towards adopting a white identity and fewer towards seeing themselves as totally and defiantly black. In these areas, the detail of being *mixed race* may have been relatively unimportant compared with the indomitable fact of being black. The 'white', 'black' and 'contrary' groups may be interpreted as corresponding to Milner's (1975) model of the identity of black British children, namely, that in between the children who have a fantasy of themselves as white and those who see themselves as black, a large group of children are unsure about whether they are 'really' white or black.

However, one qualification should be given to this comparison. It is unlikely that the children in the 'black' group, who professed to see themselves as black and who chose photographs of black children on the racial preference test, were expressing a clear sense of belonging to the black community, since their daily experience did not include any contact with black people. It is more probable that their black identification was an *individual response against racism* – perhaps even the direct result of an accumulation of rejection experiences – which was strongly encouraged by the parents.

The strength and endurance of a black identity in an all-white context must be left in some doubt, for the child who declares, 'If you won't allow me to be white, then I shall be black', has presumably less idea of what being black means than one who is well integrated into a black community and who is being exposed constantly to good models of black identity. If the parents are assiduous in providing multiracial materials in the home and if the black parent is comfortable with his or her own black identity, then the child's chances of adopting a workable identity must be considerably improved. None the less, where peer-group support and approval are entirely lacking, it seems likely that being black will remain a negative rather than a positive experience.[5]

Notes

1 Chi squared is a test of statistical significance, referring to the probability of a particular result occurring by chance. The percentages refer to *how likely* it is that the result is attributable to chance. In this case, for example, where chi squared is significant at the 5 per cent level, it means that there is a probability of only 5 in 100 that these are chance results.

2 I got to know these women fairly well, although I interviewed only two of them. One crisis I witnessed was brought on by one mother's heavy drinking. Her child was taken to another flat while she was sobered up by several friends, who had each left their children to be looked in on by another of the group.

3 When this mother says 'white friends' she means white women with white men. She does not classify white women who have black boyfriends as white.

4 A common theme in the casual comments of these women (for it must be remembered that no questions on the mother's emotional background or on the history of her courtship were asked) was a strong relationship with their father and a tense relationship with their mother – or, in at least four cases, with their *step*mother. This would be in keeping with the common clinical interpretation of interracial marriage, namely, that the woman is seeking a man who is sufficiently different from her father to pose no threat to the relationship. No particularly close relationship with their father was reported by black women in the sample, nor by many of the working-class women.

5 Some additional evidence which supports this interpretation is that the two boys in the 'black' group were each strongly encouraged by their mother to identify with their father. One mother said, 'I always

tell him, "Daddy's black and he loves being black." ' In these two cases at least, the black identity seems to have been a psychological identification with the father rather than an expression of membership of the black community.

Chapter Six

'Let Them Be Themselves':
Mother's Attitude, Children's Identity

Little is known about the part played by parents in the formation of racial identity. Research which has been conducted on children's racial *attitudes* suggests that parents do have considerable influence on the ideas and feelings which children develop about different racial groups; but the relationship is far from straightforward because the parental influence is quickly distorted by racial ideas which emanate from outside the family. The child's attitude to *self* is an even more complex matter. Parental influence is likely to be subtle and unspoken. It will also tend to be deeply enmeshed in all the other concerns which parents have about their child's physical and psychological development.

Most existing research suggests that parents' racial attitudes provide the initial bench-mark for the child's view of self. However, as the child's experience widens, with entry to school and greater exposure to the media, parental views have to be strongly held and emphatically put over to be transmitted effectively to the child.

The current investigation focused on three main areas of the mother's racial attitudes; her racial categorization system, her view of the child's 'true' identity and her general beliefs about race relations in Britain. The first two of these are considered in this chapter, and the third is looked at in the chapter following. The mother's race and her socioeconomic status were two other factors which were thought likely to influence the child's identity, but these will be considered in both chapters alongside other factors, because their influence seemed to be through and with other variables, rather than in isolation. (Also, the fact that there were only eight black women in the sample made individual consideration the most meaningful method of analysis.)

The Mother's Racial Categorization

Discussion with the mothers in the sample about racial categorization provided innumerable illustrations of the imprecision, confusion and variability of racial classification in Britain. Many women's responses exemplified both the slightly blurred nature of the white/non-white line and the vast scope which British secondary racial classification gives for regional and individual variation. The criteria for distinguishing between one secondary category and another seemed at times to border on being idiosyncratic. Focusing the mother's attention on both her own and other people's classification also elicited a variety of emotional responses. Some women were surprised at the complexity of their system and amused at its inconsistency and confusion, whereas others had thought carefully (and sometimes angrily) about the subject and were conscientiously consistent about the labels they used.

To compare the mother's view of the racial structure directly with her child's was difficult, since an adult's ability to discuss abstract concepts and to be aware of the relative and situational aspects of racial classification is greater than a child's. However, regardless of whether a direct connection between the mother's and the child's categorization system could be found, it was still important to investigate the mother's understanding and use of racial labels. Only then could her view of the child's identity and her general stance on bringing up mixed race children be placed in the context of her subjective view of the British racial structure.

All the women who were interviewed agreed about one thing, despite the general inconsistency and confusion of their secondary categories. They agreed that there existed in Britain a division between white and non-white and that the terms 'coloured' and 'white' were the ones used most frequently to express this distinction. This did not mean that all the women used these terms or that they approved of their use. They simply believed that these two categories were the most widely employed to encapsulate racial difference.

I asked all the women during the interview who they thought of when I said 'coloured'.[1] Most saw it as a collective term for all the 'non-white' groups:

Coloured? Anything from pale brown to black, really.

(Yvonne Harley, white)

Well, everybody, really. I mean, they're all coloured, aren't they?

(Jean Watson, white)

Everybody — I mean, shit! *Everybody*.

(Sibyl Finlay, white)

Oh, everybody! I class them all — West Indians, Indians, everybody — as coloured.

(Toni Ashton, black)

The mothers were also asked about the position of more ambiguous groups; were Chinese, southern Europeans and Arabs also 'coloured'? The Chinese were not generally thought of as coloured (although one or two women thought they were), and the place of southern Europeans was also doubtful. Arabs, on the other hand, were more generally thought of as coloured on the basis of the combination of a dark skin and the extremity of their perceived cultural difference.[2]

When the secondary categories of 'black', 'brown' and 'mixed race' were introduced, there was further complexity and disagreement. The terms also elicited a variety of emotional reactions. For example, some mothers found 'half-caste' a highly offensive label, whereas others regarded it as the only correct term to describe their mixed race children. To add to the confusion, many women reported that they varied the racial terms they used depending on the social situation they were in. Thus, 'coloured' may be seen as an appropriate label only in conversation with certain types of people.

To unravel the knot of conflicting views a little, it may be best to begin by looking at how the respondents related these secondary categories to each other and to the dichotomy purely as descriptive categories — in other words, what each woman *understood* by the labels, rather than how she felt about them, and whether or not she used them.

'Black' and 'coloured' were essentially understood in three ways by the women I interviewed. Some respondents saw them as interchangeable labels, referring to the non-white section of the dichotomy; a second group understood 'coloured' to be the general term and 'black' to be a label used for darker, Negroid people; and thirdly 'coloured' was seen as a term for lighter people, whereas 'black' had darker connotations (Figure 6.1). Some more sophisticated women were aware of all these meanings.

'Black' and 'coloured' were interchangeable for Liz Sanders (white): ' 'Cos when people say "black" most people in the country mean all colours; it doesn't matter whether you're light

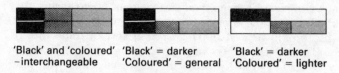

'Black' and 'coloured'   'Black' = darker   'Black' = darker
–interchangeable   'Coloured' = general 'Coloured' = lighter

Figure 6.1 The mother's meanings of 'black' and 'coloured'

brown or really black.' Yet for other women 'black' was darker skinned or Negroid:

'Black'? Yes 'black' to me means Negro, um... from basic middle brown to black... I suppose the more obviously dark they are, the more I think of them as black.

(Ruth McCarthy, white)

Negroes. Not Asians – they're not... they're dark skinned and dark haired but not Negroid.

(Linda Weaver, white)

'Coloured' – I would say 'coloured' is the whole range... 'cos 'black'... I would really think 'black' would have to be... er quite black actually, if you were to really think about it... But normally people just say 'coloured' and categorize the whole lot as coloured, don't they?

(Beatrice Turner, black)

Ilona Gould (white) said that she would regard lighter brown people as coloured and darker brown people as black. Asians she said were 'coloured... as opposed to black. I mean, there's a difference, you see.'

'What's the difference?'

'Well, I think... I regard my husband as black. And I regard Kevin [her son] as being coloured. I expect that sounds stupid, does it?'

In their understanding of the label 'brown', the women in my sample fell into four groups. Either they had rarely heard the term used as a racial category; or it was understood to refer to mixed race (black/white) children specifically; or it was a description of lighter-skinned black/coloured people; or it was a more aesthetically pleasing version (or 'baby' version) of 'black', covering all non-white people. To a minority of women, 'brown' evidently meant very little; they may have heard it used occasionally, but it brought to mind no specific category of people. Many reactions to the term 'brown' were elicited in response to statement no. 10: 'Mixed race children are neither black nor white – they are brown. They belong to a special racial category of their own.'

Jean Watson (white) was bemused by the idea: 'Oooooh... I

123

shouldn't think so. I mean, you can't sort of... go saying they're black, they're white, they're brown. I mean, life wouldn't go on like that, would it?... I don't go round sort of think they're... *brown* [laughs]. I hope nobody else does, neither.'

Kay O'Grady (white) greeted the same statement with puzzlement: 'Well, I couldn't call black "brown", could I?... As far as I'm concerned there's no such thing *as* brown, anyway.'

Lily Fisher (black) asserted that she simply did not use the term 'brown'. Ruth McCarthy (white) thought she had heard the label, but it was not a term she often came across.

For a second group of women 'brown' meant specifically *children like theirs*, and they agreed with statement no. 10 that 'brown' was a separate mixed race category:

'So who do you think of when I say "brown"?'

'Half-castes [no hesitation]' (Doreen Johnson, white).

'They *are* a thing of their own... I mean brown is not black and it's not white. So, yes, I do strongly agree that it's a special category' (Sue Green, white).

The majority of mothers, however, saw 'brown' either as a term for all lighter-skinned non-white people or else as a more aesthetic term than 'black'. Some women in the former group spontaneously extended the category of 'brown' further than they had 'coloured', perhaps because of the association of 'brown' with a tanned rather than permanently pigmented skin:

I'd include people from certain Mediterranean countries, Asian and lighter West Indian and mixed race people. You know, it would cover such a huge amount of people... Israelis, even... Arabs.

(Yvonne Hanley, white)

Half-caste children... Indians, Italians – they're brown, aren't they? Chinese.

(Mary O'Reilly, white)

Brown, yeah, mostly... Asians and that, you know. They're brown.

(Maggie Muir, white)

I wouldn't think you necessarily meant mixed. I would just think that they were a light ... brown rather than very dark or white.

(Jane Eliot, white)

If he's light, I might say 'brown'.

(Toni Ashton, black)

'Brown' was also used either euphemistically or to avoid the negative associations of 'black' which are particularly potent among children. The mothers I interviewed frequently switched spontaneously from 'brown' to 'black' when answering the 'critical situations' part of the interview as they adjusted their level of speech, imagining how they would speak to a child. Sylvia Ogundele (white) was thoughtful on the subject of her use of 'brown':

I think I might have used it, but ... it doesn't really mean much, does it? I have heard it used in schools ... yes, perhaps we do use it in school ... We say this child has got a nice *brown* skin, you see, which again is probably easier for the other children to accept than saying he has a nice *black* skin; 'cos no way are you going to convince them that it's nice to have a black one, but it might be nice to have a brown one!

In answer to the statement asking if 'black is beautiful' should be taught to mixed race children, Elaine Houghton (white) replied:

Yes ... I'm hesitating because I know a lot of people call my children black, but I ... because they don't understand – they're not at an age – they say, 'That's not black, that's brown.' I think they ought to be proud of being beautiful and *brown*. I would say I agree, it's only a matter of a word.

Similarly, Barbara Monks (white) reported: 'When my children first became colour conscious I avoided words like "black" and "white" by telling them that they were light brown, their father dark brown and I was pink."[3]

Yet for some women, the euphemism was clearly for their own benefit too. Pat Ward (white) pointed out irritably that 'that thing there is black' (indicating a black object), whereas her childen were 'brown'. The euphemistic element caused other mothers to be more cautious about the term and specific about how it should be used. Liza Hunt (black American), for example, said that she felt strongly that 'brown' should not be used to a child as a way of avoiding a black identity. This brings us to the subject of the connotations these racial labels had for the women in the sample.

The labels 'black', 'coloured' and 'brown' aroused different feelings in different women. For Beatrice Turner, a black woman originally from Jamaica, merely discussing the issue was a matter for slight embarrassment and confusion. She used the terms 'coloured' and 'black' interchangeably, but seemed to feel more comfortable saying 'coloured':

Well, 'black' is somebody who's really black [laughs] and 'coloured' would be anything from Chinese to ... if I had to think about it, but generally if people just say 'coloured' it's generally West Indian probably, or anything, but if you were to really think about what you're saying it can mean coloured people from anything slightly yellow to ... you know.

A white Englishwoman, Margaret Udoaka, was equally hesitant: 'Well, it just means to me . . . I think 'coloured' means sort of black people, perhaps. But it's not a word that I would ever use, I don't think. Not . . . it doesn't really have any . . . it only really means that they're not . . . that they're black, I think. Black, I think.' Finally, she said she preferred to say 'black' or 'brown' rather than 'coloured'.

These two respondents were in sharp contrast to the many women who felt strongly about racial labels – usually in favour of 'black' or 'brown' – and who said so with very little prompting and no hesitation, sometimes simply in response to the question 'Who do you think of when I say "coloured"?':

I think it's a euphemism by middle-class people to politely get away from saying 'nigger' . . . Yes, I think it's a euphemism thought up by so-called polite society. 'Cos after all, one can't really say . . . 'This is our nigger friend' or 'our coon friend'. They have to think of something else. So they say 'coloured'.

(Liza Hunt, black American)

Upper-middle-class and upper-class British people. They cannot face the word 'black' . . . We are still at the 'coloured' level in this country. America basically went past 'coloured' in the sixties.
(Sue Green, white English, former resident of US-influenced Caribbean island)

I don't like that word. Because if you face it, 'coloured' is black, red, pink, green and you haven't got such coloured people. You haven't. It's *black* and *white*! [Q.: So who do you think of if you hear someone say "coloured"?'] I just ignore them 'cos they ignorant. You never find my kids saying 'coloured'.

(Mathilda Spicer, black, St Christopher)

Well, the people that use 'coloured' now are what you call Uncle Toms. You know, like older black people, they say 'coloured'. Or some people when they're trying to be nice – you know? They're frightened to say 'black', you know, so they say 'coloured'.

(Chris Hastings, white)

However, Monica Finch had the opposite view. Being more used to the Caribbean colour class system, she felt nothing but outrage at the suggestion that she was black. She interrupted my questoning on categorization impatiently with the comment:

But then, you see, back home in Jamaica – and here – you get different tones of brown and you do get some . . . black people. But to use the term to cover all non-whites and say they're all black is wrong. I don't believe they're all black. 'Cos you remember all the Black Power stuff? I don't believe 'I'm black and I'm beautiful'. I'm *me*, and that's it. More often than

126

not I say 'coloured': – 'the coloured boy', 'the coloured girl', 'coloured man' as opposed to 'black girl over there'. My brother Michael says they're not coloured, they're black. But he's a bit ... well, I probaby say 'coloured'.

Most *white* women's views on these labels were expressed with less personal emotion but more from their assessment of the view of black people – in particular their husband or boyfriend. Once again, 'coloured' was unpopular, especially among the better educated and also the more radical women:

My husband doesn't like the term 'coloured'. He things it's a derogatory term which the British use for *all* non-white.

(Sally Adegbola, white)

[Q.: 'Do you ever use the word "coloured"?'] No, I've been told not to. They find it very insulting. One of the first things I learnt when I married my husband. They like to be called black even if [laughs] they look white!

(Vivian Harris, white)

I suppose it was in the sixties – was it? – when we used the word 'coloured', because it sounded polite, but I think the black Africans prefer to be called black.

(Diane Vambe, white)

Well, I used to call them coloured once because I used to think it was rude to say 'black'. But Roy's mother said 'Would you like it if we called you pale? We call you white – we're black.' Up to then I'd never heard people say 'black'.

(Ilona Gould, white)

Yet on this point, too, there was dissent. The only white non-British woman in the sample – originally from Norway – reported that 'People don't like being called black, they want to be called coloured ... Like John [her husband], doesn't like the word "black", he says his skin's not black' (Kari McClaren, white Norwegian).

Very few women introduced the term 'brown' when talking about their husband or other adults. As was mentioned earlier, most used 'brown' mainly in talking to their children. The possible significance of this for the children's categorization and identity is discussed below.

A further dimension to the usage of the terms 'coloured', 'brown' and 'black' was added by the distinction many women made between what other people would say (the classification used by others) and the labels they themselves used for racial categories. This distinction, which was carried through to a dual view of mixed race children's identity, was between such women's *public* and *private* racial classification. The first enabled the mother to understand and to be understood, whereas the second allowed her to keep the integrity of her own world view. Her public classification seemed to be derived from a certain realism about the dichotomous racial system at work in Britain and majority attitudes to non-white people, but her private categorization system was based upon her 'inside information' about how black people themselves wished to be classified; it was knowledge gained from her experience of another culture and from being the mother of mixed race children. This public/private split was a reflection of these women's marginal position in relation to the dichotomy (Wilson, 1981). Many mothers found it necessary to maintain a dual classification system in order to manage the ambiguity of their status position.

Elaine Houghton (white), for example, tried to explain why she sometimes used the word 'coloured': 'I think I use it more for other people [laughs]. So they know what I'm talking about... I would normally define what I mean, I wouldn't just say "coloured", but I do say it for the sake of other people.'

Gwen Smith (white) reacted similarly to 'black'. She used it as a collective term, inclusive of mixed race children, only in so far as she was responding to the views of others: 'Well, I always think of black as... West Indians, Asians of varying sorts... that's *myself*. But on the other hand, a lot of people would say that any person with *any* black in them – be it half or whatever – is black.'

Sylvia Ogundele (white) was highly conscious of the difference between her own and other people's classification systems. Of 'black' and 'coloured' she said:

Well, it might mean one thing to me, it might mean another thing to somebody else. To me a *black* person is a very obviously black dark-skinned person... I wouldn't use, in fact, the term 'coloured', but other people might use it in relation to people who were less dark skinned, perhaps mixed race or Asian... I know that quite a few people use the term 'coloured' to *me*, because they somehow feel it's being a bit obvious to say 'black' so they lower it down a bit and say 'coloured'. Obviously if they're South African background then I know quite distinctly that they're talking about something quite different... so I would have to know the person... There's a lot of confusion.

Another mother gave 'other people's view' as the reason why she called her children half-caste: 'If you call them what everyone else calls them, then they're not gonna feel it's horrible.'

In some cases, comments about her public and private categorization – and assessments of the private classifications used by other people – provided some revealing glimpses of where the mother's own racial allegiance and loyalties lay. The meanings of racial labels depended on where one was standing, just as the *racial structure* could look different depending upon where one was positioned within it. For example, two white mothers – Sally Adegbola and Kari McClaren – both used the term 'brown'; for them, it was a term referring to mixed race people and lighter-skinned black people. Yet both mothers commented that the *white* view would be that brown people were 'coloured' or 'black'; in saying so, they distanced themselves from the white community: 'White people see brown people as black and refer to them as being black' (Sally Adegbola); 'Well, I mean, I think the white people see the brown as black. That's how I think they look upon it' (Kari McClaren).

However, Shirley Collins, a black West Indian woman, did not use 'brown' in her private classification and she associated it not with the white mothers of mixed race children (such as Sally and Kari) but with Asians. The idea of 'brown' being used brought out some covert resentment against the exclusiveness she perceived in Asians; 'When you say "brown" I think of half-caste or, er ... some say Indians; they like to be classed as brown. *I* class them as black, 'cos they're just as black as I am ... if not blacker'.

Mathilda Spicer (also black) made the same point by telling a long anecdote about an Indian girl at school with her who was furious at being called black. Once again, what was perceived as Asians' private classification of themselves clashed with the respondent's own view of where they belonged: 'They don't *call* themselves black ... She didn't like it at all ... She was as dark as me only with straight hair ... I said I felt sorry for her if she didn't know what she was by that age.'

Curiously, one or two white women in the sample also had identified with the resentment felt by some West Indians against Asians' separate definition of themselves. I shall argue later that for some women this was part of taking on a West Indian identity. Maggie Muir (white) said of Asians, with a fair amount of scorn: 'Well, most of 'em think they're white but they *are* black. Well – brown. I used to have a landlord who thought he was white, and he was black [laughs].'

Some of the mothers, especially those who had travelled or else grown up outside Britain, were very conscious of the relativity of racial categorization from culture to culture. Two friends who had both lived in Guyana (one more recently than the other) mentioned the Guyanese classification of mixed race children as 'red skinned'. I asked Vivian Harris (white), who had recently returned to Britain, about how she classified her children. She replied:

That's something I've found very difficult since I've been in England. In Guyana it's... I mean, they're just 'red niggers' and it's not a problem, they're just part of a multiracial society, but over here... So I've always tended to think of my children as black because the black people... well, think of them as 'red niggers'.

Putting together her own classification, derived from living in Guyana and her more recent experience of British racial categorization, she had concluded that 'as far as the English society is concerned – particularly where I live [a totally white area] – my children are, *I* would say, black. *They* would probably say "coloured", "brown", "mixed". But they're certainly not white.'

Sue Green (white English), having experience of both US and Caribbean classifications, was also aware of cultural contrasts in racial categorization: 'By American definition Joanne is black, she is not brown or anything. In this country, she's brown; she's brown in the West Indies also, but she is also black.'

Lily Fisher (black West Indian) agreed that while her children were in England they were both non-white and British. But she and her husband had plans to return 'home to Guyana' and she had no doubt that 'when they go there, they'll be West Indian'.

Racial Categorization: Mothers and Children

As was noted earlier, the greater complexity of the mothers' racial categorization (and their ability to convey its complexity) made it difficult to compare their schema of racial categorization directly with those of their children. None the less, one or two broad observations can be made about the relationship between the mothers' and children's use of particular racial labels.

In general, it appeared that the category sets of the children in the sample had been influenced more by their age and peer relationships than by their mother's image of the racial structure. The children's use of the term 'brown', for example, did not seem to be linked to whether or not the mother saw it as a meaningful category nor to whom she included within it. The same was true of 'coloured' and 'black'; the meaning each mother attached to the labels did not necessarily correspond to what her children understood by them.

However, the use of the term 'half-caste' was an exception in this respect, being limited to children whose mothers freely employed the word to describe them. Out of the ten children who used the expression 'half-caste', only one had a mother who had expressed disapproval of the term. The figures for mothers and children using 'half-caste' are given in Tables 6.1 and 6.2.

An additional link between the mothers' and the children's categorization systems was that, where a mother had expressed a strong dislike of a particular label, the children were loath to use it when they categorized the photographs – even when they were specifically asked to apply the label to the photographs. (Some children winced visibly when I asked if there were any 'coloured' children; others winced when I asked about 'black' children.) The two children of the mother who said with some vehemence that 'you never find my kids saying "coloured"' did indeed only use the term 'black'. And the black Amerian mother who saw 'coloured' as highly derogatory had clearly passed this message on to her 6-year-old daughter. Yet in the main, where no clear-cut rules about racial terms had been laid down by the mother, there were no clear and simple associations between the mother's and the child's labelling system. A second glance at the children's categories (described in Chapter 5) reminds us that many children either evaded or had no real working knowledge of conventional racial labels, for they used descriptions such as 'darkest', 'blackish', 'beige' and 'sort of white' to describe the groups they had constructed.

As the next section will show, when the mothers attempted to locate their children in the racial structure they usually did so by using one of three racial contexts; they saw mixed race children

Table 6.1 *Mother's Views of the Term 'Half-Caste'*

Uses term 'half-caste'	19
Against it	12
Non-commital	8
Total	39

Table 6.2 *Views of Mothers Whose Children Used the Term 'Half-Caste'*

Mothers's view	Number of children using the term
Against it	1
Uses it or non-commital	9
Total	10

as part of a black/white, a skin colour gradation, or a black/white/ mixed category set. Yet like her general use of racial labels, the mother's choice of category to describe her children's position showed no relationship with the child's endorsement of either a simple colour scheme or a multi-criteria set. If the factor of age was controlled and only the younger children with a sophisticated set and the older respondents with a simple colour scheme were examined, there was some evidence of the more radical (black/white) mothers speeding racial awareness and the more conservative (colour gradation) mothers hindering it, but the numbers were small and the differences not statistically significant. (Out of six children under 95 months with sophisticated sets, four had mothers who used a black/white set. Five of the nine children with a simple colour scheme set had mothers using a colour gradation scheme.)

It seemed, then, that apart from when a mother made a particular point of instructing her child about racial categorization, the mother's use of racial labels had little impact on her child's classification system. Mixed race children's knowledge of the meaning and use of racial labels appeared to stem from agents of socialization outside the home.

The Mother's View of the Child's Racial Position

What has been described up to now is the adult respondents' use of racial labels, their views of the interrelationships between racial terms, their feelings about particular forms of racial terminology and the influence of these on the children's categorization systems. The next step was to discern where the mother located her mixed race child in her system of racial categorization in order to explore the influence of this upon the child's racial identity.

From the maelstrom of mixed criteria of racial classification among the women I interviewed, one thing was clear; all the mothers I spoke to agreed that mixed race children were not white. However, there was considerable disagreement about how non-white their children were and about how relevant the white/non-white line was for their social position. This variation is amply illustrated by the comments of two mothers, one black and one white. Attitudes towards the extent of the children's non-whiteness ranged from 'I think *possibly* they're more likely to be treated as coloured than white' (Brenda Jordan, white) to 'Society will see the kid as black. It's not gonna see it as white and it's not gonna see it as brown, it's gonna see it as black' (Liza Hunt, black).

It was possible to divide the women into three groups according to how they categorized their children. The first group saw them primarily as *black* within a black/white system. Although they privately recognized the individuality of the children's position as both black and white, they did not encourage this as the primary identification. These women carried through the dichotomy into their secondary category sets and saw the children *first as black* and only *secondly as mixed race*. The second group formed a strong contrast with the first; the children were 'coloured', certainly, but only just. These women tended to put great emphasis on the criterion of skin shade in racial classification (even to the extent of referring to the lighter of their children as 'white') and to play down the rigidity of the white/non-white line. The third group of women encouraged their children to think of themselves *primarily as mixed* and only *secondarily as black*. They conceptualized mixed race children as constituting a separate group between black and white (usually referred to as 'brown') which was recipient of a dual heritage by virtue of its position.

The contrast between these three attitudes is explored in detail below, before the analysis goes on to examine the relationship between the mother's 'encouraged identity' and the child's view of self. The sample was distributed over the three groups as shown in Table 6.3.

GROUP (1): BLACK IN A BLACK/WHITE SET

The first group was characterized by a no-nonsense realism about how racial categorization operates in Britain. Recognition of the primacy of the dichotomous classification system in terms of how other people would see the mixed race child was extended into the home on the basis that, although the child was mixed, he or

Table 6.3 *Mother's Categorization of Child*

Group	Encouraged identity	Category set	Number of women	%
(1)	'Black'	Black/white	13	33.4
(2)	'Coloured'	Colour range	10	25.6
(3)	'Mixed'/'brown'	Black/mixed white	16	41.0
Total			39	100.0

she was black in the context of a white-dominated Britain and should be prepared to meet that important fact. The public classification of the child as black was seen as so far reaching in its implications as to render the private view of the child as 'mixed' less urgent to convey – although some women in this group stressed the 'mixed' categorization more than others.

Five of the eight black women in the sample were in this group and these five women were notably open and positive about their own blackness. Inevitably, the black women had an advantage when it came to encouraging a black identity in their mixed race children. They could *show* the children how to be black simply by example, whereas the white mothers had to take on a conscious stance on the matter and develop a strategy for giving the identity some content. As Sally Barnard (black American) put it, 'It's more difficult for the white mothers. They have to be more conscious about it. Blackness is an unknown factor for them, so they need more support than black women do.' If a black woman is strong and confident in her own identity, passing on black pride to her children is a natural part of claiming them as her own. She has overcome, or at least learned to live with, the conflict of being black in a system which is weighted towards whites, so her children have a ready model of how to cope with racism. For these women, being black was a positive attribute; the negative side was taken matter-of-factly, as a fact of life which was unfortunate but need not destroy one's self-esteem. Sally Barnard explained, quietly and firmly, how she expressed her views on white racism to her children: 'I tell them, "There are times when we have to fight back. But there are times when we look at white people and say, well, that's just really sad for them." '

The working-class black mothers were content to convey a black identity to their children just by example, but the middle-class black mothers added the extra dimension of educating their children in an elementary political black consciousness. The two black American women were a good example of the middle-class view. They were self-conscious in promoting blackness to their children; they bought the magazine *Ebony*, had multiracial books in the house and were thoughtful about wanting their children to know what blackness meant in social and political terms. Here was Liza Hunt's answer to 'critical situation' 1, which required the mother to advise the parents of mixed race children what to do if a little girl asked if she could be white when she grew up:

We'll say, 'No, sweetheart, you'll be a lovely brown colour like you are' – brown girl, or black girl preferably because 'brown' tends to confuse them, you know, and I definitely feel they should have very much an identity of being *black* and not shirk or shrink away from the thing and say, 'Well, I'm brown' . . . I think when referring to themselves as a race . . . to acknowledge the fact that they are black is a *strength*. So that if they are called black it's not gonna be taken as, 'Oh, my God! I'm *black*, I'm not brown, oh! Oh!'

Sally Barnard had a similar view:

I would prefer that they thought of themselves firstly as non-white – 'I'm not white.' But unique in the sense that they have one white parent. Let them *be themselves*, that's the main thing, but *always*, because of the social structure and the way people react to black, they must realize that they are *not* white.

The remaining three black women – from Guyana, St Christopher and Trinidad – were less articulate in expressing their child-rearing strategies but seemed to assume that blackness was simply conveyed to their children through the family's life-style and their own behaviour. As Toni Ashton put it, 'With me being black, they are just brought up thinking more probably the black side, really. 'Cos they know that when they grow up they're black. Well, you say they're brown – but when they grow up they're black, so they have to know now.' Whereas the black American women derived strength in their identity from heightened consciousness and historical awareness, for these three West Indian women being black was treated as a matter-of-fact reality. Mathilda Spicer conveyed this feeling with a simple comment, expressing scorn for people who did not like to be described as black: 'A lot of black people think if a white person would say, "Oh, that *black* boy", he think, *oh* . . . why should he say that to *me*? It don't bother me at all. They can't call us nothing else!'

The white mothers in this group could not pass on a positive black identity by example. Some directed attention to the father as an identity model (if he was present) – 'Daddy's black and he loves being black!' – but most reported that they simply explained to the children that, because of their colour and parentage, other people would regard them as black. The main concern of these white mothers was to provide the child with adequate internal resources to meet the outside world with equanimity. As Liz Sanders put it, 'She's got to expect that certain people will class her as black, and she's got to accept it.'

The white mothers tended to put more emphasis on the *duality* of mixed race children's identity – as mixed and as black – but still their blackness was considered paramount. I asked Sylvia Ogundele, in the 'critical situation' on name-calling, what she would say if her son asked whether he was *really* black or not. She was aghast: 'Well, I'd hope he jolly well knew he was by then! You should have been preparing him all his life!... Let him think that black is beautiful all the way along.' None the less, the public/private split in the children's identity was mentioned more often by the white women than by the black:

Well, obviously they're half-caste... but they'll still be classed as black when they grow up.

(Liz Sanders)

I actually told them that they could be black, in fact... the word 'black' is going to be used of them... but technically they're very far from black... But anything that's not so-called white is black.

(Louise Forkah)

In this country, if you are half-caste, you're black.

(Jane Elliot)

Or, as one white mother said she would express it to her children, 'You know what you are, you're half-caste. You're half black and you're half white, but you know people are gonna treat you like a black person. So you're half-caste and you're black like your daddy.'

Working-class and middle-class white women held similar views about why their mixed race children were black. No class-related patterns were evident in the way they conveyed this to their children.

GROUP (2): COLOURED IN A SKIN COLOUR GRADATION

The mothers in group (2) expressed views totally opposed to those in group (1). Their main standpoint was expressed in the definite and oft-repeated phrase, 'Well, they're *not* black, are they?' Far from emphasizing the black/white dichotomy, respondents in this group bordered on denying it altogether, preferring to see racial classification as a series of fine divisions starting with white, through shades of brown, to black. Some of these mothers referred to the lighter of their children as 'white' and to the darker children as 'coloured', although they took pains to point out that it really did not matter to them what colour the children were.

A woman who stood out of this group for her denial of the importance of the white/non-white line was Monica Finch (black), who has already been mentioned in connection with her extreme dislike of the term 'black' and her endorsement of the Caribbean colour class system.[4] Despite her heightened colour consciousness, she was adamant that she did not notice colour, or regard it as important, ' 'Cos I wasn't brought up to distinguish between black and white and yellow and brown and Chinese and Japanese.' But later she said, ' 'Cos I don't even know what colour I am. You know, I sort of say I'm brown or coffee coloured or something – or chocolate coloured... "coloured"... lighter than black.' Pointing to me, she said that if I had a tan as well as dark hair, I could be called coloured, yet *'You* may have a blonde sister. Well, you don't look on her as a different breed altogether, you know.'

Monica Finch took the idea of her children wanting to be white very lightly even though she said later that she would not encourage them to think of themselves as totally white because they were obviously 'coloured'. Her answer to them wanting to be white would be, 'No, dear, you stay just as you are and you don't have to worry about a sun-tan, 'cos you've already got one.'[5]

'What if she persisted and said she *wanted* to be white?'

'Paint yourself!' (giggles).

Most extreme of the mothers who distinguished between their 'white' and their 'black' children was Vera Kano (white), who had two darker-skinned children by a former interracial marriage and two lighter children by her present (black) husband. She commented, 'Well, you see, I mean my two are literally *white*. I mean, you can't... do you know what I mean?' Like Monica Finch, she paid lip-service to the idea that they were not white, but regarded the whole situation with something approaching amusement:

Even my two little ones, I remind them that they're not white. It is *hard* when they're as white as them ... When Thadius takes Martin to school – I mean, my little boy is *completely* white – his friends say, 'Who's that black man with you Martin?' And Martin says, 'That's my dad.' And they say, 'Na... it can't be your dad. Who is he?' [laughs]

Most women in group (2) were not as extreme in their emphasis on colour, but still appeared to be placing their children on or around the white/non-white line, their precise position depending on their shade of skin:

Well, they're not black, are they? I can't encourage Paul to think black when he doesn't think of hisself as black... I suppose they'd be treated more... well, what can I say?... Paul may be treated more like a coloured and Jane more like a white because she's very fair.

(Vicki Anderson, white)

Yet once again, the concern for the children not thinking of themselves as white seemed to be somewhat superficial and often inconsistent with the mother's own feelings about blackness. Ilona Gould, for example, who had expressed such hostility about her

137

husband, exclaimed in answer to 'critical situation' 1 that her son had wished to be white on numerous occasions and that this broke her heart. She described the scenario thus: 'He used to say his prayers at night and he used to pray that when he woke up in the morning he would be white with straight hair. I think he wouldn't have minded being black or being white, but he couldn't stand this in-between bit.' She told him that, where one parent was black and one white, the children were always brown, and that God had wanted him to be brown:

And I used to say to him that his hair was so beautiful and, I mean, I *don't like* Kevin's hair, it's a curse to comb and brush and that. But I'd say his hair was so beautiful lots of white women and men go and have thir hair permed to look like that, and I'd tell him that white people spend hundreds of pounds every year going to hot countries to get brown because they wanted to be brown like that. And that seemed to . . . for a while, but it would always come up again. That when he got big, he wanted to be white – he'd like to be white now, but if he knew that when he was a bit older, he'd be white, he'd be a lot happier.

Another white woman, whom I classified as being on the periphery of this group, simply protested too much. After noting that her middle child could easily pass for white, she added, 'Well, I look on them as more black than white. I was disappointed that they were so fair skinned. I would have loved them to be really dark. I mean, the middle one you'd think was a white child.'

Whether the mothers in this group were white or black, their attitude to mixed race children's identity was the same: that although the children were nominally 'non-white', they should be brought up in just the same way as 'ordinary' (meaning 'white') children. Although, when they were talking about their views, these mothers reported that they did not encourage their children to identify as white, the covert message contained in their behaviour towards their children was clearly 'the whiter, the better'. Certainly, mothers in group 2 did nothing to counteract effectively the white bias with which their children were surrounded.

GROUP (3): 'MIXED' IN A BLACK/WHITE/MIXED SET

The women in group (3) appeared to have one main concern: that their children should clearly recognize the duality of their position (as black and white, as 'mixed' and 'coloured') and not identify totally with the race of one or other parent. Members of group (3) should not be viewed as having a distinct and different attitude from the mothers in group (1), but simply as emphasizing the *mixed* rather than the *black* element of their children's racial identity. Among the mothers in this group there was a sharp distinction between each woman's public and private system of racial categorization. Although it was recognized that mixed race children would be regarded outside the home as black, within the family they were encouraged to see themselves as 'mixed'. Most of these mothers said that they stressed to their children the importance of accepting the label 'black' without shame, but privately this was seen as an incorrect appellation, stemming from ignorance and the belief that non-white people were 'all the same'.

The women who described their children as 'half-caste' tended to be working class and to be part of a network of women with mixed race children; yet unlike the working-class women in group (1), the fact of being mixed was seen as equally important as, or more important than, that of being black. Nora Ballini explained simply that 'The white people say, well, we're white; black people say they're black, and the mixed children say they're either brown or half-caste – brown or half-caste, it's the same thing.'

Similarly, Maggie Muir said she would respond to a child asking if she could be white by replying, 'No. You're half and half. Well, you're half br— black and half white.' She saw the half-caste child as belonging *with* black people, but not being precisely one *of* them. She explained:

'I think most half-castes are accepted more by blacks ... I think they are accepted more by black people and I'd say, "Well, you're more black than you are white", sort of thing.'
'Are they accepted as black or as half-caste?'
'I think they're accepted as half-castes.'

The only black woman in this group was among these working-class mothers. She advised a parent whose mixed race child asked if he was white to 'say no, obviously. And if he says, "Am I black?" say no, 'cos he's neither one thing nor the other.'

The middle-class mothers tended to call their children 'brown' and to self-consciously encourage a pride in their dual racial group membership. They drew attention to the richness of mixed race people's cultural heritage and tried to counter any wishes to be white by presenting a positive view of the child's special position:

I think the whole thing revolves around making sure that the child is secure in the fact that they are *brown* and they're very, very lucky 'cos they've got the best of both worlds ... 'You have the privilege of belonging to both races and this allows you' – if it's used in the right way and the groundwork is laid in the right way — 'to move in both cultures *comfortably.*'

(Sue Green, white)

You have to tell them that, you know, 'Your parents are from different races and different cultures and from different countries.'

(Kari McClaren, white)

Well, that they're mixed! They're part of the mother and part of the father and so on. Well, hopefully, without being too gushing about it, 'Be proud of what you are; be *glad* that you are what you are.'

(Ruth McCarthy, white)

One mother fell in between the first and second sections in this group by combining the conscious positiveness of the middle-class mothers with the practicality of the more working-class 'half-caste' label. She said very definitely:

I don't want them to deny any of it. I don't want them to think there's a problem about being half-caste ... [Half-caste is] what everyone else calls them. If you call them what everyone else calls them, they're not gonna feel it's horrible. I know it does — a lot of people say, oh! horrible, call them brown or call them multiracial, but everyone else calls them half-caste so — it's like the 'black'. You see, years ago, it was a horrible thing to say, but nowadays they've started calling theirselves black — so now they don't like 'coloured', do they?

(Wendy Gower, white)

Like the mothers in group (1) these women thought of their children as black/mixed race, but rather than play up the 'non-whiteness' of their position, they chose to stress the uniqueness of the child's racial background. For the middle-class mothers, this meant enthusing to the children in abstract terms about the value of a dual cultural heritage. The working-class mothers took a more matter-of-fact approach. You are what you are, they said to their children, meaning that 'half-caste' was just another category in the racial classification system, no better and no worse than any other.

The Effect on Racial Identity

If one looks first at the children's identity groups, one particular link with the mothers' attitudes stands out. The children of mothers who encouraged either a black or a mixed identity were most likely to be in the two 'mixed race' groups, whereas the children of mothers who saw them as 'coloured' were more likely to be in the 'black', 'white', or 'contrary' groups (Table 6.4).

140

Table 6.4 *Mother's Categorization and Child's Identity*

Child's Identity	Mother's categorization group			
	(1)	(2)	(3)	*Total*
Black, white, contrary	5	9	7	21
Mixed race (white bias), black mixed race	12	3	15	30
Total	17	12	22	51

chi = 8.37. This difference is statistically significant at the 2% level.

It seemed that the mothers who denied the importance of the white/non-white line, at the same time as being highly conscious of it, tended to instil a similar consciousness in their children. Mothers who saw their children as unequivocally non-white, on the other hand, and then either emphasized the 'mixed' or the 'black' element of their identity, tended to have children who were more at ease with their minority-group status.

Examining the children's identity groups individually by the attitude of the mothers produces a more complex table with much smaller numbers in each cell. None the less, certain trends may be detected (Table 6.5).

Where a mother encouraged a dual/mixed black identity – groups (1) and (3) – greater emphasis on the *black* element did not appear to increase a child's chances of being in the black mixed race identity group. If anything, the reverse was true;

Table 6.5 *Mother's Categorization of Child*

Child's identity	Black (1)	Coloured (2)	Mixed (3)	*Total*
White	0	4	3	7
Black	3	1	0	4
Contrary	2	4	4	10
Mixed race (white bias)	8	3	7	18
Black mixed race	4	0	8	12
Total	17	12	22	51

although the children of mothers who emphasized 'mixture' were equally divided between the mixed race (white bias) and the black mixed race groups, those whose mothers stressed blackness tended to be in the white-bias group. However, the difference was not statistically significant.

On the face of it, it might seem surprising that a child whose mother strongly emphasized the 'black is beautiful' theme is no more likely to have a positive mixed/black identity than the child of a mother who endorses the more elusive identity of 'mixed'. This seems more understandable if the picture painted in the last chapter of the everyday identity of children in the two mixed race groups is recalled. It was suggested that *all* the children in these two groups seemed likely to be capable of feeling comfortable with a mixed/black identity, but that one would expect their lighter orientation to fluctuate according to day-to-day events. So even if a mother's emphasis on blackness as opposed to mixture *was* communicated to her child, one would still expect to see a fair number of children succumbing to the white preference our society encourages. A mother can influence the child's conception of self only up to a certain point.

Where mothers encouraged a 'coloured' identity – group (2) – and were highly conscious of the exact shade of skin of their children, the children tended to see themselves as white. Many respondents who appeared to have a particularly strong white orientation and whose conflict was most apparent (through difficulty in talking about the photographs and so on) had a mother in this group. Three of the thirty children in the 'mixed race' identity groups also had a mother who encouraged a 'coloured' identity, but these mothers were very much on the periphery of the group; they saw the children as 'more coloured' than other women in the group and encouraged some ideas of 'mixture'.

I could find no link among these children between the manner in which their conflict was expressed (that is, whether they were in the black, the white, or the contrary group) and whether they were a lighter or a darker sibling. Where the mother appears to favour the lighter children they do not seem to be more likely to escape racial identity conflict than the darker children. Presumably, though darker children have the mother's disapproval of their darkness to contend with, they are better prepared to meet adverse reactions to their colour outside the family than lighter children are, who may feel acutely the difference between their mother's view of them as 'white' and the 'non-white' classification of others.

142

The Mother's Cultural Awareness and the Child's Racial Identity

Closely related to the mother's view of where the child belonged *racially* was her assessment of where they belonged *culturally*. Items on the questionnaire which related to the subject (i.e. question 32, statements, 3, 13, 16 and 18) were intended to elicit information on two main points: first, whether the mother thought her child was 'fully British' or whether she believed he or she should 'half-identify' with the culture of the black parent; and secondly, how far this view was put into practice in everyday terms. For example, if the mother thought of her child as 'half West Indian', it seemed important to know how much effort she or her partner made to ensure that the child came into contact with aspects of West Indian culture.

The mothers were divided into three groups, according to the strength of their cultural awareness. The first group, (a), consisted of those mothers who assigned their children the identity of 'fully British' and who paid either very little or no attention to encouraging a sense of pride in the culture of the black parent. The second group, (b), expressed the opposite view: that their children should feel that they were (at least 'half') members of a different culture. Thirdly, group (c) contained the women who, although they believed the children should be taught about the black parent's culture, felt ambivalent about whether or not they should see themselves as 'half-belonging' to that culture.

Maggie Muir, a white working-class mother, was indifferent to the cultural aspects of her children being 'half-caste'. As long as they knew where they stood racially, a conscious fostering of a West Indian identity seemed to her irrelevant:

Yeah, well, they're British, aren't they, know what I mean? I don't really bother ... I've never really thought about it. I mean, they know they're not white. They know their dad's a West Indian and all this. I suppose when they're older if they wanted to know about it they could, but at the moment I don't really bother. I expect they get it taught at school anyway. Yeah, they probably get it taught by the school.

Just one of the black mothers also fell into group (a). Predictably, perhaps, it was Monica Finch, who had taken lightly the subject of her children's racial identity. She was dismissive of the whole idea of cultural awareness: 'Well, *I'm* British anyway. I don't even know much about Jamaica myself. All this thing about roots – if it wasn't for the TV programme, I doubt if anyone would want to know their roots. No, it's hogwash.'

143

The second group of women, (b), argued with equal adamance that mixed race children should be made aware of their non-British heritage. They believed that the black parent's culture should not be just a story from far-off lands that was told to the children every now and then, but should be an integral part of their identity. Some mothers, in particular the black working-class women, taught the children just by talking about what it was like 'back home':

They love hearing about when I was a child in the West Indies – because they can't just grow up thinking *white*... Well, I wouldn't say fully British. I think I say 'half' because I think it's important that they do know the other culture.

(Toni Ashton, black)

My little Carlton come home one day and he says, 'Mummy, when are you taking me home?' (I took the little one home, but she was only a baby.) And so I says, 'Maybe one day when Mummy got a lot of money.' An' he says, ' 'Cos I wanna know what colour mud huts you was living in.' Oh! My brother nearly... he was so cross. I says, 'You shouldn't be cross, that's what he was taught.' I mean, someone must be telling him that because he never heard that. He says, 'My teacher told us at school. The blacks used to live in *mud huts*!' I says, 'You wouldn't even put a *pig* in the West Indies to live in the mud huts!' And he doesn't think they got *school* in the West Indies and he doesn't think they got *nothing*... I'd love to take them to prove to them what it's like. I say it's better than here!

(Mathilda Spicer, black)

The middle-class women (black and white) were equally keen for their children to 'know their history', but they favoured a more formal approach to teaching it – using books, maps, visits to museums and so on. Both working-class and middle-class families in this group put 'a visit home' high on their list of priorities, but it was the middle-class families who were more likely to have realized the dream:

The best thing, of course, is to go on the trip of a lifetime. But we've taken Joseph to the Commonwealth Institute too, which was quite interesting.

(Sylvia Ogundele, white)

The teaching should be done at home and at school. We get books from the library on Barbados. They've always been very interested in Barbados; if it comes on the television, an advert for a holiday there, they'll always point it out, and there's a programme... they might show a palm tree and I might say, 'Well, *they're* in Barbados', that sort of thing. Jim tells them a lot of anecdotes, funny things that happened when he was a child, and I think that's good. They get some idea.

(Elaine Houghton, white)

I teach them history – slavery – things they don't get at school. I buy books and *Ebony* (which I totally agree with). The kids don't rave about it, but I know that image is there.

(Sally Barnard, black)

The women in group (c) believed that, although mixed race children should learn about, and maintain a link with, their black partner's culture, the main thing was that they should see themselves here and now as members of a *multiracial* Britain. Most of these mothers felt that it was unrealistic to expect their children to 'feel' West Indian or African while they were brought up in Britain. Some also made the more political point that an identity of black and fully British was, or should be, completely tenable. All the women in this group were white:

If they are brought up in this country, they are the same as English people – but they can be African. I mean, sometimes I worry a bit that we're bringing them up to ... to be ... too ... English ... but, you know, you have to lead the life you lead and make the best of it.

(Sally Adegbola, white)

I think it's difficult if they've never been there. If their father was here, yes, there's no reason why they shouldn't feel half Nigerian, but I think it's difficult being a single parent to do that. I think we'd probably have more Nigerian food, etc. if ... but I do try and cook Nigerian food occasionally. Yes, I think they should learn about it.

(Margaret Udoaka, white)

I want them to feel proud of their other culture, but I also want them to feel that they are fully British. It's difficult, this one ... They should be told that no one is that 'fully British' anyway.

(Wendy Gower, white)

Considered alone, the cultural awareness of the mothers showed no strong relationship with the children's racial identity. Although a child whose mother was in group (b) (strongly aware) was twice as likely to be in one of the two mixed race groups, the difference between this and other groups was not statistically significant (Table 6.6).

When the data relating to cultural awareness are combined with the information on the mothers' view of mixed race children's *racial* identity, one or two links emerge. First, many of the mothers who encouraged a 'coloured' identity – group (2) – also

145

Table 6.6 *Mother's Cultural Awareness and Child's Identity*

Child's identity	Mother's cultural awareness			Total
	(a) (weak; fully British)	*(b) (strong; half another culture)*	*(c) (strong but fully British)*	
White/black/contrary	5	8	8	21
Mixed race (white bias)/ black mixed race	6	16	8	30
Total	11	24	16	51

tended to view the children as fully British and to be unconcerned with teaching them about another culture. This combination of 'almost white' and 'fully British' seemed to be particularly associated with the children in the 'white' identity group; four out of the seven children in this group had a mother who encouraged a 'coloured' and 'fully British' identity. Secondly, where the mother encouraged a mixed identity, being strongly culturally aware increased the child's chances of adopting a black/mixed race identity. None the less, the main finding here was that the mother's cultural awareness, considered alone, was not as strong a determinant of her child's racial identity as her attitudes to his or her racial position was. The mothers who declared themselves indifferent to multicultural education still seem to have been able to foster a positive identity in their children *if their policy was to encourage a mixed or black racial identity*.

In view of the recent emphasis on the importance of multicultural education for children's identity, it may appear surprising that the mother's efforts towards fostering a pride in a mixed race child's dual cultural heritage should be so unrewarded in the child's identity response. A strong cultural awareness was influential only when combined with a mixed encouraged identity – as if an enthusiastic view of the non-white parent's culture in the home tipped the balance of ambiguity and reinforced the child's understanding of what intermediate-group membership actually meant.

It may be that these mixed race children found it hard to connect a far-away culture with their own lives and self-identity, particularly if this was not supported by a similar emphasis on cultural pride in the school. (Some of the 'strongly aware' mothers lived in white areas and had little or no support in their endeavours to engender black cultural pride in their children.)

But a more convincing explanation is perhaps that the component of these children's ethnic identity which needed the most support and reassurance from parents was not cultural but racial – concerned with having dark skin and Negroid features rather than feeling a lack of cultural roots. It is the former rather than the latter which society uses to justify the withholding of social status and the restriction of economic opportunity. At this young age the child, appreciating cultural differences only crudely, perhaps preferred the message that *it was good to be black and mixed race here and now* rather than that these racial identities were connected to a cultural background of some value.

The Mother's Identity: an Impressionistic View

It was mentioned earlier that the mother's classification system and her view of her child's racial position seemed to be linked to her own racial identity. The influence of the mother's racial identity on that of her child could not be considered systematically, since the mothers were not asked any direct questions about how they saw themselves racially. None the less, from what was said spontaneously or in response to other questions, a rough assessment could be made of how some of the mothers viewed their racial position. These mothers fell easily into four distinct types, and these types did seem to be related to the children's racial identity.

When some aspect of a respondent's attitude has not been elicited deliberately in a controlled way, there is a danger of making glib generalizations on the basis of somewhat dubious evidence. What follows, then, should be regarded strictly as *impressionistic* data – patterns derived from themes and comments which arose with persistent regularity in the course of conversations and interviews. Similarities between some of the women in experience, outlook and attitudes were sometimes too blatant to be ignored, but it must be stressed that many differences between them were overlooked in the interests of achieving a broad cartoon 'sketch'.

The white women fell into two groups in the way they expressed their identity: those who saw themselves as white and British, but who felt ambivalent about many aspects of their race and culture; and those who identified with the West Indian group, or with a subculture of women who had interracial relationships. Two types of identity could also be distinguished among the black women: those who seemed uneasy about their blackness and were

147

attracted by white status; and those who felt strong and positive about being members of the black group.

The first identity pattern was that of the white, Christian woman whose interracial marriage was part of a wider, international outlook on life, which was specifically related to her Christian beliefs. Central to this group were the six women in the sample who were married to Africans, but the description could also apply to several women married to West Indians. Predominantly middle class, the mothers of this type were usually women who had spent their childhood in quiet, white areas but who, during their teenage years, had joined an international friendship league or gone on Voluntary Service Overseas. They found themselves attracted to the African culture and had married a man they met while abroad, or an African living in Britain. Their tolerant perspective on race usually derived from a strong Christian belief in the world as one family – ideas which, for most, constituted a rebellion against a rigid or even racist family.

For these women, marrying a black man both broke the chains of a stifling family environment and also, as a psychologist might argue, served as an unconscious punishment for the repressive parents. The dangerously erotic overtones of black masculinity were contained within the sanctity of marriage and within the safety of a Christian outlook which endorsed kinship ('brother-hood') between black and white. Several of these women spontaneously mentioned the close relationship they had had with their father as a child. The psychoanalytic literature on interracial marriage would suggest that the race of the woman's partner will at once have defused and rekindled her relationship with her father. On the one hand, her choice of a black man constituted an avoidance of men like her father (that is, white); yet on the other, it meant that she had turned blatantly from her father to a man who, in terms of traditional Western stereotypes, represented the utmost in sexual competition.

An interesting adjunct to this was that the mother's admiration of African culture – for its warmth, colour and openness – was often coupled with an inability to participate in it. One imagined her presence in an African village as incongruous, for her manner often showed coldness and reserve. I felt strongly in talking to many of these women that their husband's culture represented a repressed part of themselves; they could voyeuristically enjoy *watching* it, yet they could not belong to it. They admired their husband's culture, but they also felt theatened by it. In addition, like all white women in Britain who cross racial boundaries in marriage, these women had been forced to abandon full

148

membership of the white group (see Benson, 1981). Being middle class and well educated, they had perhaps most to lose in terms of status and social advantage by marrying a black man – albeit a black man of considerable standing and education, as was the case with most women in this group.

As regards their children, this meant that although to a greater or lesser extent they wished their children to have a black identity, such mothers also tended to feel highly ambivalent on the matter. Many of the white women in my sample expressed a fear that their children would forget that they were also *part of them*; and the conscious encouragement of a 'mixed' identity was, for some, an attempt to resolve this conflict. One rather startling fact which emerged from the data was that *all the children of African fathers except one* were in the black, white, or contrary groups. To some extent, this is a spurious connection, explained by them living in a white area, having infrequent contact with other mixed children and so on. Yet I also believe that *the ambivalence about their own identity experienced by the white wives of these African men may have played a part in inducing racial identity conflict in the children*.

In contrast, some of the working-class white women married to West Indians had taken on many aspects of West Indian culture and life-style (including the West Indian woman-centred family pattern) or had established themselves in a network of interracial relationships. Women of this second type were more sure of themselves and their own cultural position. They frequently had less, in status terms, to lose in an interracial relationship than middle-class women and consequently seemed better able to foster a non-white identity in their children. These women had less fear of losing their children to the black group, for they themselves already felt part of that group – or at least members of a marginal group which had close ties with it. Working-class women of this type, who frequently if jocularly noted that they almost thought of themselves as West Indian, often had children in the mixed race identity groups.

A number of white working-class women married to West Indians reported that part of the attraction of their black partner had been his life-style: the large family gatherings in which he was involved, the relaxed and open manner of his friends and their collective ability to have a good time. This type of woman was also often strongly identified with the experience of black oppression, feeling personally the outrage of the injustices inflicted on her husband and children. One could argue that these mothers were aligning themselves not simply with a particular ethnic life-style and identity but with a black subculture which provided alternative values to the white status-quo model of happiness and success. These women fitted most closely to descriptions of the wives of black seamen found in the dockland studies of the 1950s and 1960s (see Chapter 1); severely oppressed themselves, a black life-style and the adoption of a black identity provided a welcome release from a world which offered them little hope of attaining material success.

The third and fourth types that were noticeable in the sample for their racial identity have already been mentioned in passing. The black women fell clearly into two groups: those who appeared to feel positive and confident about being black, and those who felt ambivalent about it. Monica Finch was the epitome of the latter and was quite extreme in her views; however, two other black women demonstrated milder forms of a similar conflict. These women were preoccupied with their own skin colour. Monica Finch, for example, spontaneously brought up the subject of hair straightening and bleaching, only to add that she most certainly did not believe in it. She was also vehement in denouncing the 'type of coloured person' who 'got everyone a bad name' (loud-mouthed girls, lazy youths) and dissociated herself from most 'coloured' people. She was similarly concerned to dispel any illusions I might have that she did anything the 'West Indian way'; she stressed that her household was arranged strictly in accordance with white English norms.

The remaining five black women, on the other hand, appeared to approach being black either with a fierce pragmatism or with an easy-going humour which seemed to conceal an equally deep commitment. The two black American women have been frequently mentioned as women caught up in the Black Consciousness movement who were highly articulate about black issues; they exuded self-assurance and were strong and confident in the righteousness of their cause. Toni Ashton, however, provided an example of a less vociferous approach. She recalled with some amusement an incident at the factory where she worked when the supervisor had told her to translate some instructions to an Indian woman who was with her on the assembly line; they were both 'coloured', after all, and the woman assumed that they spoke the same language. Much laughter accompanied her account, but the insult inflicted through ignorance did not go unnoticed. Toni Ashton clearly had a strong sense of self, and such incidents hardened her resolve to make sure her children also knew their true (black) identity. Despite living in a white area, both her children had a positive black/mixed race identity, and her son,

Leo, was the epitome of a child who showed candour and confidence in his discussion of racial matters.

Among the black and the white women, then, there were indications that a mother's racial identity conflict was unconsciously passed on to her child. *Where a mother appeared to have doubts about the value of her own racial identity, her child also seemed to be prone to feelings of self-deprecation.* The white mothers who were ambivalent were attracted by their husband's culture but felt indelibly trapped in whiteness; the black women had been sucked into the classic dilemma of feeling that they inhabited a despised black skin in a world where only whiteness was fully acceptable.

Notes

1   Labels were not introduced until the mother herself had used them. A large number of the mothers spontaneously used 'coloured' before they introduced the term 'black'.

2   It is interesting that Arabs were more likely to be classified as coloured than, say, Italians. This may be attributed to the more visible presence of Arabs in Britain and the conception of their 'foreignness' which has been underlined by the economic power they possess; the 'rich Arab' is a stereotype in the British press.

3   Thus, some mothers may have *reinforced* the age/categorization relationship noted earlier.

4   It is worth distinguishing between *disapproving* of the dichotomy and *denying its importance*. It is a precarious distinction. Many women expressed the view that it was a pity we had to label people at all, to show that they personally did not regard one colour as better than another. But this was very different from not recognizing the reality of the dichotomy and its effect on people's lives.

5   The sun-tan explanation was commonly used both to explain why the children were brown and to help them feel better about it, but it was particularly frequent among mothers in groups (1) and (2). As was noted earlier, the explanation seemed to encourage a white identity among the children or, at best, cause confusion. Tanned skin gets lighter and is 'really' white; some children inferred that all brown skin ultimately became white.

Chapter Seven

The Mothers' Views of Racism

The mothers' assessment of the level of racism in education and employment was included in the interview questionnaire because of its possible bearing on the identity they encouraged in their children. Whatever stance the mother claimed to have taken on which race mixed race children belonged to, the strength of her belief about how race could affect job and educational opportunities may have conveyed an *implicit* message to the child about their position in the white/non-white dichotomy. The connotations and implications of the mothers' views in this area were very complex indeed. For instance, if the mother believed that black people *were* discriminated against, it was hard for her to assign her child willingly to the black group; but, given that the child was not white, she also knew that it was crucial for her to do so, so that he or she would know what to expect. On the other hand, if the mother claimed to believe that, although her children were black, race really did not matter, the whole issue of racial identity became confused. Her child could legitimately turn to her and ask, 'If race doesn't matter, then why tell me I am black?'

Mothers were also asked to give a general overview of the amount of tension and hostility that existed between the races in Britain. Once again, this was to see if their views about racial conflict implicitly required their children to align themselves with one particular group. If the mother saw the black and the white group as locked in irreconcilable conflict, she was forced to have a firm idea of where her child should stand. This was usually linked to who exactly she believed the conflict was between: whether it involved all members of the groups, or just some 'trouble-making' segment of one or both.

The main part of this chapter attempts to unravel the intricacies of the mothers' views of racism and their effects on the children's identity. The final section looks at their beliefs about racial conflict and their predictions for the future of mixed race people in Britain.

Education and Jobs: Three Views

The mother's attitude to inequality of opportunity in Britain was gathered from her answers to specific sections of the question- naire ('spontaneous grouping'; 'critical situation' 4; statements 1, 7, 14, 17 and 19). The views expressed on this subject were surprisingly easy to categorize, since the spectrum of opinion appeared clear. The mothers were ranged along a continuum from extreme emphasis on the individual to extreme emphasis on the system. The women in the former group believed that if you work hard enough you will get the job you want, whereas the women in the latter group took the attitude that, however hard you work, racial bias in the system can and does inhibit individual achievement. In between was a group of women who held ambivalent views; they knew racism existed, but they felt undecided about its prevalence and the extent of its effects. These mothers were loath to share their knowledge of racism with their children in case it encouraged them to look for trouble – that is, to perceive bias in the system when what was needed was extra effort from the individual.

Most mothers warmed to the subject of racial discrimination with very little prompting; it was central to their worries about their children's future. Many reported that they had thought about this a lot, a fact which showed up in the clarity and articulacy of the views expressed. As with the mothers' attitude to their children's identity, class was an important influence on the mothers' views of racism – even more so because it was associated with their general outlook on social mobility and educational success. However, once again, class seemed to affect only certain aspects of the mothers' views, but not the attitude itself. Class was linked, for example, to the individual mother's knowledge of the educational system and to the articulacy of her ideas on what could be done to counter racial discrimination.

GROUP (i): STRONG EMPHASIS ON INDIVIDUALITY
The first group of mothers had a radical, left-wing approach to poverty and underprivilege generally. The women in this group were fiercely radical, community spirited and often 'grass-roots' workers of one sort or another. They snorted with derision at statement 7 – 'Britain offers equal opportunities to all races,

creeds and colours' – and they saw race as part of the far wider issues of exploitation, scapegoating and oppression, in Marxist or similar terms. Their view of discrimination ws that it was widespread, embedded in the system and part of a continuing legacy of slavery and colonization. Racism was not just a vague problem which might affect the children if they were unlucky; it was a day-to-day issue, a fact of life, an inherent feature of society.

Sue Green (white) was curt in her summary of the racial situation in Britain: 'Of course England is a racist country. In the last fifteen years it's become a *very* racist country.'

Liza Hunt (black) reacted similarly. She replied to the question of whether or not racism would affect mixed race children by saying, 'Yes, of course some people will reject them. They'll run into that as the *norm*. That's going to be part of their childhood experience.'

The working-class women tended to describe the level of racism in less abstract terms, but their message was the same: 'If you wanna get anywhere in this country you've gotta fight hard. If you want a trade and you're black, you have to work extra hard for it' (Nora Ballini, white).

The working-class women were more likely to refer to their own personal experience when talking about racial discrimination. They tended to say that they, their husband, or their friend had this or that happen and then to stress that they believed this was common, not just an isolated event in their own lives. The experiences they described were simple but stark, and most such mothers reported them with a strong sense of outrage:

I know from experience. Me and my friend – who's black, you know – we'd both ring up for a job, we'd go along, and I'd get the job and she wouldn't. And if you rang back we found it was happening in a lot of places. They'd say, 'Yeah, we've still got a vacancy', and they would have just refused her the job!

(Mary O'Reilly, white)

My husband's come across it a lot. He's a Rasta. The more black you act, the more you get it.

(Liz Sanders, white)

I mean, I work in a job where there's all white people, you know, and I see black people come for jobs, and they say the job's taken and it's *not* taken, you know! And it's just because they're black!

(Maggie Muir, white)

I've known people with *qualifications* that can't get a job an' they're black! You know, people, like, when they've been at interviews and they say, 'Oh, I'll phone you later' or 'We'll let you know', and when they go to

154

find out if they've got the job, 'Oh, sorry, you're too late.' Beatin' round
the bush to say, 'Well, we don't need *you*.'

(Nora Ballini, white)

Education was another area in which these mothers believed that
racism was rife. The working-class mothers were particularly vocal
on this point, even though their knowledge of the curriculum and
of the educational system generally was less detailed than that of
the middle-class mothers. Teachers came in for a lot of criticism,
mainly for having preconceptions about black children's ability –
or lack of it:

I think... in some cases... in school they don't worry about mixed
children that much. They just think about their own, you know. I think
mixed children tend to get left behind in school. I think myself that my
child is not doing as good as the other children. When it comes to
education, the teachers have got no time for them – they don't care.

(Nora Ballini, white)

I think the black people of this country, especially the West Indians
should, you know, get a better deal. I mean, the teachers obviously aren't
reaching them in school, are they?'

(Liz Sanders, white)

Linda Weaver (white) was more specific in her accusations. She
knew of several mixed race children who had been sent to special
schools, in her view completely unnecessarily. She also complained that schools tended to encourage black children's athletic
prowess at the expense of their academic abilities: 'Lots of
headteachers seem to think that black children are ESN fodder or
else they see them as *legs* – athletes – full stop. They think that's
all they're good at, so they make them spend too much time on
the running track and not enough in the classroom.'

On the whole, these women reported that they would represent
racism realistically to their children, so that they would be
prepared to encounter it, but that they would not encourage the
idea that the mixed race child should work *harder* than white
children in order to combat racism. Their view was that the
children should divorce personal motivation from racial issues.
They should recognize the intrinsic value of their achievements
and work to develop their individual potential rather than to
maintain a favourable comparison with white children. The
responsibility for fighting racism was implicitly placed on the
shoulders of the black/non-white community, of which the child
was a part. Liza Hunt's view of the idea of the effectiveness of
working harder than white children was that

It's just not true! I mean, working in that community centre, that kind of thing... a lot of these kids are disappointed and disillusioned because that's what they've been told. 'Oh, you work hard and you'll be recognized.' Recognized? Rubbish! If they walk into a racist bastard or bitch in their way into *anything*, no matter how capable they are, they are *not* going to get the job – no matter *how* hard they work and *how* well they've done.

When the mothers were asked how they would answer their children's questions about employment ('critical situation' 4), many responded with an instant nod of recognition. It seemed that even children as young as those in the sample had grasped the rudiments of racial disadvantage and were, by the age of 9, already beginning to question the significance of racism for their future. This may have been a direct result of the bald way these mothers represented racism to their children, but in fact a number of women in the rest of the sample also said that their children were aware of the difficulties faced by black people in getting a good job. Yvonne Hanley (white) told a particularly sad story about her 7-year-old son, Peter:

Yes, I've had that sort of question. Peter suddenly got a great interest in tramps. There were a lot of tramps near the school, and he wanted to go and look at them, talk to them and find out all about them, because, he said, *he* was going to be a tramp. He thought he wouldn't be able to get a job 'cos he couldn't read very well. He's probably heard me say to the older boy things about it being necessary for coloured children to do well in school because preference is given to white people.

Once they had told the children the bare facts of racism, most mothers in group (i) moved on to the more positive sphere of *what could be done to counter it*. The emphasis here was on the collective efforts of all black people to tackle racism through political and legal channels; this was seen as different from the child's individual struggle to do as well as he or she could at school. The fight of the black community was one for equality and racial ethnic pride. The child's fight was for personal confidence and self-esteem. Sally Barnard (black) said that she would explain it to her son this way:

I'd tell him, 'You're going to have to deal with the racist aspect of trying to get a job and it's just something with support from your friends that you get through. In Western society racism is always an aspect of it; they're more likely to give a white male a job than a black male – that's the way it works. But that doesn't mean you don't try. Equip yourself as best you can with qualifications and then go forward. That gives you the impetus to fight on because you know *damn* well that you've got whatever that situation calls for.'

Jane Elliot (white) said that she would always put the child's problem in the context of general discussions that they had in the family about how racism was being countered by black *and* white people:

I would remind him that 'If you go for an interview for a job one day and you've got all the qualifications for it and you don't get it and you think it's because of racial prejudice, there are laws making that illegal.' So we could take it to the race relations board and see if it really was that. Because if people don't use the law, then it's not going to do any good, is it?

Liza Hunt took a similar line, but she used stronger words and tacitly placed less trust in formal channels:

Racists are dangerous people and they have to be opposed and that's *why*, because some of them are in a position where they can stop people from getting *work* – not because they can't do the job, but because of the colour of their skin. If you meet people like that you must oppose them and expose them in any way you can.

Despite the careful distinction most mothers made between individual and collective efforts against racism, some women were more susceptible to the 'work hard...' set of beliefs than others. They tended to slip into the view that black children had to work harder than white children in order to gain the equivalent opportunities. Diana Vambe was one of the two middle-class mothers who took this attitude:

We worry perhaps more than most about our children's education. We don't *worry* about it, but we are realistic that they have more problems than white children and we try to stress that you should do your very best at school so you come out of school with a good education, because you'll probably need it more than the white children... They've got to be better, which is, you know, hard on them. We always keep saying, 'You've got to be better.' I mean, we don't *keep* saying it, but if it ever comes into conversation, we try to stress that they've got to be better so that they can have an equal chance.

One or two of the working-class women also tended towards this view, but one of them, Jane Elliot, was also aware of its dangers:

I'm finding that one quite difficult now. I *did* take that view, but now it's just playing along into the hands of those people, having to prove you're better, really, all the time... It's not fair. We all know it's not fair, *you* know, and really people have got to fight to be just what they are and what they want to be without having to prove they're better than so-and-so who's white. I don't think I'm going to push that one.

In summary, this first group of mothers believed that the system was heavily biased against non-white people and hence against their children. The solution for most mothers was to prepare the children to meet racism, but not to represent the individual struggle to achieve goals as the struggle against systematic racial bias. The former was a personal affair, whereas the latter was a battle to be fought collectively by all non-white people.

GROUP (ii): AMBIVALENT

The second group of women seemed to be very much in conflict over their beliefs about the extent of racial discrimination and how far it could affect the individual. The main characteristic of this group was that the mothers, while placing enormous emphasis on the power of education for achieving material success, still harboured a secret fear that racism may be rife. Radical beliefs about racial disadvantage were at war with status-quo educationalism. These mothers knew that racism was a fact, but they were loath to tell their children about it for fear that this would discourage them from their work in school.

The women in this group were unsure of how much discrimination existed in Britain. Take, for example, the view of Ilona Gould, a white mother:

Well ... I dunno. I s'pose if you're prepared to work extra hard if you're coloured to get those few more O levels and A levels, I s'pose you would be equal. But I've not really had a chance to find out what's gonna happen to my son. I hope it's gonna be equal, but, well, I don't think it will be. I don't really know.

Sally Adegbola (white) was equally doubtful. Asked how she would describe the racial situation in Britain to someone who knew nothing about it, she said hesitantly, 'I'd tell them that *overall* ... outwardly, this is a tolerant society, but ... that if they want to come and settle here – get a house and a job – they might start to come across some hostility.'

The reaction of these women to statement 7 – 'Britain offers equal opportunities to all races, creeds and colours' – was in marked contrast to that of the mothers in group (i). Rather than being outraged at the suggestion, they gave it serious consideration and then tentatively either agreed with it or rejected it as unlikely:

It should do, shouldn't it? Whether it does or not I wouldn't like to say. I suppose it does ... compared to other countries probably.

(Pat Ward, white)

That's a difficult one. Because if I looked at my friend's children, who are

158

black, they've all achieved what they set out to. And yet I know this chap who wanted to get an apprenticeship and he didn't have the opp— well, it *looked* as if he didn't have the opportunity because he wasn't a British subject. So if I cast my friend's children aside I would say no, it isn't equal.

(Lily Fisher, black)

Despite their misgivings about the fairness of the system, group (ii) mothers placed their faith wholeheartedly in education as the key to their children's future. Although this type of mother had seen evidence of discrimination, she still believed that under most circumstances, and for most people, 'certificates talked'. Sybil Finlay (white) was adamant on this point: 'I agree being black can't really stop you getting a job. If you've got a stupid white person and a brilliant black person they've *got* to choose that black person for the job.'

Normo Ojo (white) agreed: 'If you've got the right qualifications you can usually get what you want no matter what your colour is.'

The mother's view that a good education could override colour was in some cases in direct contradiction to her statements about the prevalence of discrimination. Ilona Gould (white), who hoped all would be equal for her son but did not think it would be, still had this to say about black people generally: 'I do think they bring a large amount of it on themselves. I mean, if you have the qualifications to get a job you should get it – if you're good enough.'

Some women appeared to try to resolve their ambivalence about racism by seeing it as something which went on elsewhere – that is, outside the area in which they lived. This, together with the idea that the situation would have improved by the time the children were older, helped to place discrimination *outside the mother's personal sphere*. The diversity of the comments about which areas had the worst reputation for discrimination suggested that these were not objective assessments; they were the mother's attempt to deny the effects of racism on her own life, to place it out of reach and to protect her child from its clutches:

I suppose it depends on whereabouts you are, I mean area. In London you get a lot of that, don't you? I don't think it is round here and I hope it isn't where I'm moving to, anyway.

(Jean Watson, white)

I think there is in some parts, but... not widely so. I just put 'agree' because I think it's in *some* parts. I can't disagree because I think it's there somewhere.

(Toni Ashton, black)

I believe that in Hammersmith and Shepherd's Bush it's supposed to be relatively good in relation to the rest of the country.

(Louise Forkah, West London, white)

I live very much in my own little world and I don't really know what is going on elsewhere... As far as it affects me, it's all right... I know it *happens*, but...

(Doreen Johnson, South London, white)

As regards jobs for the children, many women avoided confronting the possibility of racial bias by being optimistic about the future. Vicky Anderson (white) commented, 'By the time Paul gets older, I'd like to think that he'd have the same chance as any English kid. Opinions change all the time, you know.'

Kari McClaren (white) was also hopeful: 'It's there now, yeah. But who knows what it will be like ten years from now? There's no point anticipating it. You have to be optimistic.'

For the black mothers in this group, the conflict between a belief in the individual and a belief in the system was even more acute than for the white mothers, because their views had a direct bearing on *their own* successes and failures as well as those of their children. Despite initial disclaimers of any personal experience of racism, all four black women in this group cited examples of discrimination which had been directed against them. They evidently knew only too well what it felt like to be on the receiving end of racism. Toni Ashton, for example, began her assessment of the state of race relations by saying, 'I can only speak personally – not what you read in the papers – and I mean I haven't really *found* prejudice... I *know* it's there... but I haven't had it personally.' Yet Toni went on to relate the racial tensions at the factory where she worked and to describe the ignorance and tacit racism of the supervisors which *had* affected her personally. Lily Fisher summed up the racial scene in Britain very similarly: 'Well, I'd be talking personally and, because I haven't come up against a lot of trouble, I would say, well, everything is all right.' But she added, 'But then you listen to the news and hear different things... *Personally*, I would say that it's not very tense; but unless something is done it could, you know, get out of hand.'

The conflict of these black women was exacerbated by the closeness of racism to their view of themselves. If they saw the system as *fair*, then the discrimination they had encountered must be taken as personal rejection. Yet to see the system as *unfair* would be to contradict their strong belief in the possibility of individual achievement through education. These women in

160

group (ii) were torn between the two extremes of the black mothers in groups (i) and (ii). The black women in group (i) saw discrimination as an issue totally separate from their own self-esteem, a stance which allowed the possibility that being rejected for a job could be due to racism rather than to personal inadequacy. Those in group (iii) took completely the opposite view. They believed that, although *some blacks* might be discriminated against, *'you and I'* (because of our personal qualities) will be immune, leading to the idea that *only a certain type of black person* encounters racism.

The black women in group (ii), however, wanted neither to blame the system for the failure of blacks to get on, nor to dissociate themselves from 'blacks as a whole' and declare themselves immune from racism. This conflict seemed to engender doubts and contradictions over what to tell the children. Three of these four black women were mentioned earlier as being open and confident about their own and their children's blackness. Yet when race was linked with the possibility of restricted economic opportunity, their confidence was considerably diminished.

The train of thought of one black woman caught in this dilemma is worth following through; it is full of contradictions. This was Mathilda Spicer's answer to the open question on the state of British race relations:

A lot of blacks not working is not because they not educated – I must say, some of them is useless – but some of them is well educated, because I know this for a fac', you know? A lot of these Rastafar – whatever they call it – a lot of them is well educated, but they just can't get a job. Why? They won't tidy they heer up, that's why! That's what I think, anyway.

Yet she went on to relate her own experiences while looking for a job:

I mean, I can remember leaving school an' I was ringing up for these jobs an' they said, 'Oh, yes, come along.' An' then I'd go, and they'd see my face and they say 'Oh, it's just gone' or 'Oh, we'll write to you' – not being interviewed or nothing, so I thought this is no good. At first I used to hold out, hold out, hold out, and think, oh, I will get a letter in the post, and then I say, 'No! Why should I keep waitin' and waitin' and waitin'?' This happened a lot of times. An' I says, 'No!' I usually *go*, I don't phone up. I see it in the paper or in the agency and I just go straight there. Then they see you straight there and make their mind up. I mean, I'm not bein' funny but it's true, it happens a lot. I mean, if you ask a lot of black people they'll say, 'Oh, it's because I'm black', but it's not the case all the time. Not *all* the time; sometimes it is.

Both the black and the white mothers in this group reported that they underplayed the effects of racial discrimination when talking to their children. Despite their doubts about the fairness of the job market, they encouraged their children to believe that qualifications were the ticket to success and that any amount of racial discrimination could be overcome by hard work. Jean Watson (white) put it to her son this way: 'I say, "As long as you study hard you'll get a job" – that's what I drum into him. If he won't do his work, I say, "Well, how are you gonna get a good job?" He wants to be rich, he says, so I say, "Well, you're not gonna be rich unless you work hard."'

Most of these responses came in answer to 'critical situation' 4, which posed the problem of a child who wondered whether being mixed race would stop him or her from getting the job he or she wanted. Sybil Finlay (white) became heated about this question, as she thought of her own failure to do well in school: 'I'd say no. No bloody way. 'Cos he can. If he's got the bloody brains and he studies at school he can do it. 'Cos, I mean, I never got anywhere. I never did sod-all at school ... If he's ambitious, he'll get on.'

Margaret Udoaka (white) felt the same way, although she expressed it in more restrained terms: 'Tell them, "It's what you make of your life that's important, not what you look like. If you work hard at school and you want to do something badly enough there's no reason why you shouldn't do it."'

Another white mother, Wendy Gower, thought that the children should be left to find out about racism on their own, ' 'Cos otherwise they're gonna go looking for it and I say, well, if they look for it, they're gonna find it.'

However, despite underplaying the existence of racism and stressing the efficacy of hard work, many of these mothers also told their children that they would have to work *harder than white children* in order to get on. The contradiction of their attitude did not seem to present a problem, although a few mothers expressed misgivings about telling the children this when they were very young. Toni Ashton (black) was firm in her attitude on this point:

I've told him he has to work that bit harder than a white child to succeed. I don't know if it's right or not, but I have. Yeah, I've said, 'You have to be that bit better', which might be wrong at that age, but I think ... it's a fact! But I tell him, 'You can do whatever you want as long as you work hard.'

The view of a white mother, Gwen Smith, was similar:

I would say, 'You will be able to do what you want when you grow up if you really set your mind to it and work.' But I have, in fact, said to Nigel that whatever he does he will have to be good at it, because in some jobs if there was a choice between two candidates of equal intelligence, it would be weighted for the English one. Perhaps he was too young to hear that, but I said it to him.

The only class difference among the mothers in group (ii) was the minor, but expected, one that the working-class women were less knowledgeable than the middle-class mothers about the educational process. Their attitude was more of a hope that the magic formula of 'working hard' would prove potent for their child, and learning was seen as something which happened if a child was placed in close enough proximity to learning artefacts. The middle-class mothers were more specific in their ambitions for the children – to take O- and A-levels and perhaps go on to college or university. They were also aware that discrimination was worse in some areas of employment than in others. Some believed that the higher up the professional scale one moved, the less a person's race mattered – a view which provided yet another incentive for encouraging their children to do well in school.

To summarize: both middle-class and working-class mothers in group (ii) felt ambivalent about what they should tell their children about racism in the economic system. Ultimately, they encouraged the children to do well at school and not to worry about the extent of discrimination, but at the same time they hinted that racism could affect their chances once they were 'out there', in the open job market.

GROUP (iii): STRONG EMPHASIS ON INDIVIDUAL ACHIEVEMENT

The mothers in group (iii) placed extreme emphasis on the possibilities of personal qualities and of individual endeavour, both in their own views and in what they told the children. From this type of woman emerged the view that only a particular kind of coloured person encountered prejudice or discrimination, because they were, in reality, either *inventing* it as an excuse or *provoking* it by their behaviour. The emphasis on the individual was not just a means of enforcing educational values; it was also central to the mother's theories about why discrimination occurred. Aggressive and assertive behaviour was seen as attracting real or apparent discrimination, and thus, to some extent, black people were to be seen as 'bringing it upon themselves'. It was sometimes conceded that there *could* be an element of luck in this process – if one was unlucky, one might come across a prejudiced person within the system – but generally if one mucked in and worked hard one would find the system fair. There was occasionally a hint that the prospect was not all rosy for black people, but knowledge of such things was far removed from the respondent's own experience.

The two black women in this group were clear about their view of racism. It was a device used by 'certain kinds of coloured people' to get sympathy and to provide an excuse for not succeeding. They completely denied any experience of discrimination; unlike the black women in group (ii), these mothers maintained throughout the interview that their lives had been untouched by any kind of racism. Monica Finch had this to say about the state of British race relations:

Personally, I've never had any trouble at all. It's a case of having a chip on your shoulder. If you look for trouble, you'll find it. I remember when I first started at the bank, there was another coloured girl there, and she sort of walked around as if she was Miss High and Mighty, and if an English person asked her something, she'd snap. You get these people who say, 'So-and-so's doing that because I'm black.' I don't look at it that way. If you go looking for trouble, you'll find trouble.

Shirley Collins felt that race was completely unimportant and irrelevant to what one achieved in life: 'I've never met anyone in the council that was prejudiced ... I've never been turned down for a job because I was black – although in the job I'm in they're mainly black [laughs]. Oh, I dunno ... colour, it's neither here nor there.

The answers of the two women to statement 7 ('Britain offers equal opportunities ...') were similarly unhesitant. Monica Finch declared, 'Oh, I *strongly* agree with that.' Shirley Collins also agreed: 'The opportunities are there. It's just up to the individual, black or white or coloured or pink with purple spots, to just get out and do it.'

The white women in this group were slightly less adamant about the fairness of the system than the two black mothers, but their view was essentially the same: that if black people worked hard they had every chance of succeeding, but that racism was all too often used to mask individual inadequacy. Vera Kano argued that this was particularly true of 'black youths': 'I think some of these youths hide behind their colour, to say that they can't get jobs when they don't *want* jobs. I *do* think they blame their colour for not getting jobs. I *don't* think it holds them back if they really wanted a job.' She stated emphatically that she had never encountered racism and she implied that the white people in Harmony (to which she belonged) were oversensitive to it:

I've never come across prejudice. I mean, I can't say I've come across prejudice from any white person *at all*. I've lived in London eleven years and before that I lived in Sussex, which is an all-white area, and I have never, never, never come across colour prejudice. *Surprise* that my children are coloured, yes – but never prejudice. I'm always surprised that people in Harmony come across it so much. Perhaps they're just looking out for it.

The view that 'if you look for it you'll find it' was common among the women in groups (ii) and (iii). It seemed to have three meanings. Some women appeared to use the expression to mean that racism was 'out there somewhere', either in a different area or in a different social sphere from their own, but that they were personally not affected. A second meaning ws that 'it' (prejudice) could be found in most white people if you dug deeply enough. The implication was that one should take people at face value and not push their 'tolerance' too far. The third meaning, which was the most common among the women in group (iii), was that if you acted in an assertive or aggressive way, or if you emanated suspicion of white people's motives, you would *provoke* trouble where none existed. *Anticipate* it, said these women, and you *precipitate* it.

Both the black and the white mothers in group (iii) had a well-defined message about racism to convey to their children; if you work hard, every opportunity is there. They were adamant that a person's colour could not lessen their chances of getting a job. This is how Monica Finch would explain it to her son if he asked whether being black would mean that he might not get his ideal job:

I'd say, 'No, it won't mean that. If you . . . learn what you have to learn and do your schooling, complete your schooling, apply for your job, you'll get your job.' Because if he wants to be an engineer I don't see anything stopping him from being an engineer, I don't think colour comes into it . . . I think if one is determined to get a job, then you'll get the job, but if one wants to skive and they get up in the morning, get dressed and say, 'I'm going down for an interview', and they do not turn up for that interview, then they can't expect to get the job.

Brenda Jordan (white) was another mother who had little time for children who 'blamed their colour'. She said brusquely, 'I'd say that would depend on how well he used his education, not as much on the colour of his skin, and if he used his education properly then he's got as good a chance as anyone else.'

Shirley Collins (black) was willing to admit that prejudice was there, but she stressed that it was up to the individual to overcome it:

I say to Marcus, who is black [child of a previous relationship with a black man], 'If you try hard enough you'll get anything you want', and I believe that. You know it's got nothing to do with the colour of his skin. I think if you settle down and you're prepared to work, you should get it. So I don't think racial prejudice has got anything to do with it. Admittedly, you do go into some jobs and you meet biased people, but it's up to you to prove your ability, as good as anybody else.

To summarize the view of the mothers in group (iii): racism was viewed as minimal; where it did exist, they felt that the onus was on the individual to battle through on the strength of his or her ability. Both the black and the white mothers believed that some black people used their race as an excuse for not being successful. Those with the wrong attitude brought racism upon themselves.

The Children's Identity

The extent of the mother's emphasis on racism, and her view of whether responsibility for discrimination lay with the individual or with society, did appear to be related to the child's identity. The children whose mother strongly believed that the system was biased tended to be in the 'mixed race' identity groups; the children of the ambivalent mothers were evenly spread between the 'mixed race' and the 'in conflict' groups; and those of the mothers who played down discrimination were concentrated in the 'in conflict' groups: 'white', 'black', or 'contrary'. Thus, *the more politically left-wing the mothers were on the subject of race and opportunities, the more likely the child was to have a strong mixed/black identity* (Table 7.1).

One might think that the influence of the mother's attitude to racism on her child's identity could be explained by her view of

Table 7.1 *Mother's Attitude to Race Opportunities and Child's Racial Identity*

Child's identity	Mother's attitude to race and opportunities			
	(i)	(ii)	(iii)	Total
Black/white/contrary	4	12	5	21
Mixed race (white bias)/ black mixed race	13	15	2	30
Total	17	27	7	51

the child's racial position – that, for example, a mother who encouraged a black identity would automatically stress racial inequality to the child, whereas a mother who saw her child as coloured (or 'almost white') would play down the unfairness of the system. This was true to an extent; but it applied to only about half the sample; the mother's attitude to discrimination seemed to influence the child's racial identity even when 'encouraged racial identity' was controlled. Regardless of which racial identity a mother encouraged, *the more forcefully she represented systematic racial bias to her child, the less likely her child was to experience a racial identity conflict.* (Although, of course, cell numbers were very small.)

At first glance, one might have imagined that the relationship between these two variables should have been the reverse – that to draw the child's attention to the advantages of being white would have made racial identity conflict more acute. But if one looks more closely at the situation from the child's point of view, there are several possible reasons why open recognition of racial inequality might encourage a secure black/mixed race identity.

Whatever a mother tells her child about his or her racial identity, her assessment of the level of racism and her view of the way it operates is bound to affect the final message he or she receives about which group is 'really' his or hers. The mother's statement to her children that he or she belongs to this or that racial group is contradicted or confirmed, underplayed or underlined, by the messages she conveys in other areas. Her view of racism is particularly important in this respect, because it says something about how seriously she takes the whole matter of race and racial identity. It may be the difference between telling the child, 'You are black, but it does not matter', and telling him or her, 'The fact that you are black affects your whole life.' Inevitably, the mother's view of racism afffects the content and salience of the child's racial identity.

If the mother underplays the amount of discrimination her child is likely to suffer – or denies the existence of racism altogether – but still encourages a black identity, then the child receives one of two messages. He or she either reasons that blackness is unimportant, and so may be safely disregarded, or else understands his or her mother to mean that racism, though it exists, does not apply to him- or herself. Either way, the child comes to the conclusion that he or she is not really black; they may have a black father, they may have brown skin, but they are not really part of that community which is oppressed and disadvantaged by the actions of white people.

167

Why does the mother's denial of racism seem to undermine her encouragement of a black identity rather than vice versa? This is probably because a denial of racism *contradicts the child's own experience*. Several studies have shown that even very young children associate whiteness with 'having a nice house', 'wearing pretty clothes' and so on, and most researchers in this area have concluded that children have by the age of 6 a rudimentary understanding of the connection between whiteness and success (e.g. Radke and Trager, 1950). Some additional evidence on this is available from the present study. When the children in the sample were asked to match certain jobs with the 'fathers' in the photographs, the dirty/manual jobs such as road-sweeper and dustman were given to the black and Asian men, and the job of businessman was allotted to the white man. (Sixty-six and 70 per cent respectively matched road-sweeper and dustman to a black or Asian man; 68 per cent matched businessman to a white man.) Yet most mothers who underplayed racism believed that their children were too young to be aware of racial bias.

Ilona Gould was a mother in group (ii) who underplayed racism to her son, Kevin. She told him he could get any job he wanted as long as he worked hard; racism would not affect him. But she also told him that he had to be *better* than most white children to 'get on'. Ilona thought of Kevin as 'definitely not white' and she encouraged him to adopt a 'brown' identity, but she was ambivalent on the subject of blackness. She complained that Kevin's Afro hair was 'a curse to comb and brush'; she had a very low opinion of her husband and his friends; yet at the same time she claimed to be incorporating 'black pride' into her strategy for dealing with Kevin's identity. One can hardly be surprised that Kevin was in conflict over his racial identity, unsure of whether he was white or not. The messages he received from his mother about his racial identity, combined with what he already knew about race from his own experience, must have presented a highly confused picture. How could race be unimportant for jobs if you had to be better than white children? How could being black be unimportant if all the most successful people in the world seemed to be white? How could black be beautiful if Afro hair was a curse to comb?

For many children such as Kevin, who received conflicting messages about racism and racial identity, there seemed to be only one appropriate response: to identify as white. The children knew the system was unfair, they knew that being white made life easier, yet their mothers refused to acknowledge this as a reason for lack of success. These children were expected to tackle the contradictory task of both ignoring racial bias and challenging the system single handed. To succeed, they had to beat the white opposition, yet the white opposition had every possible advantage. No wonder that the temptation to join them rather than beat them overwhelmed them and led them into the fantasy that they too were white.

Children whose mothers denied racism altogether, and claimed that only a 'certain type' of black person 'attracted' discrimination, had an additional fear: that being the victim of racism meant that they were 'bad'. Some mothers gave the impression that only bad black people were discriminated against because they were the ones who went looking for it. This reinforced the idea that, if one was black, all failures had to be blamed on the self rather than on the system. In the minds of the children whose mothers took this attitude, blackness must have been linked indelibly with the risk of failure and disapproval. Much easier, then, to dissociate oneself from blackness and to cast off the burden of having to be 'good' against the odds. White children clearly had a better chance of succeeding, and *their* goodness was not dependent on avoiding the guilty trap of racism, into which it was all too easy to fall.

The children whose mothers represented racism to them realistically were presented with a more manageable task in terms of individual achievement. Although their knowledge of racial discrimination was expanded by the mother's explanations of the unfairness of the system, and although their worst fears were confirmed when she said that racism *would* apply to them, these children were offered two ways of coping with racial bias. First, they were encouraged to see themselves as part of a non-white/black community that was fighting back collectively against white oppression. Racism was shown to be not just a personal problem but also a public issue. Secondly, the children were taught to divorce the experience of racism from their own self-esteem. Being discriminated against was not a personal slight, related in some way to their actions or personality, but an objective reality which existed independently. This firm placement of racism in the public rather than in the personal sphere left those children free to pursue their own goals, without being expected to grapple with the elusive spectre of white opposition.

Racial Conflict and the Future

The final variable to be cross-tabulated against the children's racial identity was the mother's assessment of the level of racial tension which existed in Britain and her view of how race relations would develop in the future. The hypothesis behind linking these two variables was that the more the mother saw race relations as a state of irreconcilable conflict between black and white, the more likely she would be to encourage her children to align themselves with one group or the other.

The mother's view of the level of racial tension did not in fact seem to have a strong relationship with her children's racial identity. Although mothers who believed that racial hostility was rife tended to have children with a black/mixed race identity, this relationship could be accounted for by the link between the mother's attitude towards inequality and the child's racial identity. These were the same mothers who represented the economic system to their children as heavily biased, and it was this, rather than their view of racial tension, which seemed to have a greater effect on the kind of identity they encouraged (Table 7.2).

The mothers who were classified as having a 'high' emphasis on tension and hostility were those who recounted experiences of racial violence, expressed fears for their own or their children's safety, or saw racial tension as both extreme and inevitable. It was noted in Chapter 6 that several families had first-hand experience of racial violence – mothers and children who lived in multiracial areas who had been attacked verbally or physically – but a larger number of women seemed to be aware and fearful of racial harassment, even when it was not a feature of their area. Jean Watson, for example, lived in a white area of Essex where race was not a local issue, yet she described the racial situation in Britain as very tense: 'It's getting pretty bad, I think, meself, isn't it? You see so much fighting and everything going on, you get quite frightened really. And I worry about these when they're

Table 7.2 *Mother's Emphasis on Tension and Child's Racial Identity*

Child's identity	Mother's emphasis on tension and hostility			
	High	Moderate	Low	Total
Black/white/contrary	8	10	3	21
Mixed race (white bias)/ black mixed race	17	9	4	30
Total	25	19	7	51

170

grown up, what the world's gonna be like. I mean, I do worry a lot over them. Especially now they haven't got a dad.'

The mothers who assessed the tension as 'moderate' were those women who represented racial prejudice as cyclical ('it flares up now and again'), as partial ('some white people are prejudiced, some are not') or as dual ('it's extremists from both sides that cause the trouble') – or else who, though claiming not to have experienced prejudice personally, were none the less highly conscious of its existence. Chris Hastings (white) had this to say about race relations in Britain: 'Well, I couldn't really say from first-hand experience, but what I would surmise is that it's not particularly tense at the moment but it will build up because, you know, things just aren't getting better. There's nothing being done to help, you know, so things will get worse.'

Some 'moderate' mothers, like Ruth McCarthy, were tentatively optimistic about the future, but none of these mothers was wholeheartedly hopeful:

I would say that among younger people – particularly people who've mixed and been educated – I should think it probably will get better. If things don't get worse before that, if you see what I mean ... On the face of it, it doesn't seem to be as bad as it has been in the States, but there are a lot of strong undercurrents.

(Jane Elliot, white)

A further small group of women rated racial tension in Britain as 'low' or non-existent. Monica Finch (black), in keeping with her general denial of race as an issue of conflict, felt that apart from 'a few trouble-makers', the feeling between the races was amicable: 'I wouldn't say it's very tense. I would say it's on an even keel. There's give and take on both sides.'

Wendy Gower (white) agreed:

People here are not racialist. Some of them are patriotic and they don't like it – especially Asians – if they come here and they're different. But I say it's not really a racialist country. Some people are, but then some people are pigs, aren't they? I mean, you *do* get it, of course. I've had arguments with people who say, you know, they ought to be strung up and send them all back home and this, that and the other. But the way I look at it is they'd say that about anybody. If it weren't the blacks it would be the Welsh and if weren't the Welsh they'd be saying it about people from Manchester.

One possible reason why the mother's feelings about racial tension did not appear to affect her child's identity was that the difference between the three levels of emphasis on racial tension was not that great. One could generalize about the sample as a whole and say that *none* of the mothers I interviewed was entirely complacent about race relations in Britain. Most women described the situation as consisting of some degree of tension between black and white. Their views about who were the main protagonists varied – older people, younger people, the media, Asians and the government were all targets of blame – but there was general unease about the level of racial conflict in Britain today, and overall pessimism about relations in the future.

If one looks at some of the incidents recounted by the mothers, this unease is hardly surprising. Most women experienced some sort of racial harassment on a regular basis, even if it was only being stared at by strangers, gossiped about by neighbours, or generally treated as objects of curiosity. The mothers interpreted all these incidents matter-of-factly; none the less, they contributed to the overall view that racial tension was a pervasive force in Britain. A number of women mentioned that they could never relax in their neighbourhood. They had to be cautious about trying to make friends, for fear of being rejected:

When you go out into the street, you get the odd Irishman who's drunk, you know, and he'll say something to you. 'Nigger lover' – something like that, but, well, I don't really take much notice.

(Maggie Muir, white)

I usually keep myself to myself, really... I mean, I never bother with people round the street. I don't like to cause arguments. I mean, sometimes they can say nasty things, so rather than go out and argue with them I keep the children in. I find just keeping myself to myself and just ignoring the remarks they make at you or anything is the best thing to do. Other than that, you'd always be arguing with people, so I just don't bother.

(Mary O'Reilly, white)

For black women the fear of rejection had a double edge; the fact that they were black and the fact that they were in an interracial relationship. Mathilda Spicer, who lived in a multiracial area but not a multiracial street, was highly conscious of both:

Around here, well, the people over the road say hello, but I don't start saying, 'Oh, good *morning*' and so on, because I don't wanna be insulted. I don't know how they gonna react. I don't get involved. I hate someone to shout or show me up. I feel so embarrassed. I'm the only Negro living in this road. Five doors up there's an Indian family, and over the road there's an Indian/white couple, but that's about it.

The future of British race relations, from where many of these women stood, looked bleak. Liz Sanders believed that the relative position of black and white had become more polarized in recent years: 'I think there'll be more violence before ... I don't know how it will all end. But it's definitely building up.'

Despite this, some mothers still believed that interracial families were the key to future harmony between blacks and whites in Britain. They echoed the 'melting-pot' vision of the 1960s that racial conflict would disappear as interracial marriages increased. The role of the interracial family as a bridge between the two communities provided the one note of optimism in these women's thoughts about the future. As one mother put it, 'In my own view, in twenty years or so there'll be so many mixed marriages and mixed people that, hopefully, all the tension we're getting now will go.'

Chapter 8

Conclusions

A study based on a sample of only fifty-one children cannot discuss its conclusions without first adding a note of caution about possible sources of bias in its results. The sample used in the study was small; it was not recruited randomly, and there was no guarantee that it was representative of mixed race children as a whole. The study was also limited to a small area of investigation which left a number of key areas unexplored. For example, the father's influence on identity was not investigated, and the child's school life was studied only at second hand, through the mother. These limitations do not invalidate the study as a piece of preliminary research, but they should be kept in kind when its findings are considered.

Sample Bias

There were three sources of bias, stemming from the way the sample was selected, which seemed particularly likely to affect my results. The women who were interviewed tended to be candid and concerned about racial matters; they regarded their children as 'mixed race' rather than as wholly black or wholly white; and, because this was a 'snowball' sample, they were likely to know at least one other interracial family.

Although the women I interviewed varied in how voluble and how articulate they were, they were all concerned with, and willing to speak openly about, racial matters. Some of the mothers had already demonstrated their concern by being actively involved in Harmony; others illustrated their openness simply by agreeing to be interviewed. This meant that my sample may not have adequately represented women who had difficulty in acknowledging their racial feelings and attitudes, those who were deeply ashamed of having mixed race children, mothers who denied any racial difference in their children, or those who were simply shy of talking to a stranger about topics which they considered intimate. Since the mother's attitude to race was found to be an important determinant of the child's racial identity, this may have biased the results. One could not suggest that every member of the adult sample was an extrovert, well-adjusted woman with her racial consciousness fully raised, but a tacit prerequisite of the interview was a fair degree of candour about race and a certain amount of interest in racial politics.

An even more specific selection bias (which could be even more directly related to the results obtained) was that the women in the sample, by agreeing to take part in a study overtly concerned with mixed race children, were implicitly concurring with the idea that such a category of children existed. Whatever their personal categorization system and reported view of their children's identity, all these women clearly acknowledged that, on one level of social reality, their children were different from both white and black children. In other words, *I may have selected a sample of women who were not only highly reflective about racial issues, but who were also in some measure of agreement with the sociologists about defining their children as being 'of mixed race'.*

Because this was a 'snowball' sample, beginning from the central, formalized network of Harmony, *the women I interviewed were inevitably in contact with at least one other interracial family.* Although this connection was not necessarily a close one, there was an unavoidable risk of interviewing a disproportionate number of mothers who belonged to a network of interracial families maintaining frequent day-to-day contact between themselves. As a consequence, the numbers of children having other mixed race children as friends may also have been high in comparison with British mixed race children as a whole.

All of the above factors suggest that the sample may have over-represented mixed race children who had a good chance of developing a secure and positive mixed race identity.

Both the literature and my own experience in meeting interracial families suggested that there were at least two groups of children missing from my sample: those who maintained a viable black identity and those who saw themselves as white. The respondents closest to the former position were those in the 'black' identity group, but it will be recalled that this was viewed as a defensive reaction because it did not appear to be socially viable in the context of their everyday lives. Although some mothers and children approximated to the latter stance of seeing mixed race children as white, the mothers still paid lip-service to the idea that, on one level, they could not be regarded as full members of the white group.

In defence of the risk that was taken in over-representing children with viable mixed race identities, it must be noted that previous research tended to concentrate on 'problem' families or on mixed race children who were in situations where their identity problems were likely to be particularly acute. For example, the mixed race children mentioned in the dockland studies (Chapter 1) were usually the children of prostitutes living in particularly poor areas; and where mixed race children have been included in studies in recent years, they have often been children who were being adopted or fostered or who were in care.[1] The present study appears to have avoided this type of bias, and if it has inadvertently sought out well-adjusted mixed race children this is perhaps a useful counterbalance to previous research.

Summary of Findings

If the main findings of the study had to be summarized in a single sentence it would be that mixed race children do not necessarily conform to the stereotype of the social misfit, caught between the social worlds of black and white. Not all mixed race children are torn between the ethnic loyalties of their parents and not all spend their lives trying to make themselves acceptable to *one* ethnic group. Some interracial families (and some areas) seem conducive to the development of a positive mixed race identity, where the child is content to be both black and white without perceiving a contradiction between the two.

The data collected in the study related to three subject areas: mixed race children's image of the racial structure; their view of themselves within that structure; and the influence of the mother's attitudes on their racial identity. By putting all this information together, one can gather some idea of how mixed race children's identity develops and is maintained and of the conditions under which a positive identity seems most likely to thrive.

MIXED RACE CHILDREN'S VIEW OF THE RACIAL STRUCTURE
The racial structure, seen through the eyes of a mixed race child aged between 6 and 9, contains many imponderables, many incomprehensible inconsistencies. It is good to have a tan, but not

to be black; black skin is not black at all, but brown; if your skin is very light brown, it could pass for white except if your hair is very curly or very straight or if you speak a different language. The sheer number of racial labels is confusing, but when one adds the wealth of nuance and meaning contained within them and the way their usage varies from situation to situation, the complexity is overwhelming. Racial labelling must seem to mixed race children like a cacophony of sound from which it is possible to pick out only one or two basic themes.

If any single feature of the system stands out it will be the material, educational and occupational differences between white and non-white people, reinforced by the symbolic content of the colours 'black' and 'white'. These will be understood as the constant features of racial categorization. Whatever else the child learns about race, he or she will remember that white skin gets rewards in our society and that the colour white is associated with all things good. White dresses are beautiful; blonde hair is the ideal. Rich and powerful people – kings and queens, prime ministers and princesses – are nearly always white. Those that are black are depicted frequently as 'baddies' or as 'not quite one of us.' By the age of 6, all children in Britain are aware that society makes a distinction betwen white and non-white and that it values the white above the non-white group.

Within this white/non-white distinction, younger children see racial categorization as series of skin colour gradations, ranging from very dark to very light. Black merges into brown and brown into white with no hard-and-fast rules about where each category begins or ends. The young mixed race child in Britain seems to absorb – perhaps wishfully, perhaps not – the *vagueness* of where whiteness ends and non-whiteness begins and applies this vagueness throughout the racial structure. The extremes of the continuum – black and white, light and dark – are clear, but in between lies an area about which the child is unclear, which could equally be counted as one racial category or as many.

It may be that this system of vague skin colour gradations represents an intermediate stage of a cognitive transition from colour to fully fledged *racial* attitudes. The early infantile experiences of night and day, light and dark, may be transformed at a very early age into culturally sanctioned feelings towards *colours*; these in turn become socially reinforced attitudes towards different shades of skin. Colour retains its importance until the more abstract themes of 'culture', 'nationality' and 'race' are understood; these are then incorporated into the colour classification system which already exists in the child's mind.

As the child gets older, he or she becomes aware that the rules of racial classification are more complex and more rigidly enforced than they first appeared. The child begins to understood *cultural* divisions between people and to appreciate their subjective importance. The link between these cultural differences and certain physical characteristics is made also – for example, between being 'Indian' and having straight as opposed to curly black hair. The older child realizes that the criteria of parentage, skin colour and culture are combined in a number of ways and then used racially to classify people in various social situations. From this time on, the mixed race child is striving to reconcile the labels heard at school, at home and in the street, in order to develop a racial classification system which is socially viable and appropriate to his or her area of Britain.

At this stage, different children see different criteria as paramount in the way the racial structure is organized. Some see 'culture' as the important feature and so understand society to consist of a number of cultural groups, such as West Indian, Indian and Pakistani. The more sophisticated children also have some understanding of what these differences in ethnicity entail, such as eating particular kinds of foods, speaking different languages and embracing another religion. Other children feel that parentage defines one's place in the racial classification system and that, for example, all 'mixed' West Indian children belong together because only one of their parents is black. However, it is interesting that the division between Asians and West Indians/Africans still tends to intrude into this system; the fact of being 'mixed' cannot usually override the distinction between being of Indian and being of Afro-Caribbean extraction.

Although mixed race children's understanding of the whimsical subjective technicalities of racial categorization improves with age, the amount of classificatory detail they assimilate, and the rate at which this learning process progresses, to a large extent depends on where they live. Systems of racial classification vary from area to area. Regardless of age, children who live in multiracial areas seem to develop relatively sophisticated secondary category sets, which take account of a wide range of criteria. Children in white areas, on the other hand, tend towards simple, colour-scheme sets and appear to be more concerned with the white/non-white dichotomy.

For the children in multiracial areas, whose life is played out as part of an intricate mosaic of ethnic groups, knowledge of all kinds of ethnic difference comes fast and early. The discovery and questioning of visible differences between people are an integral part of the young child's exploration of the social world. As soon as children in multiracial areas are old enough to articulate observations about their expanding circle of social contacts, knowledge of ethnic difference rapidly increases. One 7-year-old in the study, referring to the photographs in the identity test, said, 'I knew those people were Indian because I see lots of Indian people.'

'Indians all have straight black hair,' said another child; 'at least, the ones that I know do.'

In areas where racial hostility is near the surface of people's consciousness, ethnicity forms part of the currency of everyday conversation and racial categorization is stark, vivid and to the point. Racial insults are often the first lesson in racial labelling that a child in a multiracial area receives; name-calling defines sharply who is who in the ethnic pecking order. These insults may be negative but they are also clear. The child learns immediately where he or she stands in relation to the white group and moves on to learn more abstract and more positive terminology. Ironically, it is the children in multiracial rather than in white areas whose knowledge of race is consolidated and reinforced through formal channels, for they are the most likely to receive multiracial education in their schools.

Children in white areas are more reliant on the efforts of their parents to provide multiracial and interracial experiences to transcend the ethnic restriction of their daily lives. They are highly unlikely to receive any such training in school. For these children, racial categorization is simply a matter of whether one is white or not. An appreciation of the finer points of ethnic categorization is unnecessary because it is irrelevant to their playground politics. The children in the study who went to all-white schools found the categorization test more difficult than those in multiracial environments and had less to say about the categories they constructed. 'They're black, they're brown and they're white' was the stock description of the photo groups. Precipitous understanding of the abstractions of cultural and physical differences was not there unless the parents had taken pains to encourage it.

In white areas, older children seem to cling to the 'colour continuum' type of categorization long after their cosmopolitan counterparts. This may be partly because the information to construct more detailed sets is simply not available; the charac-teristics of Indian/African/West Indian people are not part of their everyday experience, nor do they have a reference-point in mixed race people like themselves. But children may hold on to simple colour categories for another reason; this type of classification maintains a reassuring fiction that the black/white line is ill defined and negotiable, long after the child knows intellectually that this is not so. Mixed race children in white areas are slow to abandon the 'colour scale' idea because it contains the classification 'almost white'. To think of yourself as different but equal is hard unless you have a group to support you in your difference. It is easier to minimize the importance of ethnic difference and to place yourself as near to white as possible on a fluid colour scale.

Regardless of the type of secondary categories mixed race children use, they are all aware that white skin gets rewards. All British children are exposed to this message nationwide, from books, comics and television and from the preponderance of white faces over black ones in almost all areas of responsibility and power. Yet, having internalized that in the long term and in the context of the wider world whiteness is an asset, the young child turns, for further information, to his or her own experience of the world – that is, the world of playground, home and neighbourhood. Confirmation or contradiction of the value of whiteness and of feelings about other racial groups is sought locally through day-to-day encounters. Here, once again, the children's perceptions vary from area to area.

In areas of ethnic diversity, the children's experience dictates that every shade of skin has its own advantages, depending on the context in which it is being viewed. Neither being 'brown' nor being 'half-caste' means *per se* a playground life of rejection and withdrawal, for the identity of brown (like black and white) may be used to construct, break down, bend, stretch and otherwise manipulate ethnic boundaries, depending on the wishes of the individual and the social demands of the situation. Some children in the study belonged to black friendship groups; they gained acceptance by playing up the Afro-Caribbean element of their identity. Others moved in a more 'mixed' environment, using the fact that they were brown to find bonds with all kinds of children. Still others chose mixed race or brown-skinned friends and so defined themselves either as part of an intermediate skin colour group (which included Asians, southern Europeans and Middle Eastern children as well as those of mixed race) or, more specifically, as part of a mixed race English/Afro-Caribbean group. In terms of finding, keeping, or changing friends, the children found strategies to use each of their identities to advantage. These young mixed race respondents had probably concluded that although 'out there' it was better to be white than black, *in their experience* brown and black children, too, were considered attractive and popular.

Multiracial areas also bring local forms of ethnic alignment within the 'non-white' group. For example, many of the older children in the study seemed prone to the prejudice against Asians which has been noticed in their West Indian counterparts (Davey and Norburn, 1980). They stereotyped Asians without guilt and saw them as undesirable companions. There are presumably intricate pecking orders in different areas which depend on how many and which ethnic groups are represented. One would guess that an 8-year-old schoolchild in, say, Hackney, could give a detailed analysis of where Greek Cypriot children stand in relation to blacks in the playground hierarchy and of how these two groups relate to their white, Jewish, Indian and Pakistani peers.

To the children in white areas, the values inherent in ethnic divisions are theoretically more clear-cut – white is positive, anything else is not – but in reality the situation is not so simple. White people vary in the extent to which they enforce the white/non-white division and also in the way they express their racial feelings. The mothers of white friends may react in any number of bewildering ways (ranging from overt hostility to exaggerated affection) depending upon the extent of their racism and the amount of subtlety they use to express it. Mothers of mixed race children in white areas related incidents of school-mates who befriended their child, only to be drawn away by disapproving parents. They were loath to let their children visit the homes of schoolfriends until they were sure of the parents' attitudes. Mixed race children in white areas have to build up their social contacts with people who can be relied upon to give them an ethnically neutral reaction. This takes time and can involve many sharp disappointments.

Mixed race children in white areas are aware that there there are other people like themselves in the world, in terms of being black/mixed race, but their everyday experience dictates that such people are few and far between and that one must manage as one can without relying on their support. When conflicts occur between peers, racial insults are available for use only against oneself. They assume a potency which they do not have in an area of ethnic diversity because the child endures them and must defend him- or herself against them alone. All black children everywhere have to contend with the negative view of blackness which is perpetuated by the white group, but those who are isolated in white areas have the added burden of being the sole representative of a negatively defined category of people. They must either set out alone to define the category positively, or else claim immunity from the derogatory stereotypes and draw

181

attention away from their ethnic group membership.

To summarize: by the age of 6, mixed race children have acquired an image of the racial structure as a continuum of skin colour groups. As they get older and in particular if they live in a multiracial area, this simple form of categorization progressively takes on the confusion and complexity of adults' racial classification. Thus, by the age of 9, awareness has dawned that criteria other than simply colour of skin are used to construct racial categories. More significantly, the mixed race child has learnt that being white entails all kinds of emotional and material advantages. The fact of belonging to a locally based, positively viewed mixed race group cannot overcome the disadvantages of being black in a society dominated by whites, but it can protect the child's self-esteem against the insinuation of white racist ideas.

THE MIXED RACE CHILD'S VIEW OF SELF

Knowledge of the racial classification system of Britain and its value connotations is not knowledge for the mere sake of it. It helps the mixed race child to make sense of the world as an observer and, more centrally, to understand his or her own place within it. An independent, cognitive understanding of racial categorization, and of the extent to which society values different ethnic groups, is a prerequisite for the development of racial attitudes and identity. However, from a very early stage, emotions concerning the child's own ethnic group membership are able to affect his or her 'knowledge' of ethnic difference.

The process of racial identification appears to consist of two stages which involve placing oneself, first, in the societal and, secondly, in the local context. Initially, people decide whether they are white or non-white, and thereafter they proceed to detect and organize all the secondary categories to which they belong, in order of importance. For younger children, secondary racial identification is a matter of comparing their own skin colour with that of others. The secondary racial identification of older children takes account of criteria drawn from a growing knowledge of the racial classification system current in the locale.

Mixed race children under the age of 8 years normally envisage the secondary racial structure as being composed of a range of skin colour groups from white to black, so their self-identification within this structure involves an attempt to judge how others would classify their particular shade of skin. Having, for the most part, decided that they are non-white, they assess their level of 'non-whiteness' in terms of either broad or fine colour category distinctions. Broad distinctions are such categories as black, brown and white; examples of finer distinctions are terms like 'pale', 'whitish', 'quite light' and 'dark brown'.

Older children take account of a larger number of criteria in making their secondary racial identification. Their self-alignment may be based on cultural characteristics ('I am West Indian rather than Asian'), on parentage criteria ('One of my parents is white, therefore I am of mixed race'), or on both ('I am mixed race rather than totally black or totally white and I am mixed race West Indian rather than mixed race Asian'). Some aspect of physical appearance may also be included in the classification; this usually amounts to the child distinguishing him- or herself as having Negroid rather than Caucasian characteristics.

Regardless of age and despite their awareness of secondary racial categorizations, some children go little further than viewing their racial identity in white/non-white terms. This is because they find the application of society's racial value system to themselves an insurmountable obstacle, which makes secondary identification irrelevant. Mixed race children in white areas are particularly prone to this difficulty in overcoming the pressure of white hegemony – although, conversely, living in a multiracial area by no means ensures that the problem is avoided.

The children in the study who had this kind of identity were usually very resistant to talking about race. They approached the identity test furtively, perhaps with their eyes cast down, their voice kept to a whisper, or their hands firmly hidden. This suggests that, although on one level children *believe it* when they say they look like the blond(e), blue-eyed pictures in the photographs, they do not really delude themselves. It is simply that the all-pervasive white bias of the world around them makes white the only identity of any worth; society makes these children want to be white so much it simply *has* to be true. Mixed race children who live in white areas are particularly prone to the idea that they can become white by ignoring the black side of their identity. Just as infants believe that covering their eyes makes them invisible, these children feel that, if they do not draw attention to the fact that they are black, others will forget it also. The result is a fragile fantasy of being white, clung to tenaciously until it is ultimately torn away.

A second group of children is similarly preoccupied with the white/black division, but they hold on tightly to the idea that they are black. This identity probably means very little to them in social or cultural terms, unless they are completely absorbed in a black social world. They have little sense of black community, only a vague understanding of the cultural richness of the black group and no appreciation of the continuing, developing dynamic of the contemporary meanings of blackness. If the child lived in a family where the parents were firmly rooted in a black friendship network and where siblings were actively involved in a black British peer group, they would have a life-style to attach to the concept of being black; but for a mixed race child outside such a community, the label 'black' has all the emptiness of an arbitrary world, pinned to a set of intrinsically unimportant physical characteristics.

Without community support and shared symbolic meaning, 'black' is simply a defensive device – perhaps either the produce of, or a pre-emptive measure to avoid, white rejection. If I tell myself I am black, then if others use the label as an insult I cannot be hurt by it, just as if I tell myself I am fat it causes less distress if others call me so. Yet this self-description may bear little relation to my core sense of social identity. I do not necessarily define my place in the social world as one of a number of overweight people, and I have still not replaced the negativity of the label imposed upon me with a positive view of self.

A third type of black/white identity conflict experienced by mixed race children is between the first and second type and comes closest to the classic marginal dilemma. These children are ever conscious of feeling and wishing to be both black and white. Their basic conception of self may be either black or white, with their wishes or ideal directed to the opposite group of their self-conception. Possibly, the group of identification veers from black to white, depending on time and circumstance. Some situations may encourage a white identity with black as the ideal, whereas others favour the opposite.

When they identify as black, the children are painfully aware of all the advantages of being white and are beset by feelings of longing towards the white group. As soon as they are old enough to have a crude understanding of the concepts of success, prestige and power, they associate these with having a white skin and so idealize membership of the white group. Typically, these were the children in the study who stereotyped the white group positively and the black group negatively; whites were 'clean', 'good' and 'neat', whereas blacks were 'naughty', 'dirty' and 'always picking fights'. Children caught in this kind of conflict openly admired white Caucasian looks and deprecated their own hair, skin and colouring. Unlike the group mentioned earlier, who maintained a fiction of being white, these children knew that they were black. But they knew equally well that, for all kinds of reasons, they would prefer to be white.

When mixed race children who are in conflict identify as *white*, they often set up the black group as their ideal. There are two possible reasons for this. The first is that the child wants to 'appease' the black group because he or she feels guilty at having denied belonging to it. The second is that this may be a way of keeping a black identity as an 'insurance policy' against white rejection. When mixed race children deny that they belong to the black group, they are not just ignoring one part of their cultural heritage, they are rejecting one of their parents. The psychological implications of doing this can be enormous, and the guilt engendered may considerably complicate the issue of racial identity. One 8-year-old girl in the study seemed to typify this kind of struggle. She was very white in appearance, whereas her father was black. When he took her to school, her friends refused to believe he was even related to her, let alone that he was her father. In her identity test, she gave black as her ideal identity – saying that the black children looked 'very nice' – but she placed herself in the white group. Neither choice was made with ease. When she was asked to which group she would rather belong, her hand moved from white to black and from black to white until at last she looked up and said, 'It's hard.' Intra-psychic feelings weave in and out of the social pressure on identity. It is hard indeed to reconcile wanting to be white with wanting to belong to your father, who is black.

All black children in Britain probably experience some degree of identity conflict, but some children seem to overcome their uncertainty more easily than others. This was the case with the mixed race children in this study; a sizeable proportion of respondents got beyond the black/white conflict to a more positive secondary categorization and chose to identify with an intermediate ethnic group.[2] Some of these children were more white oriented than others, but all appeared to have a clear and positive view of themselves.

The younger children saw themselves as belonging to a large skin colour group, situated between the two extremes of light and dark, black and white. In terms of the still photograph which was the test – attitudes frozen in time – the children were ranged along a continuum from exhibiting wishes to be white (although they knew they were brown) to being content with an identity as both brown and black. In real life, one may imagine that all these 6- and 7-year-olds were juggling with their brown identity and striving to come to terms with it in the context of their social environment.

Brown is a flexible concept. It may be considered nearer to

white, nearer to black, or exactly in between; it may be a nice thing to be because it is almost white, because it is a highly prized colour within the black group, or because it is neither white nor black and so better than both. As a colour, too, brown is versatile in its connotations, and on balance children appear to find it positive. The aesthetic virtues of a tanned skin and good things to eat (nuts, chocolate, cake) seem to outweigh the negative connotations with excrement and dirt. In replacing 'black' with 'brown', the horror of the link with evil, fear and night is shed, and although some connection with dirt and disapproval remains, it is possible to overcome this with the white-sanctioned ideal of the tan.[3]

The older children expressed their racial identity in terms of a more complex set of categories. The label 'brown' recurred as an apt and central self-description, but alongside it came ideas of being mixed race, half from one culture and half from another, and the concept of being black West Indian rather than Asian. The blanket identification of brown gave way to greater detail in describing ethnic characteristics. Whether it was the mother or the father who was black, whether the child had straight or curly hair, the place of origin of the black parent – all these were deemed to be important in self-identification.

Once again, although the children ranged along a continuum of white orientation in the test, one may imagine that in real life they were all involved in exploring the potential of a mixed race identity. Some mixed race children appear to conquer the negative overtones of the label 'half-caste' and treat it as a matter-of-fact and acceptable identity. The larger number of criteria in use brings a greater range of possibilities for ethnic boundary construction. Links may be forged with West Indians on the ground of one parent being from the West Indies; with Asians because they, too, are brown; with all mixed race children (regardless of culture) because they are all mixed race; and with white children because having a white parent makes one 'almost white'. Like the secondary category of brown, that of mixed race lends itself to almost any kind of social end; the child invests it with the significance merited by time and circumstance.

Many children discover that, of all the possible ways of using a mixed race/brown identity, there are great rewards to be gained from reinforcing links with a black peer group. Acceptance of the idea that mixed race children are also black brings the strength of belonging to a community which has its own goals and ideals. For mixed race children in multiracial areas, acceptance within a black friendship group offers a real alternative to the frustrating road of white orientation. As the child gets older, and particularly when adolescence demands a more rigid choice of racial membership group, the attractions of black youth culture probably increase. The new black British style provides a secure environment within which normal adolescent insecurities may be faced, although it is possible that the 'private' view of self as 'being of mixed race' asserts itself again later, when adulthood allows individuality to re-emerge.

Living in a multiracial area favours intermediate identification, because, in such a locale, secondary ethnic classification involves a large number of categories, and there is a greater potential for describing one's ethnic identity, as it is subjectively perceived, with more 'precision'. In white areas only the crude 'white or not' division is seen as being of any significance, whereas in more heterogeneous neighbourhoods there may be sufficient numbers of mixed race people to make 'mixed race' a viable racial identity. Frequent contact with people of a similar ethnic background gives a reality to the concept of being both black and mixed race and provides support for the maintenance of this dual view of self.

To summarize: mixed race children's views of their own position in the racial structure appeared to be of two main types. They were either preoccupied with a conflict concerning their place in the black/white dichotomy or else they accepted a definition of themselves as non-white and were involved in exploring the potential of a black/mixed race identity within the context of the local classification system. The children who appeared to be experiencing identity conflict expressed this in one of three ways. They either fantasised that they were white, retreated defensively into a black identity, or else were unable to choose between the two. The children who adopted a black/mixed race identity showed differing degrees of white orientation. It was suggested that, like all black children, they were subject to the effects of white institutional bias, so that a mild preference for white skin would appear and disappear according to time and circumstance.

THE MOTHER'S INFLUENCE

The mother's attitude to race and her view of the child's racial position were an important influence on racial identity construction. From the complex pattern of associations which emerged from this study, it is possible to piece together a rough pattern of how the mother helps to formulate her mixed race child's image of their position within the racial structure.

The mother's racial categorization system does not appear

greatly to influence that of her child. To a large extent, mixed race children's socialization into a system of racial thought which is appropriate to the area in which they live is carried out independently of the mother. Like her child, the mother is caught up in the process of negotiating ethnic boundaries and of finding her own ethnic identity amongst the maze of racial categorization labels which are current in the locale. Her influence is potent only if she comes to feel strongly about a particular racial label and if she lays down clearly articulated rules about its use. If the mother believes that to say 'black' is wrong, to say 'coloured' is derogatory, using 'half-caste' is insulting, or describing someone as 'brown' is inaccurate, only if she spells this out in unequivocal terms does it affect her child's categorization system. The mother's main influence is on her mixed race child's *racial identification* – both directly (through her assessment of the child's position in the racial structure) and indirectly (through impressing on the child the various gains and losses at stake in deciding which racial identity to adopt).

The mothers in the sample described the racial position of mixed race children in one of three ways: either as predominantly black, as coloured ('only just' non-white), or as predominantly mixed. The encouragement of both a black and a mixed identity was associated with the children adopting an intermediate racial identity, whereas the attitude that the child was coloured seemed to be linked with black/white identity conflict.

The women who see their children as black and those who describe them as mixed race are at different points on the same attitudinal scale, for both sets of mothers believe that 'in reality' their children are both black *and* mixed race. The former have decided to emphasize the *public* categorization of the child, seeing this as the most pragmatic solution, whereas the latter prefer to stress the child's *private* classification and to make duality the focus of identity. Whether it is the public or the private categorization which is stressed does not appear to influence the child's racial identity, for the children of both sets of mothers tend to see themselves as belonging to an intermediate group which is also black. However, it is possible that the effects of this difference in parental attitudes on the children are hidden at this age and that they have an influence in later life. Children whose mothers see them as predominantly black may be more likely to align themselves with a black peer group in adolescence and adulthood.

The mothers who encouraged a coloured identity are generally more concerned with skin colour than with race. Sensitized to variations of skin tone either by the niceties of Caribbean skin-related status or by a white desire to have their children 'just like them', they resent any suggestion that their children are considered black. Inherent in this attitude (whether held by a white or by a black mother) is a collaboration with the idealization of whiteness and feelings of unease about being black. These women are truly part of the tradition of the white-over-light-over-dark hierarchy and have been untouched by black militancy and pride. Their mixed race children reflect this preoccupation with white skin and all approximations to it, and their identity rarely gets beyond attempting to resolve the dilemma of fervently wishing to be white yet being frustrated in their efforts to attain white status. In particular, the children of these mothers are prone to *seeing themselves* as white – or, at least, as lighter skinned than reality allows.

The mother's decision about which aspects of her child's identity to encourage is a complex one which can be fraught with difficulties. Primarily, she wishes to be realistic about her child's identity *vis-à-vis* the white society. What this means is that her knowledge of the world informs her assessment of the amount of prejudice her children are likely to encounter, and she tries, on the basis of this information, to encourage an appropriate racial identity. She may believe that racial prejudice is rife and so feel that the children must know they are black in order to face the inevitable slurs from a position of strength; or she may think that racism is a figment of the imaginations of its 'victims' and train her children to believe that it does not apply to them. But she may equally be *unsure* of how much her children are likely to suffer from racism and so remain indecisive about what she should be telling them.

More secretly, the *white* mother has an added consideration. She does not want to see her children as fully black because to do so is to deny her own motherhood and to alienate herself from both her husband and her children. For the latter problem, encouraging the children to be mixed race or brown offers an attractive compromise, for to tell the children that they are part of, but different from, both the mother and the father prevents either parent from claiming the prerogative of including the children in their own ethnic group.

The cross-pressures which influence the mother's choice are perhaps most acute in relation to her educational and economic aspirations for the child. Unless her attitude is at one of two extremes – either beliving that the system is inherently *un*fair or else being convinced that it is scrupulously fair – she is caught between a wish to be realistic and a desire for her child to succeed in life. Some mothers are unsure about the price their children might have to pay for the psychological 'safety' of a black identity and so have an ambivalent attitude towards teaching the child about racism. To tell a child that being black can be an economic handicap may be to implant a mistrust of the system within which that child must achieve his or her success; moreover, these mothers are loath to rear a child who is defensive against the world in case the racial bias of that world proves not to be as bad as feared. On the other hand, the signs that racism is rampant are sometimes too blatant to be ignored, so that the mother is left wondering whether her children are ill prepared for the injustices which await them. The identity of the children of these ambivalent mothers is equally likely to be in conflict as mixed race or brown; factors other than the mother's attitude to economic opportunity can tip the balance one way or the other.

The women who whole-heartedly believe that the system is unfair tend to have children with a strong black/mixed race identity. It appears that to present the economic and educational structure as biased against black people – yet to continue to offer academic encouragement – has the effect of urging the children to gain success for their own sakes as individuals, rather than for the purpose of proving that they can do as well as whites. If the link between whiteness and success is presented to the child as real and as due to racial injustice, and if in addition the mother makes it clear that black people are attempting to oppose this kind of injustice, then the child's potential for racial identity conflict seems to be minimized. This explanation releases mixed race children from the frustration of feeling that they are forever competing with white children on unequal terms, and losing.

The children whose mothers represent the system as fair and see success as a matter of individual effort are more likely to experience identity conflict. This is not surprising when one considers the bewildering battery of contradictory messages that such a child receives. In the child's eyes, the kind of academic success which is so highly prized appears to come through whiteness; yet the mother vehemently denies that skin colour has any bearing on achievement and states categorically that success comes from constant application and sustained hard work. Some mothers add a further contradictory twist to this message by occasionally suggesting that black children need to work 'extra hard' to prove that they are 'as good as white children'. In the midst of such confusion, the child experiences uncertainty about where he or she belongs and anxiety about the pressures of an unfair system.

The inducement of racial identity conflict is even more likely if the mother combines the 'individual effort' approach with ambivalence about blackness generally and the encouragement of a 'coloured' identity in the child. Colour is openly declared to be unimportant, even to the central issue of educational achievement, and yet colour categories ('fair', 'light', 'virtually white', 'dark', 'black') take a prominent place in the mother's conversation, which suggests that they are, in fact, of considerable significance. The mother makes it clear to the child that he or she is not 'officially' white, yet her negative attitude to black relatives, to generalized black groups ('lazy youths', 'Rastafarians', 'West Indians') and perhaps even to her black husband indicates to the child that a black identity is not to be encouraged. If success, beauty and parental approval are on the side of whiteness but the weight of social opinion points to a black identity as the most appropriate, the mixed race child is unlikely to escape at least some degree of painful internal conflict.

Although the identity which the mother encourages in the child and her attitude to systematic racial bias are important factors in the development of the child's identity, their influence can apparently be tempered by other variables. For instance, the woman's attitude to the non-British culture with which the family has links can affect the child's view of self, particularly if she also encourages a mixed race or a brown identity.

A mixed race identity, though believed by many women to be the only appropriate self-description for their children, is none the less a difficult one to encourage with conviction. A dual racial identity, in a society where many people are concerned only with whether one is white or not, may easily appear ambiguous and confusing for the child and so create a potential for white orientation. However, this problem appears to be forestalled if the mother stresses that the child is not simply of mixed race but also from two cultures. The attraction of all things white is slightly diminished if the mother is knowledgeable and enthusiastic about the black parent's culture. Supplementing the British bias of the children's education by locating them in a second cultural tradition provides a series of images with which to link them to their black 'half' and gives added content to the mixed race identity. Parental cultural awareness alone is not enough to induce any particular racial identity in the child; but if it accompanies the encouragement of the somewhat ambiguous mixed race identity, it can tip the balance towards a viable view of self.

A further, more intangible aspect of the mother's influence on her child's racial identity is her attitude to her own racial and cultural position. This is one area in which more research is needed. From the results of this study, it seems that whether the mother is black or white the strength of her security about who she is and the value she puts on that definition of herself can be communicated to her children and can affect their racial identity. Tentatively, it can be said that the mother who takes pride in her own blackness or who, as a white woman, is secure in her position *vis-à-vis* the black group is more likely to have children with a black/mixed race identity. On the other hand, black women who are prone to feelings of self-deprecation and white women who are ambivalent about both the white and the black group are more likely to have children who suffer racial identity conflict. Future research will need to operationalize this nebulous idea of coming to terms with one's own racial position in order to make a more precise assessment of its effect on children's racial identity.

If the mother is sure of her own position either as a member of the black group or as part of a network of women with interracial relationships, she is better able to convey a strong black element in the mixed race child's position. A black mother of this type is open about, and proud of, being black. Regardless of the extent of her political militancy, she appreciates the emotion behind the slogan 'black is beautiful' and is determined that her children will share the same sentiment. Both the positive aesthetic aspects of blackness and the strength of the black group are forcefully represented to the children. For this type of white mother, her entry into an interracial/black social world meant finding an ethnic identity which she felt was more truly hers, so that her children's blackness is welcomed as the seal on her own new identity. For this reason, she encourage them to explore freely the possibilities of alignment with the black group.

If the mother is ambivalent about blackness, then she is less able and less willing to convey the advantages of a black identity to her child. If she is black, she may be caught up in her own colour conflict and white orientation. Her child by a white man may represent her own aspirations to whiteness, in which case the white side of the child's heritage is likely to be stressed to the exclusion of all else. A similarly ambivalent white mother may be unable to free herself from despising the low status of blackness, or, more nebulously, her partner's blackness may perform the function of expressing externally a set of values and emotions which she cannot own as hers. In both cases the mothers are unable to reverse the negative connotations of minority group status for their children and to encourage a black identity. Despite any rhetoric they may hear about the beauty of blackness, these children are more vulnerable to the establishment of a negative view of self and are less able personally to resolve the problems posed by living in a system of white exclusiveness.

The mother's influence, in summary, is exerted in several ways. The identity she encourages her children to adopt, her aspirations for their educational achievements and her awareness of the non-British side of their cultural heritage can all affect the children's racial identity. The overt encouragement of a black or a mixed race view of self seems to help foster a positive black/mixed race identity, whereas the view that the children are 'coloured' or 'only just' non-white is more conducive to racial identity conflict. In terms of their attitudes to educational opportunity, the mothers who present racism as a reality to their children seem to allay anxiety and minimize racial identity conflict; mothers who stress individual effort, on the other hand, tend to heighten their children's desires to be white. Finally, a strong cultural awareness or enthusiasm for the black parent's culture can strengthen the child's mixed race identity if the mother is simultaneously encouraging a mixed race identity.

The Needs of Mixed Race Children

Social workers, health visitors, teachers and parents have to make decisions daily about the welfare of mixed race children. They have not only to decide on their problems and needs as individual children, but also to find the best environment for the encouragement of a positive racial identity. How should a social worker assess a mixed race child's identity and decide on their parenting needs in this respect? What special needs of mixed race children should a teacher be aware of when designing an anti-racist or a multiracial curriculum? A small-scale study such as this, conducted by one person with limited resources, cannot provide definitive answers; but it can provide some general guidelines of areas to consider. One can at least identify the factors which seemed to be important for the identity of the children in the study, with a view to teachers considering whether they also apply to the children in their care.

ASSESSMENT OF MIXED RACE CHILDREN'S IDENTITY
One thing that may have surprised 'carers' of all kinds when reading this study is the knowledge and sophistication of the young respondents. Even some 6-year-olds, if they lived in a multiracial area, could give a detailed account of the confused and

illogical criteria which govern racial categorization in Britain. The children may not have been able to articulate how various ethnic groups differed culturally, and they knew very little of the home background of the groups, but they were well aware of the ethnic pecking order in their locale and of the characteristics and values attributed to each group.

In all kinds of assessment of mixed race children's requirements – whether of their parenting needs in an adoption placement or of their educational needs to be met in the school – the first question to ask is: what is the ethnic vocabulary of this child? Children over the age of 5 or so are almost certain to know something of racial difference, but adults cannot assume that their view of the racial structure is the same as their own. Even parents cannot be sure that their children speak the same racial language as they do. This study showed that children go through different stages of ethnic categorization according to their age and also that the labels they use are influenced by the area in which they live. So before trying to communicate with mixed race children about racial identity, an adult should first establish the child's own racial terminology. The labels which the adult considers appropriate may not be current in the child's social world or they may have negative connotations of which the adult is aware. So racial labelling should be guided by the child, with the adult asking questions to discover as much as possible about the child's knowledge of racial terms.

Some clue as to children's racial vocabulary may be gained by considering their experience of different ethnic groups in relation to their age. A child who has had no contact with black or mixed race people is unlikely to categorize beyond the black/white dichotomy, regardless of his or her age; whereas a 6-year-old who has been exposed to a variety of cultures will probably have at least some notion of the criteria which define ethnicity.

When talking to children about race it is worth remembering how vast a learning task we set our children with our vague, arbitrary ethnic boundaries, our ever-changing definitions of labels and our subtle disapproval of certain terms. Even when children use the simple black/white/brown scheme, they still have problems understanding the exact nature of racial difference. Is it any wonder? Few of us understand it ourselves. Discussing race with young children is a useful exercise in questioning our own assumptions. Why exactly *is* having a tan different from being 'brown'? Are Spanish people brown in the same way as mixed race people are? (Why?/Why not?) Are all black people 'really' brown, or are brown people 'really' black? Silenced behind a wall of tacit taboo, which either outlaws race as 'not quite nice' or else dismisses everything in black/white terms, children ponder these questions. And they are right to do so, for, inconvenient as the questions are for adults, they are often crucial to the child's understanding of who they are in the local context. We must be critical of our own view of the racial structure. We should take pains to analyse the assumptions which underlie our system of racial classification before conveying it, implicitly or explicitly, to children. The variable subjectivities of all our racial categorizations might be a useful starting-point for racism awareness training.

The second question which someone concerned with mixed race children's identity needs to answer is: how does the child feel about his or her subjectively defined categories and where do they place themselves within the system? This is more difficult to elicit from the children than the labels *per se*, but any method (such as pictures or photographs) to get the child to talk about race should yield some information. The important thing is not to anticipate a particular set of responses (or interpret responses in one particular way) just because the child is of mixed race. The 'betwixt and between' image of mixed race people is a stereotype and one which has not, so far, been supported by empirical research.

The identity patterns distinguished in this study show some of the possibilities for mixed race children's identity. They are by no means exhaustive; it was mentioned earlier, for example, that one group which is conspicuously absent from the sample is those mixed race children who are brought up, unmabiguously, as black. However, the study suggested five patterns of mixed race identity to which mixed race children might conform: white identity, defensive black identity, black/white conflict, mixed race identity with white orientation and mixed race identity with black orientation. These five patterns were summarized as being of two types: children who were preoccupied with the black/white dichotomy and who had difficulty choosing between black and white; and children who had a secondary system of categorization and who saw themselves as black/mixed race. The proportion was roughly 2:3; 40 per cent of the children showed some degree of identity conflict, and 60 per cent did not.

Even this figure masks the extent to which the children in the study identified themselves accurately as mixed race and reacted to the photos of mixed race children in a highly positive way. Eighty per cent of children pointed to a mixed race West Indian figure as looking 'most like them', and the mixed race West Indian photographs were chosen overwhelmingly as companions for imaginary activities. If the caring professions bear in mind that it appears to be possible to maintain a positive mixed race identity which is also compatible with a black identification, they may be less likely to define mixed race children's racial identity *per se* as a problem. Individual mixed race children, like members of other minority groups, may well have identity problems, *but these are not the inevitable result of having one parent black and one white.*

PARENTING NEEDS

The debate about the necessity of placing black and mixed race children with black families rages on. Some people argue that black children cannot develop a viable racial identity in the context of a white family; others counter that white families are as able as any to provide the children with self-esteem and a pride in all aspects of their identity. Still others point to the difficulty of finding sufficient numbers of black families for placement and argue that, from the child's point of view, any family is better than none. Transracial adoption is often as much a moral/political question as one about the parenting needs of the children, and it is not proposed to enter the fray here. But, clearly, some of the results of this study are relevant to the issues involved in the debate. In general, the results from the study support the idea that a black mother *who has a positive black identity* is in the best position to encourage a black/mixed race identity in her child. However, for the mother *just to be black* is not enough to override the other factors which influence identity. The black mother has to be completely at home in her blackness to develop a positive self-identity in her child.

Although there were only eight black women in the sample, there was a considerable amount of impressionistic data to support the idea that black mothers who were comfortable with their blackness transmitted that feeling to their children. Whether middle class or working class, in a white or in a multiracial area, black mothers who referred to themselves as 'black', and who had a clearly defined culture or life-style to attach to that identity, seemed better equipped to foster a black/mixed race identity in their children. One black woman in the sample – Toni Ashton – was a perfect example of a mother who had managed to bring up her children as black/mixed race, apparently against all odds, simply by example. She lived in a white area, her children went to an all-white school where there was no multiracial education, yet they were among the most open and black-oriented children in the sample. Toni made the Caribbean come alive for them with stories of her childhood and she impressed on them constantly the importance of taking a pride in being black. Of her two children's identity she said, simply, 'With me being black, I suppose they just *think* black.'

On the other hand, the black mothers who felt ambivalent about being black – in particular those who were influenced by the Caribbean colour class system – tended to pass on their ambivalence to their children. Black mothers who were too concerned with whether their children were 'dark' or 'fair', who encouraged their children to think of themselves as 'coloured' and who held a secret contempt for their Caribbean origins appeared to encourage identity conflict in their children. For example, the mother who declared vehemently that she was not 'black' but 'coloured', who discussed at length the exact shade of her own and her children's skin and who took pains to show that her life-style was no different from that of white people, had a daughter who was ambivalent and confused about her racial identity.

What these impressionistic findings might do is introduce a note of caution into the idea that black families are always best for black children. It cannot be taken for granted that a black or mixed race child who is placed in a black family will emerge with a strong, positive black identity. The child's racial identity will depend, to some extent, on the parents' own identity and how they transmit the meaning of being black to their children. However, the value of a good model of black identity should not be underestimated either. Black parents who are proud of being black transmit a positive racial identity to their children effortlessly and unselfconsciously. They do not simply *tell* the children they are black; they *show them how to be black* with confidence.

The other factors in the study which were found to encourage a black/mixed race identity were also more likely to be found in a black family than in a white family. But, unlike the provision of a black identity model within the family, it is theoretically possible that a white family could provide them. The factors which were associated with a positive racial identity were the encouragement of a black or black/mixed race identity; a 'strong' line from the parents on institutional racism; involvement in the black community; and contact with other mixed race people. This suggests that white families who adopt black or mixed race children should be encouraged to involve themselves in the black and mixed communities, to educate themselves about racism and to support a black identity in their children.

197

More research is needed to investigate how white parents of black and mixed race children may best do this. The aim is to transmit a black identity which is neither too abstract nor 'taught' self-consciously – a black identity, in other words, which has content and meaning for the child. In this study, the white mothers who were most able to do this combined a number of characteristics. They were sure of their stance on race and racism, they were happy with the idea of their children being black and they tended to be involved in a subculture of women in interracial relationships. The key element seemed to be the white mother's *own* racial identity. These women had abandoned full membership of the white group in favour of an intermediate group which had sympathies with both black and white. They did not wholly identify with either; they belonged in a separate marginal culture which had a foot in both camps. The white mothers who encouraged their children to be black were sufficiently removed from mainstream white culture to be able to see white institutional racism, but not so immersed in the black reaction to it that they viewed that reaction without criticism. These mothers could not *show* their children how to be black, but they seemed to be able to provide an environment in which a black identity could flourish.

The one parenting characteristic which perhaps needs underlining for both black and white parents is that racism should be represented realistically to the child. Once again, more research is needed to confirm the relationship between the parents' view of racism and the child's identity, but on the basis of this study it appeared essential that parents do not deny the white bias which surrounds their children. A balance must somehow be struck between acknowledging the unfairness of the system and encouraging the children to fulfil their potential *as individuals*. It is not an easy task. The parents in this study who seemed most successful at achieving such a balance were those who separated the black community's struggle against racism from the child's personal struggle to get on in life. They encouraged their children to strive for success for their own benefit as people, rather than to prove that they could do as well as white children. The unfairness of the system was admitted freely, but the children's frustrations were channelled into black people's fight against injustice, rather than being allowed to damage their motivation and self-esteem.

A New Perspective

From a litany of tentative statements, based sometimes on scanty evidence, one theme has emerged from this study with certainty: that the view of mixed race children as a 'problem', unable to find security and acceptance from any ethnic group, is outmoded. The idea that mixed race people are, by the very nature of their position, torn by spiritual uncertainty and racked by *malaise* is an oversimplified anachronism in the multi-ethnic mosaic which Britain has become. The inadequacy of this 'problem' approach to mixed race children has highlighted a general lack of flexibility in the modern approach to racial identity. A dichotomous black-or-white view of racial categorization, which is an adequate tool for analysing the racism of white institutions, is too blunt an instrument with which to dissect the intricate contents of a child's racial identity.

Future research will no doubt increase our knowledge of the variability of mixed race children's identity and of the conditions under which a positive identity thrives; but whether or not the gathering of empirical sociological data can oust the 'problem' stereotype in the popular imagination is another matter. Books, newspapers and televison programmes all tend to reinforce the image of mixed race people as misfits, for reasons that were discussed at the beginning of this book. The continuation of white superiority demands that interracial relationships be discouraged, and one way of doing this is by presenting the children of such relationships as the victims of intolerable psychological pressure.

None the less, for those concerned with reinforcing a good self-image among mixed race children, the overall picture presented by this study is a hopeful one. These fifty-one children were a long way from the archetype of the tortured personality split between two conflicting cultures. If any unarguable conclusion can be drawn from this study it is that mixed race children can be themselves without suffering psychological disintegration. Given the right environment, they can make full use of their distinctive dual cultural heritage and assert their individuality in a multiracial society.

Notes

1   According to Beth Day (1974), it is a frequent complaint of interracial families that only 'problem' families are ever studied:

The stereotype of the troubled mixed race child is so fixed that a British mother reported that when a television staff was looking for participants in a study of interracial marriage, they interviewed her teenage son, then turned him down because he was 'too normal'. 'The people were chosen because they had difficulties'. (Day, 1974).

2 The secondary identification is often more positive simply because the dichotomous classification system is *inherently* negative for children who are not white (defined as it is in terms of *white* or *not white*). The secondary identifications open wider horizons, giving scope for a view of self which is defined positively.

3 The concept 'brown' also allows the endorsement of the old story-book adage of being neither too much this way nor too much that, but being 'just right'. Some mothers reported that they told their children, 'Daddy thinks he's a bit *too* black and Mummy thinks she's a bit *too* white, but you're *just right.*'

Appendix 1

The Photographs

The photographs of the children were taken by a professional photographer at a junior school in West London. The school must remain anonymous, but I would like to thank Ealing Education Authority for its co-operation and to note with pleasure how the occasion of taking the photographs was used by the school as an informal lesson in the multiracial composition of Britain. Most of the adults in the photographs were students or staff at the London School of Economics. The children were photographed individually and smiling, whereas their 'parents' were asked to adopt a 'pleasant but neutral' expression and were pictured sitting side by side. From a large number of frames, fourteen photographs of different children were chosen; the Asian, West Indian and white pairs were selected on the basis of looking unequivocally like members of those groups, but finding mixed race children was much more difficult because of the wide variety of skin, hair and eye colour combinations. An attempt was none the less made to find eight mixed race children who represented at least some of the various different 'looks'.

The photos of the fourteen children and seven adult 'couples' were arranged on seven large cards in families. The picture of the 'parents' was stuck firmly to the card, but the individual photos of the children which were placed beneath it were easily removable. Each child was numbered, and the same number was marked on the card where the photo should be placed so that it was clear which child belonged to which set of parents.

Appendix 2

Test and Interview Procedure

In the pages following the children's racial identity test and the mothers' questionnaires are reproduced. First, some explanatory comments on each may be helpful in conveying exactly how each encounter was conducted.

The Children's Test

The children's test consisted of four main stages. First, I chatted to the child, normally with the mother present and then, at the appropriate moment, either the mother withdrew or the child showed me to a quiet room in their home where the test could be carried out. The tape-recorder was switched on before the test began, with some play or chat about the recorder if the child was interested in it. Even if the child was self-conscious at first, the tape machine was very quickly forgotten once the test had started. Respondents usually remembered with surprise that the tape was on at the end of the session and asked to hear some of the recording. During this period the child's name, sex and physical appearance were noted. The child was reassured that this was more like a game and that there were no right or wrong answers. The subject was then asked to name his or her three best friends (or fewer if they could not think of three). After this the photographs were introduced, and the child was told that all he or she had to do at this point was to look at the photographs. With both the child and myself seated on the floor, the large cards were produced one by one and handed to the child, who looked at them and placed them in full view on the floor. The respondent was then asked which one looked most like him or her, and the number of the indicated photograph was noted. Throughout the test the photographs were referred to by number to eliminate the necessity for me to use any racial labels.

In the second stage came the party and activities test, where the respondent was asked to choose children to invite to a party and to participate in various activities. Following these, the ideal identity was elicited and then further preference questions (stereotypes) were asked. The third section was the racial categorization test. The child was asked to put the photographs into their racial groups: 'Put all the white children together and so on.' Here particular note was taken of the child's reaction: how long he or she took to understand the request, difficulty over any particular photograph, any hesitation or verbal comments. If the child appeared not to understand immediately, the instruction was repeated in a slightly different way. When the groups were completed I asked, pointing to each group in turn, 'Who are these children?' This question was to elicit the label the respondent attached to each group.

At this point the idea of 'the spaceman', the third stage of the test, was introduced. The child was asked to imagine that a spaceman came into the room and wondered what he or she was doing; how would they explain to the spaceman how they knew the right groups for the children? (The term 'right group' was used deliberately so that the children would not see this request as a challenge to the accuracy of their grouping.) If the child could not think of any reason here, probes were used – 'Did you look at the hair? Did you look at the parents?' – and questions about specific photographs were sometimes included: 'How would you explain to the spaceman why number 4 belonged in *this* group?' Occasionally, too, if the respondent had hesitated over one photograph I attempted to pursue it: 'You didn't seem too sure about number 2; why was that, I wonder?' When as much information aas possible had been elicited without losing the child's interest or attention, the self-identification criteria were explored. The children were asked to which of the groups constructed they belonged and *what it was* about the photograph chosen on the self-identification question that looked like them. The race of the three best friends was also requested at this point.

In the fourth stage, the 'non-spontaneous groupings' were investigated. That is, the child was presented with some common racial labels which had not appeared in the spontaneously constructed sets and asked if they applied to any of the photographs: 'Are there any coloured children in the photographs? Are there any mixed race children?' ('Half-caste' was not included here because so many people had told me before constructing the questionnaire that children considered it an abusive term. With hindsight, this seems to have been only a middle-class reaction; many working-class children described themselves as 'half-caste' as a spontaneous identification.) To conclude the test, I asked the child to help me put each photograph back with its parents, and this exercise was done together; this short period provided space for additional comments from the children and also time to ask them what they thought of the test and to thank them for doing it. The test took about an hour.

Several factors were taken into account in the ordering of the questions on the test schedule. On a general level, the racial categorization sections were placed after the racial preference and identification sections in order to make the latter results comparable with previous research. If the racial categories had been constructed before identification and preference were elicited, thereby drawing overt attention to race, the results could not be considered alongside Milner's (1975) and other British research. More specifically, the question asking for the child's three best friends was put first in order to take advantage of the preliminary moments when the child was not aware that the test was concerned with race. If the photographs had been shown before this question was asked, they may have influenced the children's assessment of who their three best friends were. However, as soon as the photographs had been produced, it also seemed important to elicit self-identification straight away, from the respondent's first reaction to the pictures. Although every effort was made to make the photos similar in expression and attractiveness, so that the most obvious differences between them were sex and race, the more closely the photographs were examined the more other minor details may have intruded to affect this crucial choice.

The ideal identity question was placed in the middle of the preference section in order to separate it a little from the real-self identification. If a contrast existed between the mixed race child's real and ideal group membership, it did not seem necessary to place the questions in such stark contrast as perhaps to stifle its expression. A further advantage in placing the racial categorization section last was that it was the part which needed the most input from the children; it was hoped that by this point in the test, they would have lost any shyness and would be more likely to comment freely on the photographs.

The small pilot study had suggested that this was a feasible practical task for young mixed race children. However, an additional comment should be made about the decision to use the test. I was aware that a task of this kind could be upsetting for mixed race children who were particularly sensitive about their racial identity. Before embarking on the study in the first place, I had had to resolve certain moral issues; none the less, I was naturally determined to be as sensitive as possible to the children's reactions during the test and not to pursue relentlessly points which were being defensively resisted. This involved maintaining a careful balance between closely watching for any sign of distress and encouraging a relaxed atmosphere for the test. There was always a danger of perceiving sensitivity where none existed, of being furtive in manner and thus conveying the impression that the subject of race was taboo.

The Mothers' Questionnaire

The mothers' questionnaire consisted of five sections: items asking for factual information, those tapping frequency and quality of contact with other people, and finally, three sections attempting to elicit racial categorization and attitudes. The tape-recorder was switched on before the beginning of the interview, and the mother was reassured that no one would hear the tape but myself.

The first section of the questionnaire was a quick battery of questions requiring simple factual answers, such as name, age, occupation, marital status and country of origin. Two items also dealt with whether or not the respondent's parents were alive and living in Britain, and similar information was sought for the child's father.

The second section contained questions concerning the frequency and quality of contact the mother had with neighbours, friends and relatives. She was asked to name all the people she saw regularly, her closest friends, her children's friends in the area and also anyone in the neighbourhood who was particularly *un*friendly to her or her children. An attempt was made to get the fullest possible idea of the family's social network within a short space of time. The respondent was asked to specify frequency of contact as closely as possible (e.g. once a week or every few months), and probes were used to try to establish the importance of each relationship to the mother and to the child. All the names mentioned in this section were noted; then, at the very end of the interview, the mother was asked to go over each name and specify the race of the person concerned.

The third section — 'spontaneous grouping and dichotomy emphasis' — served as a preliminary general orientation for the mother to the more specific attitude questions to follow. Up to this third section, no racial labels had been mentioned by the investigator (except 'mixed race' in asking for the interview). Now the respondent was asked to describe the racial situation in Britain, in her own words, as to someone who knew nothing about it. The two main areas of interest here were the racial labels used to designate different groups and the mother's view of the amount of hostility and discrimination that existed in Britain. The question was deliberately vague and unspecific so that I could obtain a superficial idea of the mother's racial categorization system and viewpoint before asking the more detailed questions; she had, at this point, no idea of any particular type of answer being required and had been given no clue as to which racial labels she should use. The probes used in this section were mainly concerned with categorization: 'Who is it you are talking about here?'; 'So who would you say the main situation is *between*?' Usually at the end of this section (but at a later time if it seemed more appropriate) I asked the mother to explain the racial terms she used; I attempted to elicit quick, spontaneous answers to such questions as 'Who do you think of when I say "coloured"?' and 'Who exactly do you mean when you say "black"?' (In the mother's questionnaire the label 'coloured' is used most frequently because the majority of mothers preferred it. As far as possible, I tried to follow the mother's own categorization system; once the meanings of labels *for them* had been established, labels which seemed likely to jar or cause offence were abandoned, regardless of what was written in the questionnaire.)

The fourth part of the interview dealt with 'critical situations'. The mother was asked to advise the parents of mixed race children what to do in four commonly experienced situations where there was often no clear right or wrong thing to do or say. Each question was read out as many times as the mother wished, and she was allowed to think carefully about the problem before replying.

The first question — a mixed race child expressing a wish to grow up white — was designed to encourage the mother to talk about the child's racial identity. If her first response to this question was that she would tell the child he or she was *not* white, an attempt was made to get her to go further by using such leads as 'And would you say anything else?' and 'What if the child said, "If I'm not white, what *am* I?" What would you say then?' I also tried to sound out whether the mother made a distinction between the mixed race child's *real* identity (what he or she *is*) and the *imposed* identity (what he or she will be treated as by others).

The second question – putting the case of a mixed race child claiming that white people hated coloured people – introduced the idea of hostility between the races. Here I wished to discover the mother's assessment of how tense the racial situation was and also of how far she would consciously make her views known to her children. The third question kept this theme of hostility, but drew the mother back to the matter of racial identity: she was asked how she would respond to a mixed race child's distress at being called a (black) racial name at school. Of all the situations, this one most often elicited a true-life story from the mother about an incident with one of her own children, and she was always encouraged to relate this in full. The fourth and last question switched the subject to discrimination in the economic system; a mixed race boy had heard that black children could not get a good job when they grew up and wanted to know if this applied to him. Once again the mother was asked to distinguish between what she herself believed on this issue and what she would tell the child.

Although they had different emphases, all four of these 'critical situations' were designed to gather information pertaining to the same three variables: the mother's level of awareness (amount of consciously conveyed information on racial and cultural matters); her view of the racial dichotomy as reality and also as represented to the child; and her racial categories and categorization of the mixed race child.

In part five of the questionnaire the mother was read a list of nineteen statements, covering various aspects of her racial attitude, to which she was asked to give her level of agreement. If the statement seemed ambiguous to the mother, or did not adequately describe her true opinion, she was given time to express her views on the subject more fully; otherwise, the given response was checked by the investigator repeating the statement with the prefix, 'So you think ...?' – to make sure the statement had been understood as it was meant and to give the mother a chance to say more if she so wished. Finally, mothers who were Harmony members were asked briefly about their level of involvement with the organization, and then every respondent was asked to give the race of each person mentioned in the earlier sections.

Questionnaire (Child)

Name ....

Age ....

Sex ....

Who would you say are your three best friends? ....

....

(A) PARTY TEST + SELF-IDENTIFICATION
This isn't at all a test, so there are no right or wrong answers to the
questions. It's really more like a 'pretend' game where I ask you to
imagine all kinds of things. Don't worry if you get confused. OK? Let's
begin, then.

In a moment I am going to show you some photographs. They are
photos of seven families, each with a mother, a father and two children —
one son and one daughter. So each of the seven families has one boy and
one girl.

(Hand photos, one card at a time.)

1. Which child looks most like you?
2. Now I would like you to imagine that you can invite four children to
    a party at your house. Which four children are you going to invite?

        (1) ....

        (2) ....

        (3) ....

        (4) ....

(B) ACTIVITIES
Now would you choose two children with whom you would like to do
these things I am going to read out to you. You may choose the same
child as many times as you like — you don't *have* to choose every child
once if you don't want to. Think about each activity carefully before you
choose two children to do it with.

Which two children would you like to —

1. Sit next to in class ....

2. Travel to school with one morning ....

3. Share your sweets with. ....

4. Come on holiday for two weeks with you and your
    family ....

5. Have in your team for a game   ....

6. Play with one day in the playground   ....

7. Invite home to tea with your family   ....

8.   Lend a pencil to in class. ....

9.   Stay the night at your house. ....

(C) REAL IDENTITY

If you could actually *be* one of these children (as if by magic) which one
would you rather be? ....

(D) RUDIMENTARY STEREOTYPES
(Use same sex as respondent)

1.   Which boy/girl looks clean and neat?   ....

2.   Which boy/girl looks lazy?   ....

3.   Which boy/girl looks dirty?   ....

4.   Which boy/girl looks nice and friendly?   ....

5.   Which boy/girl looks naughty?   ....

6.   Which boy/girl is good-looking?   ....

7.   Which boy/girl is always picking fights?   ....

8.   Which boy/girl never needs telling off?   ....

(E) JOB STEREOTYPES
Can you guess what the men in the photos do? *(Read complete list first)*

1.   Which man is a businessman?   ....

2.   Which man is a mechanic?   ....

3.   Which man is an electrician?   ....

4.   Which man is a road-sweeper?   ....

5.   Which man is a doctor?   ....

6.   Which man is a dustman?   ....

(F) SPONTANEOUS GROUPING
What I would like you do to now is a bit different. Sort out the children in
the photographs into their proper groups, putting all the children that
belong to the same 'race' together. Put all the white children together and
so on. If you think they are all from the same race put them all on the
same pile. Do you see what I mean? Put all the white children together
and so on.
   (Record numbers).
   (Pointing to each group in turn:) 'And who are *these* children?
   (Record group names)
   Do you think you could imagine that a man from outer space has
suddenly dropped in on us who doesn't know the first thing about people

on earth? Try to imagine that a spaceman is here now. He sees you sort out the photographs and wonders what you are doing. Then he says to you, 'How did you *know* which children to put in each group?' He wants to learn about everything you thought about when you grouped the photos so that if I asked *him* to sort them out he would do it right too. How many reasons can you think of why you knew the children went with which? Remember, the spaceman would need as many reasons as you can think of.

(Speak numbers of every photo referred to into tape.)

Probe check-list
Try to think of the connections beteen the children in each group.

(*Physical:*) • Did you look at the hair (texture/colour)?
                                    eyes (shape and colour)?
                                    head shape?
                                    nose?
                                    mouth?
             • Are the children connected by skin colour?
               (Check position of photograph no. 4.)
(*Racial:*)   • *(Check for ideas of mixture.)* Is each half equal? Is it more white or more non-white?
             • Did you look at the parents?
             • What would you tell the spaceman in general about parents and children, whether or not they look alike?
(*Cultural:*) • Did you think about the customs
                                  the religion
                                  the dress
                                  the language (how they speak)
                                     of any of the children?

(Take each group in turn and re-check criteria. Group a, b, c, etc.)

(G) SELF-IDENTIFICATION CRITERIA
Which group are you in?
   Remember you said that number .... looked most like you?
What exactly is it about number .... that looks like you?
   Did you look at the parents?
   Which group are your three best friends in?

(H) NON-SPONTANEOUS GROUPING
Are there any • coloured children? How do you know *(Say numbers.)*
              • black children? How do you know?
              • Indian children?
              • half-black children? How do you know?
              • Pakistani children?
              • brown children?
              • West Indian children?

209

- mixed race children? How do you know?
- Harmony children? How do you know?

GENERAL TEST REACTION

APPEARANCE OF CHILD

APPEARANCE OF SIBLINGS

COMMENTS

Questionnaire (Mother)

1. Name .... Number ....
2. Date of birth ....
3. Country of birth ....
4. Marital status: M / S / D / Single
5. Number of children .... Ages ....
6. Date of birth of child respondent ....
7. Mother's parents: *Alive*   *In this country*
                    YES / NO   YES / NO
8. Education:Age on leaving full-time education ....
       Educational history ....
       ....
9. Do you work?   YES/NO   P/T or F/T? ....
    What is your job? ....
10. Husband (father if single):
    Date of birth ....
    Country of birth ....
    Parents: *Alive*   *In this country*
                  YES / NO   YES / NO
    Age on leaving full-time education ....
    Educational history ....
    Occupation ....

(A) NEIGHBOURS

Now I'd like to ask you a few questions about your neighbours and the people you know in this area.

11. How many (a) families and (b) single people do you know in your street or within 10 minutes' walk of where you live?

Families											*Single*

1   2   3   4   5   6   7   8   9   10   more than 10   1– 5

6–10

11–20

more than 20

Could you name the families and single people that you know:
    Families   *Single*

12. Is there anyone in your street (or near by) who regularly looks after your child (respondent child)? How many people   NONE
   (a) 1–5   What about occasionally?
   (b) 6–10
   (c) 11–20
   (d) more than 20

13. Who would that be? ....

....

14. Do they have any children of their own?   YES / NO
    Near the age of your child?   YES / NO
15. Are there any adults or children living in your neighbourhood who are unfriendly to either your or your children   YES / NO

16. In what way are they unfriendly? ....

....

17. Does your child have any friends living in this street (or near by): Could you name them:

   (1) ....(5) ....

   (2) ....(6) ....

   (3) ....(7) ....   NONE

   (4) ....(8) ....

18. Who would you say was your child's best friend in the area?

....

19. Thinking about the child seen most often, how often would you say your child visited at their house, if at all?

   (a) more than once a week   (b) about once a week

(c) once every 2 or three weeks (d) once a month
(e) once every few months

(B) FRIENDS
And now about your own friends.

20. Try to cast your mind back to last week. Starting with Sunday could you tell me which of your friends you saw, visited, or spoke to during the week. Could you name them as you go.

SUN ....WED. ....

MON. ....THUR. ....

TUES. ....FRI. ....

SAT. ....

(*Probes:*) • Was that a normal week?
• (*Note all new names mentioned. Check for indications of closeness, frequency of contact, etc.*)
• Did your child go with you on any of these visits?
• Would your child have been at school when X called?
• Was there anyone you didn't see last week that you normally would?

21. Who would you say was your closest friend/your three closest friends? ....

22. How often do you see her/him/them?

23. What about your husband (*man present*) – who would you say are his closest friends? ....

(*Probes:*) • Do they ever visit the house?
• Is child respondent ever in contact with them?
• How close is close? Would you/he confide in them about intimate things?

24. And what about friends of both of you?

....

How often do you have people round in the evenings?
(a) once a week
(b) once every 2 or three weeks
(c) once a month
(d) once every few months

(*Probes:*) • Who usually comes round?
• How close are you to them? How important are they to you?
• Do your children see the friends you go out with?
• Who do you go out with?

212

(C) RELATIVES

25 Which relatives (*state relation and to whom*) does your child see most often?   m.m./m.f./f.m./f.f./   m.s./m.b./   f.s./f.b.

        Others ....

26. How often does he/she see these relatives? ....

27. What other contact does your child have with relatives (letters, phonecalls, etc.)? ....

28. Which particular relative (if any) would you say your child felt closest to? .... /NONE

(D) SCHOOL

And now one or two questions about your child's school life.

29. Who would you say are your child's three best friends at school?
      'best friend'

    (1) ....(2) ....(3)................................

30. Do you happen to know anything about the attitude of your child's school to teaching children about different cultures and religions?

    D/K ....

    Name of school ....

31. Has your child ever suffered from any form of racial prejudice from other children at school? (*Detail*).

    ....

32. Does your child visit the homes of any children from school?

    Who? ....

33. Thinking of the one most often visited, how often does your child go to the house of schoolfriends? Who are you thinking of?
    (a) more than once a week
    (b) about once a week
    (c) once every 2 or 3 weeks
    (d) once a month
    (e) once every few months

34. Which children from school have recently visited your house (if any)?..

35. Does your chiild ever meet with or play with any other children of interracial parents? (Do you know?)   YES/NO

    (*Probe:*) • At school?
              • Harmony?

36. How often?
    (a) more than once a week

(b) about once a week
(c) once every 2 or 3 weeks
(d) once a month
(e) once every few months

SPONTANEOUS GROUPING AND DICHOTOMY EMPHASIS
A person who knows very little about Britain asks you about the racial situation here. How, in your own words and giving your own view, would you describe it?
  (*Probe: look out for spontaneous mention of all cultural, racial and physical labels.*)
    (*Ask:*) • Who are 'they'?
           • Who are you talking about here?
           • So who would you say the racial situation was between in Britain?

  (*Use non-specific probes.*)
  (*Write all labels used here for reference later on.*)

'CRITICAL SITUATIONS'
Most interracial parents whose children are at school have at some time or other to deal with questions or situations which have begun with perhaps a cruel – or just a casual – remark passed by another child. This type of situation can vary from being a bit embarrassing for either the parents or the child to being very upsetting for both and often there seems NO CLEAR RIGHT OR WRONG THING TO DO OR SAY. I would like you to say what you would advise parents to do in the following situations, basing what you say on what *you* would do (or have done) in a similar situation.

1. A child says to her white parent, 'When I grow up, can I be white like you?' What would you advise the parent to do or say?
   (*Probe: looking for perceived identity and encouraged identity. Explore in detail any identity mentioned.*) (*e.g.*) What does it mean to be 'mixed'?
2. A child becomes rude and naughty whenever he is looked after by the white parent. Finally he says that some kids at school had said that white people hated coloured people. What would you advise?
   (*Probe: the dichotomy reported as reality to child.*)
   (*Ask:*) • How *exactly* would you explain this to the child?
          • Where do you think a child might get this idea from?
          • Do you think it is common?
   (*Also bear in mind: perceived and encouraged identity dichotomy as reality to parent.*)
   (*I.e.*) • Is the child 'really' coloured?
          • *Do* white people feel this way?
3. A child has been called a racial name at school. Obviously upset, the little girl asks if she is really a 'wog'. What would you advise?
   (*Probe: encouraged identity.*)

4. A little boy comes home and reports that someone said that 'racial prejudice' meant that coloured children couldn't get a good job when they grew up. He asks if this means that *he* won't be able to be what he wants when *he* grows up. What would you advise?

   (*Probe: dichotomy as reality to child and parent with the focus on opportunities.*)

THE STATEMENTS
I would like to know what you personally think about these statements. Please say whether you
strongly disagree / disagree / agree / strongly agree / don't know

1. 'Some coloured people use their race as an excuse. In Britain being coloured cannot stop you from getting the job you want.'
   (*Probe: focus on opportunities. Also cover the term 'coloured'; find respondent's own meaning, then explain meaning of 'non-white' here.*)

   SD/D/DK/A/SA

2. 'Mixed race children living in Britain are going to be treated as coloured when they grow up. It is wrong to bring them up to think otherwise.'
   (*Probe: encouraged identity:*) • How *do* you encourage them to feel coloured?
   • How should you bring them up, then?
   (*Dichotomy as reality:*) • What does it mean to be coloured?
   • What should you tell child?

   SD/D/DK/A/SA

3. 'Parents of mixed race children should just love their children and let them be themselves. They should not try to talk to them about what race they belong to.'
   (*Probe:*) Why do you think this?

   SD/D/DK/A/SA

4. 'I sometimes think that white and coloured will never live together in peace in Britain.'
   (*Probe: Focus on white/non-white conflict.*)

   SD/D/DK/A/SA

5. ' "Black is beautiful" is a good slogan to teach mixed race children. They should be proud of being black.'
   (*Probe:*) • What do *you* understand by 'black' – who do you think of?
   (*If yes:*) • To what extent should you encourage this?
   • How do you teach a child to feel black (what does it mean?)
   (*If no:*) • Why not?

   SD/D/DK/A/SA

6. 'There is no real conflict between the races in Britain, and if people

215

would only stop drawing attention to race, there would be no conflict at all.'

(*Probe: dichotomy as reality to mother-focus on white/non-white conflict.*)

SD/D/DK/A/SA

7. 'Britain offers equal opportunities to all races, creeds and colours.'

(*Probe: any groups more advantaged/disadvantaged than others?*)

SD/D/DK/A/SA

8. 'Mixed race children are not immigrants or foreigners, or coloured. Their parents should help them to have enough confidence to think of themselves as white children.'

(*Probe:*) • Why/why not: • (*If yes:*) How would you do this?

SD/D/DK/A/SA

9. 'We all know that if you are coloured, it is harder to get a council house.'

SD/D/DK/A/SA

10. 'Mixed race children are neither white nor black. They are *brown*; they belong to a special racial category of their own.'

(*Probe: explore racial identity – perceived and encouraged.*)
   • How do you get over the idea of brown? What does being brown entail?
   • Who would you think of if someone referred to brown people?
   • Is brown nearer to black than white?

SD/D/DK/A/SA

11. 'My advice to other parents is – if your child "looks" more coloured, then encourage him or her to "feel" coloured. If he or she looks more white, then encourage him or her to *be* white.'

(*Probe:*) • Do you think the hue of skin makes any difference as to how a child is treated? What about how the child himself feels?
   • What would you tell a child about this?

SD/D/DK/A/SA

12. 'Racial tension is definitely building up in Britain. I often wonder how it will all end.'

SD/D/DK/A/SA

13. 'Mixed race children should be taught as much as possible about the culture of the parent who is not originally from Britain.'

(*Probe:*) • Should they themselves feel *more* from that culture: Equally from both? Should they be taught the language, accent, etc.? How should the teaching be done – by whom? Why should it be done at all?
   • If not – why not?

SD/D/DK/A/SA

14. 'Parents of mixed race children should not try to hide the fact that white people and coloured people are not equal in Britain. They should know what to expect.'

(*Probe:*) • Are they coloured, then? Will they experience inequality? Should you prepare them? How?/Why not?

SD/D/DK/A/SA

15. 'There is no race problem in Britain. It is just a few from both sides
that cause all the trouble.'

SD/D/DK/A/SA

16. 'Loving your children and giving them confidence is the main thing.
But with mixed race children it is also important to make them feel
part of a racial group.'
    (*Probe:*) • Which racial group should they feel part of?
             • How do you help them with this?
             • If not – do you think they will feel part of one even if
               you do nothing?

SD/D/DK/A/SA

17. 'There *is* racial discrimination in Britain today. It is pointless to deny
it.'
    (*Probe: dichotomy as reality.*) • *How do you know?*

SD/D/DK/A/SA

18. 'It is important to help mixed race children to feel fully British and
not confuse them by telling them they "half" belong to another
culture.'
    (*Probe:*) • What does being British *mean?* How do you encour-
               age it?
             • What do you tell them about this? Are they 'really'
               British?

SD/D/DK/A/SA

19. 'Even if you believe that racial discrimination exists in Britain you
should still encourage mixed race children to feel that they have an
equal chance.'
    (*Probe:*) • *Have* they got an equal chance? (*Encouraged identity
               + dichotomy as reality to child.*)

For Harmony members:
1. When would you say you began to think about the sort of things
   we've been talking about? (Had you thought about them?)
2. Would you say that being a member of Harmony has influenced you
   at all?
3. How much contact do you have with other Harmony members?

Meetings	*Social functions/outings, etc.*
(a) every meeting	(a) every meeting
(b) about every other meeting	(b) about every other one
(c) occasionally	(c) occasionally
(d) rarely	(d) never
(e) never	

Contact outside meetings, etc.
(a) often (specify)

(b) rarely (specify)
(c) never

4. How important would you say being a member of Harmony is to you?
5. What about to your husband/family?

Finally, I would just like to ask you:

• What do you think is the best way to refer to children with one parent white and one non-white? I have called them mixed race children, but what do *you* think is the best name? Why?

Lastly, can we just go back to all the people you have mentioned, saying which racial or national group they belong to. Clarify if necessary:

Families near by ....

Single people near by ....

Unfriendly adults/children ....

Child's friends in street ....

Child's best friend (in street) ....

Child's friend in street visited most often ....

People seen during week ....

....

Closest friend of mother/three closest ....

Husband's closest friends ....

Friends of both of you ....
(Who comes round?)
(Who do you do out with?)

Child's three best friends at school .... (+ best)

Racially prejudiced children ....

Child most often visited from school ....

Children from school visiting ....

Other interracial children and parents ....

.... Which is which, etc.?

Others ....

Do you know any other interracial families who may be willing to be interviewed?

Appendix 2

AREA

COMMENTS

219

Appendix 3

Sample Characteristics

From October 1979 to May 1980 I recruited the full sample of fifty-one children and thirty-nine mothers (some of the children being siblings). A description of two events will serve to illustrate the process by which the sample was recruited.

A member of my local Harmony group who appeared at a meeting one evening after a long absence happened to mention a friend of hers with a mixed race West Indian child. I told her about the study and asked for her address. Nora Ballini was sent a handwritten letter explaining that Madeleine Troy had suggested I write to her asking for her help with a study I was doing of mixed race children and their mothers. Madeleine had said that she had a child of the age I was looking for and that she might be willing to take part; I then explained exactly what was involved.

Receiving no reply within two weeks, I called round at Nora's flat on an estate in West London. Nora remembered the letter, apologized for not replying and said she 'wouldn't mind' being interviewed the following day. I asked her if she knew anyone else who had mixed children aged 6 to 9. She replied that she didn't know anyone personally, but that she had noticed a woman over the other side of the courtyard with a child; she pointed out the window of the flat where she thought the woman lived.

I called immediately at this flat she had indicated and quickly explained to the white woman at the door about my study and how I had found her flat. I offered to leave a form letter (which I carried with me) explaining about the study, but this woman, Chris Sanders, said she was free there and then and that I could interview her. I fetched my tape-recorder and did so, arranging to interview her daughter later on. Chris Sanders gave me the address of a woman on another estate as well as that of her sister in Luton; the former contact resulted in another interview.

Ruth Ademola, whose address was given in a Harmony newsletter, was married to an African and lived in a town on the south coast. She replied to my letter within a week, agreeing to the interview, and gave me a number of dates on which she would be free. Two or three letters were exchanged negotiating dates, and on the day agreed, Ruth drove to the local station to meet my train. I completed the interviews and then spent the day with her and her children, chatting about Harmony, her job and anything we had in common.

Ruth used to run a Harmony group for the area – spanning a considerable distance since mixed race families were few and far between – but not many of the families she knew had children of the right age. However, she found three addresses of women she thought might be eligible. One of them was Mary Asante, who lived in a town fifty miles away. I wrote to her that week, rang her the week after and arranged to interview her the following month.

Throughout this eight-month period, I was given perhaps one hundred addresses, to which I sent personally addressed, handwritten letters. Outright refusals from women whose children were within the age range numbered nine. At least three of these refusals were on the grounds that the woman's husband had found out about the interviews and strongly disapproved (two of these refusals were personally threatening and abusive); three thought it might be bad for the children, and the remainder did not give a reason. Forty-one women (including the three pilot interviews) took part in the study, and the remaining fifty were either uncontactable, or did not reply (twenty-two), or were ineligible (twenty-eight) (Table App. 1).

Table App. 1 *Non-response*

	Refused	No reply or non-contactable	Ineligible	Interviewed
100 addresses personally contacted	9	22	28	41

Some of my contacts had only a casual acquaintance with the people whose addresses they gave me, so some were out of date or inaccurate; also, a fair number of women replied to my letter but were ineligible, having Asian husbands, adopted children, or children outside the age range. The rate of response is very difficult to calculate, for in a 'snowball' sample a high rate of non-response may be concealed. Women I interviewed and ineligible women asked friends to participate, some of whom refused; yet it was impossible for me to keep track of how many refused since they were personally unknown to me. However, it was my impression that for a study so controversial the non-response rate was surprisingly low. Once a contact had been made, at least one of her friends or acquaintances usually agreed to take part.

The Sample: Race, Class, Place of Origin, Harmony

I cannot say with any certainty how representative my sample is of mixed race children and their mothers in Britain, for a 'snowball' sample may be subject to any number of unknown, unseen biases. None the less, a few features of the sample may be pointed out.

First, there were those mothers who belonged to Harmony. Of the sample used in the actual study (thirty-nine women), twenty-one belonged to Harmony, committed in various degrees, and eighteen were non-members. (Seven of the latter were contacted through a Harmony member, and the remaining eleven were either entirely unconnected or could be traced back only to a tenuous link with a Harmony contact three or four times removed.) Within the sample, there were inevitably sets of friends who had both agreed to be interviewed; this applied to seven pairs of women and one chain of three women who knew each other. None of the other women in the sample were friends, although some may have had a distant knowledge of each other through Harmony.

The rough class-wise split of the sample was twenty working-class and nineteen middle-class families. That is, eight women were unpaid and alone or living with an unemployed man; twelve women were in the Registrar General's classes V, IV, or III (manual); nineteen women were in classes II or III (non-manual). There were no class Is. Race-wise, the sample was divided into eight black and thirty-one white women. The small number of black mothers was not due to non-response, but to the lack of black women contacts; however, this is in keeping with the commonly noted preponderance of black man/white woman bonds in Britain. The middle-class interracial family has not figured largely in any studies of Britain up to the present. This may indicate that there are now more middle-class mixed families or that my sample over-represents the middle class as a proportion of all interracial families due to the Harmony connection; or else both of these may be true to some extent (Table. App. 2).

Table App. 2   *Race-Wise Split/Class-Wise Split*

Middle class	Working class	*Total*
19	20	39
Black women	White women	
8	31	39

Table App. 3   *Marital Status of Sample*

Status	Number	
Married	22	
Single	4	
Separated	5	} 17
Divorced	8	
Total	39	

Appendix 3

There was a high proportion of single, separated and divorced women in the sample (almost half). This too may be a general characteristic of the interracial family; it was noted in Chapter 1 that interracial relationships sometimes adopt the more transient, working-class, West Indian pattern. But as I noted in the text, some of these women were seeing or living with men other than the father of their children, so some may have been part of a new couple (Table App. 3).

References

Antonovsky, A. (1956), 'Towards a refinement of the "marginal man" concept', *Social Forces*, vol. 35, no. 1, pp. 57–62.

Arbuthnot Lane, W. (1939), *The Modern Woman's Home Doctor* (London: Odham's Press).

Asher, S. R., and Allen, V. L. (1969), 'Racial preference and social comparison processes', *Journal of Social Issues*, vol. 25, pp. 157–66.

Banton, M. (1955), *The Coloured Quarter* (London: Cape).

Banton, M. (1967), *Race Relations* (London: Tavistock).

Banton, M. (1979), 'Its our country', in R. Miles and A. Phizaklea (eds.), *Racism and Political Action in Britain* (London: Routledge & Kegan Paul).

Bastide, R. (1967), 'Colour, racism and Christianity', *Daedalus*, Spring, pp. 312–26.

Battle, E. and Rotter, J. (1963), 'Children's feelings of personal control as related to social class and ethnic groups', *Journal of Personality*, vol. 31, p. 482.

Benson, S. (1981), *Ambiguous Ethnicity* (Cambridge University Press).

Berger, P., and Luckmann, T. (1966), *The Social Construction of Reality* (Harmondsworth: Penguin).

Brand, E. S., Ruiz, R. A., and Padilla, A. M. (1974), 'Ethnic identification and preference: a review', *Psychological Bulletin*, vol. 81, no. 11, pp. 860–90.

Brody, E.B. (1963), 'Color and identity conflict in young boys: observations of Negro mothers and sons in urban Baltimore', *Psychiatry*, vol. 26, pp. 188–207.

Clark, K. (1955), *Prejudice and your Child* (Boston: Beacon Press).

Clark, K., and Clark, M. (1939), 'The development of consciousness of self and the emergence of racial identification in Negro pre-school children', *Journal of Social Psychology*, SSPSI Bulletin, 10, pp. 591–9.

Clark, K., and Clark, M. (1947), 'Racial identification and preference in Negro children', in T. M. Newcomb and E. L. Hartley (eds.), *Readings in Social Psychology* (New York: Holt).

Collins, S. (1957), *Coloured Minorities in Britain* (Guildford: Lutterworth).

Cooley, C. H. (1902), *Human Nature and the Social Order* (New York: Schocken).

Davey, A., and Norburn, M. (1980), 'Ethnic awareness and ethnic differentiation amongst primary school children', *New Community*, vol. VIII, nos. 1 and 2, Spring/Summer.

References

Day, B. (1974), *Sexual Life between Blacks and Whites* (London: Collins).

Dover, C. (1937), *Half-Caste* (London: Secker & Warburg).

Durojaiye, M. (1970), 'Patterns of friendship choice in an ethnically mixed junior school', *Race*, vol. XII, no. 2, pp. 189–99.

Gitter, A., Mostofsky, D., and Satow, Y. (1972), 'The effect of skin colour and physiognomy or racial misidentification', *Journal of Social Psychology*, vol. 88, pp. 139–43.

Golovensky, D. (1951–2), 'The marginal man concept: an analysis and critique', *Social Forces*, vol. 30, no. 3, October–May.

Goodman, M. (1952), *Race Awareness in Young Children* (Cambridge, Mass.: Addison-Wesley).

Greenwald, H. J., and Oppenheim, D. B. (1968), 'Reported magnitude of self-misidentification among Negro children – artifact?' *Journal of Personality and Social Psychology*, vol. 8, pp. 49–52.

Gregor, A. J., and MacPherson, D. A. (1966), 'Racial attitudes among white and Negro children in a Deep South metropolitan area', *Journal of Social Psychology*, vol. 68, pp. 95–106.

Hill, C. (1965), *How Colour Prejudiced is Britain?* (London: Gollancz).

Horowitz, E. L. (1936), 'Development of attitudes towards Negroes', *Archives of Psychology*, no. 194.

Horowitz, R. (1939), 'Racial aspects of self-identification in nursery school children', *Journal of Psychology*, vol. 7, pp. 91–9.

Hraba, J., and Grant, G. (1970), 'Black is beautiful: a re-examination of racial identification and preference', *Journal of Personality and Social Psychology*, vol. 16, pp. 398–402.

Hughes, E., and Hughes, H. M. (1952), *Where Peoples Meet* (Glencoe, Ill.: Free Press).

James, C. L. R. (1981), 'An accumulation of blunders', *New Society*, December.

Jones, J. M. (1972), *Prejudice and Racism* (Reading, Mass.: Addison-Wesley).

Kannan, C. T. (1972), *Interracial Marriages in London* (London: C. T. Kannan).

Katz, P. A., and Zalk, S. R. (1974), 'Doll preferences: an index of racial attitudes?' *Journal of Educational Psychology*, vol. 66, pp. 663–8.

Lasker, B. (1929), *Race Attitudes in Children* (New York: Holt).

Little, K. (1972), *Negroes in Britain*, revised edn (London: Routledge & Kegan Paul); first published 1954.

Long, E. (1772), *Candid Reflections* (London).

Luckiesh, M. (1967), quoted in K. J. Gergen, 'The significance of skin colour in human relations', *Daedalus*, Spring, pp. 390–406.

McCarthy, J. D., and Yancey, W. C. (1971), 'Uncle Tom and Mr Charlie: metaphysical pathos in the study of racism and personal disorganization', *American Journal of Sociology*, vol. 76, p. 648.

Mead, G. H. (1934), *Mind, Self and Society* (University of Chicago Press).

Milner, D. (1975), *Children and Race* (Harmondsworth: Penguin).

Morland, J. K. (1958), 'Racial recognition by nursery school children in

Lynchburg, Virginia', *Social Forces*, vol. 37, pp. 132–7.

Park, R. (1937), introduction to E. Stonequist op. cit.

Porter, J. (1971), *Black Child, White Child* (Cambridge, Mass.: Harvard University Press).

Pushkin, I. (1967), 'A study of ethnic choice in the play of young children in three London districts', unpublished PhD thesis, University of London.

Radke, M., and Trager, H. (1950), 'Children's perceptions of the social roles of Negroes and whites', *Journal of Psychology*, vol. 29, pp. 3–33.

Richmond, A. (1954), *Colour Prejudice in Britain* (London: Routledge & Kegan Paul).

Shepherd, J., Westaway, J., and Lee, T. (1974), *The Social Atlas of London* (Oxford University Press).

Simon, R. J. (1974), 'An assessment of social awareness, preference and self-identification among white and adopted non-white children', *Social Problems*, vol. 22, October, p. 43.

Stonequist, E. (1937), *The Marginal Man* (New York: Scribners).

Teplin, L. (1977), 'Preference vs prejudice: a multi-method analysis of children's discrepant racial choices', *Social Science Quarterly*, vol. 58, p. 390.

Verma, G. K., and Bagley, C. (1979), *Race, Education and Identity* (London: Macmillan), ch. 12.

Verma, G. K., and Bagley, C. (eds.) (1984), *Race Relations and Cultural Difference* (Beckenham: Croom Helm).

Wallman, S. (1979), *Ethnicity at Work* (London: Macmillan).

Walvin, J. (1973), *Black and White* (London: Allen Lane).

White, R. (1979), 'What's in a name?' *New Community*, vol. VII, no. 3, pp. 333–47.

Williams, J. E., and Morland, J. K. (1976), *Race, Colour and the Young Child* (Chapel Hill, NC: University of North Carolina Press).

Williamson, J. (1980), *New People* (New York: Free Press).

Wilson, A. (1981), 'In between: the mother in the interracial family', *New Community*, vo. IX, no. 2, Autumn.

Index

227